THE CIVIL SERVANT
IN PAKISTAN

THE CIVIL
IN

SERVANT PAKISTAN

By MUNEER AHMAD

A STUDY OF THE BACKGROUND AND
ATTITUDES OF PUBLIC SERVANTS
IN LAHORE

OXFORD UNIVERSITY PRESS · 1964

KARACHI LAHORE DACCA

PUBLISHER'S NOTE

This book is a Monograph
prepared under the auspices of the
Social Sciences Research Centre
of the University of the Panjab.

OXFORD UNIVERSITY PRESS
Amen House · London E.C. 4

BOMBAY CALCUTTA MADRAS KARACHI LAHORE DACCA
GLASGOW NEW YORK TORONTO MELBOURNE WELLINGTON
CAPE TOWN SALISBURY NAIROBI IBADAN ACCRA
KUALA LUMPUR HONG KONG

printed by
THE INTER SERVICES PRESS LTD., KARACHI-4

PREFACE

The purpose of this study is to 'get to know' the public servants in Pakistan. Or to be more precise, it is to know the public servants in the upper tiers of the administrative hierarchy of the government.

It is a sociological study. That is to say it studies the public servants as a social group. The field of inquiry may be divided into three broad aspects.

The first part relates to the social background of the average public servant in Pakistan. In this section an attempt has been made to find out from which social classes the public servants are generally and mainly drawn. What attracts them to public service? Why do they prefer it to the independent professions or service in private enterprise?

The second part of the study deals with the attitudes of the public servants. According to the theory of democratic government the functioning of a modern state depends upon the team-work of the triumvirate of the public, the legislators and the public servants. We have tried, therefore, to ascertain the attitude of the public servants towards the other two components of the triumvirate.

The third part is devoted to an investigation of in-service relations. The effectiveness of any social group in the long run depends upon the co-operation and the understanding which exists among its own members. In this section of the study attention has been focused upon the relationship between the superior and the subordinate at different levels of the chain of command. As the inter-personal relations inside the office tend to vary from those outside the office, the two types of interactions have been examined separately.

What may be described as a sub-section of the third part of our study spotlights the views of public servants about a number of in-service issues which are peculiar to Pakistan. In this category fall the evergreen controversies about the generalist versus the specialist tradition in the public service, the role and position of the Civil Service of Pakistan, representing as it does the elite class of public servants and the successor to the celebrated Indian Civil Service, the government policies in regard to the transfer of officers from place to place and post to post and certain other related matters.

This is the first study of its type about the public servants in Pakistan. That, however, is not the only justification for its appearance. A more plausible reason may be found in the prevailing intellectual climate in Pakistan, which, as in other developing states, has stimulated the desire to evolve a new concept of public service patently suited to a developing society in order to effect with speed an all-round development in every aspect of the body politic.

The years following the Second World War have witnessed a considerable expansion in the role of the public servant. It is not the characteristic of any particular form of government. It is a world tendency. Presumably this trend is the direct result of the extension of the scope of activity of the modern State. The additional responsibilities which the State decides to take upon itself oblige it to increase the number of its already numerous, permanent, salaried employees or to enhance their powers and functions in order to look after the additional areas of State enterprise.

The emergence of the new states, whose society in most cases is passing through a period of transition, has given new dimensions to the role of the public servant. The governments of these young states under the impulse of ambitious nationalism are eager to catapult their backward societies into the age of modernity. A task of so great a magnitude undertaken on such a large scale and at such a fast rate makes heavy demands upon the traditional role of the officials of the State. The new states feel obliged to modify the classical concepts of public service in order to evolve a new system which has a greater relevance to their peculiar circumstances.

A painful fact of the history of the new states is that the long spell of foreign rule has left them ill-prepared to meet this situation. For reasons of security and for other reasons, colonialism has generally denied indigenous talent the opportunities to move into positions of responsibility. As a consequence this policy has not allowed the requisite body of locally recruited, trained manpower to develop in the new states.

The colonial era has also bequeathed to the new states a peculiar tradition of 'public service'. The salient features of this tradition are that it is authoritarian in spirit and negative in purpose. Whereas it served the alien rulers well, it is utterly unsuitable to achieve the objectives of a free people. These considerations make the problems of public service an issue of immediate concern to any developing state.

On achieving independence Pakistan faced such a situation. Conditions following independence were of the nature of an emergency which prevented the governmental leaders from giving due thought to the development of a new administrative order. All their energies were devoted to a struggle for survival. As conditions stabilized the government was able to direct its attention to this subject. In the first instance a number of committees were appointed to review the existing office procedures and to examine the grouping of departments and their functions. Later on some foreign experts were invited to make a thorough inquiry into the entire existing system and to make suggestions for reform. These probes set in motion a train of thought, both within and without government circles, regarding the reform of the public service system.

In more recent years this process of inquiry has received further impetus. The government has initiated a strong campaign to effect a radical change in the attitudes of the government officials towards the public. Administrative commissions have been appointed with terms of reference to attack the fundamentals of the system. The Pay and Services Commission of 1959 was charged exclusively with the investigation of public service matters.

Our study is an attempt to examine the same problem from another angle. The difference is that, whereas the other inquiries mainly concern themselves with the stage and stage arrangements, our study concentrates on the actors of the play.

A word of explanation is in order regarding the way in which the tables have been presented in this study. It is customary in sociological studies of this nature to include in the text almost all the tables to which reference is made. Although the advantages of this method are realized yet it is felt that too many tables generally cause an unpleasant interruption in the continuity of reading. Wherever necessary tables have been given but their number has been kept as small as possible.

Another word of explanation is due about the title of this book. The main title carries the term 'civil servant' and not 'public servant' simply because the former is better known in the English-speaking world. It has been used in the singular, implying a concept, the public servant as such. The subtitle carries the term 'public servant' in the plural because this is the term ordinarily used in Pakistan for any member of government service—indeed nowadays the two terms are virtually interchangeable. The term civil servant should not be confused with a member of the Civil Service of Pakistan (Civil Servant), which is only one of the many career services in Pak-

istan within the public service as a whole and is roughly equivalent to the administrative class in Britain.

Another aspect which often invites controversy is that the
writer should ensure an absolute freedom from value judgements.
Although this is a highly laudable objective it is extremely difficult to achieve in practice. No such claim is, therefore, made
about this study. The data have been interpreted with material
drawn from sources other than the data upon which this report
is based. In interpretations the writer has on occasions set up
his own criteria. These criteria may or may not obtain the reader's
agreement or full agreement, yet they do provide him with a
base from which he can proceed to his own conclusions.

ACKNOWLEDGEMENTS

In the course of work on this study the writer has incurred many a debt of gratitude. It is, therefore, but appropriate to acknowledge here all the help and support received.

First of all my thanks are due to Dr. Karl Heinz Pfeffer, 1959-62 Director, Social Sciences Research Centre, University of the Panjab, Lahore, who was my original and main source of inspiration and guide in initiating and completing this study. His guidance and help have been so encompassing that it is difficult to single out particular areas. His most valuable advice, gratefully accepted, came in clarifying basic concepts at all stages of the investigation and especially during the stage of report-writing.

I am most heavily indebted to my friend and former colleague, Mr. Shan-i-Raza Zaidi, M.A. Mr. Zaidi worked with me for the major part of the period during which the study was in progress. He helped me in preparing the dummy tables, interviewing, editing the filled-in questionnaires, code-making, codification and in transferring the data to IBM cards. Without his support and devotion, my work might have taken a far longer time to complete.

I must also offer my sincere thanks to Mr. Muhammad Khalid Hayat Khan, Director, Social Sciences Research Centre, without whose help it would have been impossible for a statistically untrained mind like mine to choose a sample.

My thanks are also due to Mr. Jamil Ahmad Zaidi, M.A., who helped me in interviewing the public servants, to Miss Shamim Dil, M.A., who, in spite of her own pressing research assignments, very kindly agreed to extend voluntary help in codification, to Mr. Saghir Ahmad, M.A., and Mr. Abdur Rehman Rizwani, M.A., whose valuable help, based on their experiences in field research, was most ungrudgingly offered, and to Mrs. Olga B. Fuller, M.A., who very painstakingly edited the language of the first draft.

I must also thank the Director of the Agricultural Census Data Processing Centre and its Technical Officer, Mr. Muzaffar Ali, for processing the data of this study on their IBM tabulators.

I acknowledge my gratitude to Mrs. Satnam Mahmud, Mr. Hasan Habib, Dr. Ralph Braibanti and Mian Afzal Hussain, whose advice and support I had to seek at different stages of the study.

The Government of West Pakistan is entitled to my unqualified gratitude for granting me permission to interview the public servants, and so are all the public servants who very graciously co-operated in this venture.

Lahore, July 1962   *Muneer Ahmad*

CONTENTS

CHAPTER 1

INTRODUCTION TO THE THEME

Pakistan is committed to the ideal of building up a welfare state. The achievement of this ideal involves development work of an immense magnitude. It calls for the mobilization of the resources of the country under the leadership of the State.

In order to realize this ambitious mission the State needs a suitable apparatus. In other words it requires an administrative structure and machinery which is geared to the realization of the national ideal. It also needs administrative methods and procedures which are fashioned in the same spirit. Above all, this enterprise demands men, first-rate men, who are not only well equipped to work for the achievement of the national goals but also possess complete faith in and sympathy with these goals.

The problem is not only that of the creation of a new administrative order. It also demands the demolition of the old. The old order is the inheritance of the British rule over India. In the case of the public servants with whom we are primarily concerned here, the spirit of the old order still persists in their attitudes. Attitudes are a tenuous substance, therefore they are difficult to plant or to uproot. But for the same reason it is of basic importance to weed out the old attitudes.

In British India the bureaucracy occupied a paramount position
in the scheme of government. Except for the brief period during
which the constitution of 1935 remained in operation, bureaucracy
had known no political superior. The popular governments which
were installed in office in the provinces for the first time in 1937,
following the constitutional reforms of 1935, enjoyed no control
over disciplinary matters and the conditions of service of their
principal permanent officials. As late as 1919, the executive heads
of the government departments were also responsible for the
initiation of government legislative measures. After 1919, constitutional provisions were made to pass on to popularly elected
ministers the power to formulate policy and to determine the
general direction of the administration. But during the periods of
constitutional breakdown, which were not infrequent, the effective
authority remained with the civil servants. No wonder British
India is commonly described as a large bureaucracy.

As the civil servant of British India was not legally accountable
to the public he developed a habit of working independently,
countenancing no interference from public representatives. The
inherent contempt of the civil servant as a trained expert for the
amateur politician was immensely reinforced due to the weakness
of the popular institutions. Any suggestion for the transfer of
effective power to the popular governments was violently opposed
by the bureaucracy. In 1919, under the Montagu-Chelmsford
reforms, certain 'safe' government departments were handed over
to the popularly elected Indian ministers. In the following few
years 345 officers of the Indian Civil Service resigned their jobs. [1]
They had enjoyed unquestioned and unlimited power for many
years. It was not so easy for them now to accept a secondary
position.

Similarly, the attitude of the politician towards the civil servant
also developed on unsound lines. The politician as a nationalist
stood for the liberation of his country from foreign rule. As such,

[1] N. S. Pardasani, *How India is Governed*, Bombay, 1942, p. 314.

on many an occasion he stood opposed to the established authority. As things were then in British India, the civil servant was
the embodiment of that authority. It was he who came into
immediate conflict with the political worker. Therefore he was
quite often the instrument for the perpetration of unpopular
measures. Accordingly in the mind of the politician he represented
oppression, tyranny and reaction.

As a minister the politician assumed the position of the political master of the civil servant. But he possessed no control over
his recruitment, appointment and dismissal. He looked upon this
arrangement as a serious affront to his authority. The ministers as
the leaders of aggressive nationalism represented new values. The
civil servants were the products of the old order. Sometimes they
would fail to appreciate the schemes proposed by the popular
ministers. Any criticism by the civil servants no matter how well-
intentioned was taken by the politician as obstructionism by the
bureaucracy. In some cases, partly due to inexperience and partly
due to enthusiasm for speedy reform, the popular minister would
design ambitious schemes which may have been impractical in
view of the limitations of the government resources. A counsel
for caution from the principal executive was very likely to be
interpreted as an attempt by the bureaucratic reaction to stop
the wheel of change. The ultimate effect was that a relationship
of mutual trust and understanding between the politician and
the public servant failed to develop.

British rule also left its stamp on the relations between the civil
servant and the public. Note has already been taken of the
influential place which the civil servant occupied in the Indian
policy under the British. This situation developed in him an
exaggerated self-concept. His attitudes towards the public were
shaped and conditioned by this self-image.

Throughout this essay the phrase civil servant and not public
servant has been used to describe the permanent professional
servant of the State in British India. It has been done deliberately.
He was a civil servant in the sense that he served the civilian as
contrasted to the military establishment. He was, however, no

servant of the public. The concept of service to the public figured neither in government policy nor in the minds of the officials.

The dominant feature of British India was that it had colonial status. It was ruled by a foreign government. That foreign government had established its authority by force in opposition to the previously established authorities. Therefore, the primary concern of the British was to preserve their supremacy. This consideration provided the main content to the civil servant's role in that period.

In the earliest phase of the evolution of modern bureaucracy, the civil servant started his career as the king's personal servant. The creation of his office was necessitated in order to project the reality of the royal presence in all corners of the realm. He was not an agent for the distribution of goods and services among the royal subjects. He was an 'outpost of royal authority' entrusted with keeping the king's peace in the royal provinces. In essence, that was the role of the government official before Independence.

If at its worst, the official concept of government in India was that of a police state, at its best it was that of a patriarchal empire. The British rulers did not credit their Indian subjects with intelligence or enlightened self-interest nor did they consider it worthwhile to consult their subjects in ordering their affairs. They were looked upon as simple, artless children, who were just learning to walk and therefore had to be led by the hand. Participation by the people in the processes which determined policies and decisions affecting their own lives was considered to be unwarranted. The government knew what was best for the people and ruled them accordingly.

For this policy the government found strong allies in the socio-economic conditions of the country. The social scene which British India presented was that of a village society. The life in a village society is inextricably bound to the land. The tie with the land has the quality of producing a society which proceeds at a leisurely tempo. Being self-sufficient a village economy discourages new enterprise. It also fails to develop in men a spirit of adventure such as, for instance, the urge to go beyond the frontiers of the little world which a village society is. Due to the lack of mobility in the population, social and professional divisions take the shape of permanent caste marks. The cumulative effect of all these factors is that it engenders an attitude of resignation and false contentment.

This attitude was reinforced by the military-feudal form of government which had prevailed in India under one foreign royal house or the other. The official had always represented the might of the State. In many cases he also represented a conquering race. Therefore, the official was surrounded by an aura, so to speak, of traditional authority even before the British arrived. These conditions had developed in the people an attitude of dependence upon the official. It nurtured a psychological make-up of great respect towards the holder of power and a willingness to accept him as a leader.

The British, very conveniently for themselves, accepted this supplicating attitude towards authority as a trait of the Indian character, without admitting that it was no more than a symptom of that particular phase of Indian history. They carefully fostered such behaviour in the people and discouraged, as far as possible, a questioning attitude towards authority.

The outstanding characteristic of the British political system in the home country is the firm tradition of holding the bureaucracy accountable to the popular will. On the national plane this effect is obtained by vesting the supreme authority in the popular chamber of the Parliament. On the local level, a robust system of local self-government holds in check the bureaucratic excesses. The British avoided, as far as they could, the introduction of similar self-governing institutions in India. Some administrators did not approve of establishing such institutions for security reasons. Some honestly believed Indians to be incapable of self-government.

As a consequence, the people's participation was rigorously held in check. Parliamentary institutions were introduced grudgingly under the strong pressure of the rising Western-educated

urban class. The franchise was subjected to so many complicated
contortions that it defeated its own purpose. For the most part
the representative assemblies were not given the power to influence
the fortunes of the government. The local self-governing institutions were kept in a state of impotence. In addition they were
placed under the overriding control of the bureaucracy.

This authoritarian climate provided the soil on which were
cultivated the habits and behaviour of the official. He assumed a
grandiose style of carrying himself in his official as well as in
his private life. He adopted high-sounding titles such as 'Sahib',
'Sahib Bahadur' or 'Janab Sahib Bahadur'. 'The access of the
people to the office was through cards and there would be a
huge peon with a big red turban standing in the door to prevent
entrance.' A trivial matter such as offering a chair was regarded
as a special favour. On the visits of higher civil servants flags
and bunting were displayed, ceremonial gates were erected, school
children were collected on both sides of the route of the visiting
official and he was welcomed with garlands. The attitude of 'the
Sahib' towards his subordinates was equally snobbish. The approved behaviour in this respect was to keep 'them' at a distance
and to develop in them a submissive attitude towards their
superiors. In order to show that this attitude was not the result
of individual idiosyncracy but the result of deliberate policy we
may quote as an illustration the Punjab Government Circular
No. XXI of 1860, corrected up to 1939, which reads: ' . . . and
the custom universal on the first acquisition of the country according to which on arrival of a district officer at a village the
headmen at once waited on him and paid their respects, should
still be insisted upon.' The subordinate was not trusted. The same
attitude extended down the line. Therefore, human relations inside
the bureaucracy were in a state of serious sickness.

It is easy to detect traces of the Mogul tradition in the high-
sounding titles adopted by the British functionaries in India. For
instance, the East India Company styling itself as the 'Company
Bahadur' was an obvious though awkward attempt to imitate the
Mogul court. This and other high-sounding titles adopted by the

British rulers were, however, more than mere imitation. They were rather a manifestation of a deliberate effort on their part to emphasize the majesty and the might of the conquering race.

A fantastic prodigy was the Western-educated Indian bureaucrat. As a part of the bureaucratic machine he shared the overbearing attitudes and manners of his European masters, but as a member of a conquered and subjugated people he was also supposed to show proper respect to his superiors. These pulls in opposing directions gave him a dual personality of wide contrast. In the words of a senior civil servant, who had entered service more or less in the same old days, he adopted a 'hectoring and bullying attitude towards his inferiors and practised abasement before his superiors'.[1]

Indians had been admitted to the top echelons of bureaucracy in British India in response to persistent agitation. But perhaps it was not much of a gain. The Indian-born bureaucrat was Indian in blood and colour, but English in tastes, in opinions, in morals and intellect. As a cog in the huge bureaucratic machine he had hardly any choice. The complete transformation was a concrete tribute to Macaulay.

The Indian member of the superior services in India provided 'good hunting' for the nationalists. He has often been criticized and railed at in Indian literature for imitating the ways and attitudes of the English gentlemen. The thing to marvel at is not that he did it but how perfectly he did it. The standards before the Indian candidate for the civil service were those of the English upper class. In order to achieve success he had to conform to those standards as closely as possible. Its logical extension was for him to acquire the social attitudes and even the physical appearances of that elite group. This process began during the preparation for the qualifying examination, long before the actual assumption of office.

Here we can quote with profit, from an Urdu novelette, the travails of an Indian student which he experienced in attempting

[1] Address by the Governor of West Pakistan, Mr. Akhtar Husain, published in the report on the *Seminar on the Expanding Role of the Public Servant in Pakistan's Democratic Structure*, Lahore, 1960, p. 4.

to obtain that effect in his personality.[1] This Indian, as a candidate for the civil service, had come all the way to England at the expense of his parents because his stay there was to enable him to make better preparation for the competitive examination. He wanted to be one of the rulers of India. This idea had been put in his mind by his parents right from his childhood. Other Indian students went dancing or indulged in politics. Our hero refrained from such activities regarding them as a waste of time. He took great care to dress as much like an English gentleman as possible. He practised speaking English with a perfect English accent. In order to converse with ease he laboriously acquired information about English movies, about the private affairs of the Hollywood actors and actresses, their marriages and divorces and the like. He was one of those who took pride in the fact that they could not speak well their own mother tongue, and who looked upon themselves as more of a 'pucca sahib' than the English.

He was looking forward to the time when, after passing the ICS (Indian Civil Service) Examination, he would become the ruler of hundreds and thousands of men and when a single frown of his would be enough to strike terror in the hearts of poor Indians.

He knew that they asked queer questions in the interview for the ICS Examination. Therefore it was necessary to read newspapers every day. Exactly for that reason our Indian candidate used to read *The Times* with punctilious regularity. Sometimes he took down cryptic sentences from *The Times* in a copy-book with a view to memorizing them and using them in conversation with his friends. He hoped that it would not only improve his mastery of the English language but would also ingrain in his mind the views of *The Times*. This paper was supposed to represent the ideas of the English aristocracy and it was considered to be a semi-official organ of the government. His endeavour was to identify his own ideas so closely with the official policy that,

[1] Sajjad Zaheer, *London Ki Ek Raat*, Lahore 1943. The above account is a free translation from the Urdu.

at the time of the examination, the examiners would not find a single remark of his out of tune with their own imperialist policies.

The *raison d'etre* for the overbearing attitude of the Indian-born civil servant towards the public and subordinates has been admirably explained in a recent paper by one of the new generation of civil servants in Pakistan.[1] He says:

As long as the English were dealing with the public there was no difficulty in getting their order accepted. Their blue eyes and brown hair and white skin marked them out as the rulers. Society accepted them as rulers and could make no mistakes about it. Society knew that behind the kindly facade lurked the power of the British military might. Therefore, kindness was more gratefully received and generosity more easily accepted.

When the Indians entered the services they did not carry those visible symbols of authority which made legal definitions almost unnecessary for the British officers. If the Indian officer was to be effective he had to be insulated from accepting influence from the society in which he had lived and in which he would die. To fit the role of the rulers he had to bear as close a resemblance as possible to the rulers. He had to dress like them, eat their food, play their games, live amongst them, bring his wife out of veil, speak their jargon. He was not to mix with the masses and with benefit avoid his relations.

How much of the officer described in these statements is still lurking in the new officer in Pakistan? This study is an attempt to find an answer to this question.

In the paragraphs above an attempt has been made to identify what is generally described as the colonial heritage. The main content of the public discussion to which reference has been made in the beginning of this essay is to disown that heritage. For the public servant it means destroying the old concepts of his inflated role in society. The destruction of the past implies the evolution of the new to replace the former. That is the real challenge for the planners of the new Pakistan.

Things are still in a fluid state in Pakistan today. It is difficult to say with any amount of certainty what role will be assigned to the public servant in the new society. However, it is possible

1 Masih-uz-Zaman, 'Public Service Tradition in Pakistan: A Case for Revision', a paper published in the report on the *Seminar on the Expanding Role of the Public Servant in Pakistan's Democratic Structure*, Lahore, 1960 p. 11.

to take note of the direction in which the movement is progressing.

The indications are that the patriarchal tenor of the administration will still be kept intact. One possible explanation is that
traditions die hard, but other considerations might have been
more influential. The history of Pakistan has been marked by
political instability. The politician has been weak or inept or
altogether absent from the scene because of the frequent supres-
sion of constitutional machinery. This situation has enabled the
civil servant to step in to fill the vacuum. In the words of an
observer: 'today in the Government of Pakistan the civil servants
often play an even more powerful role than that of their imperial
predecessors. This ascent to power has been both steady and
dramatic.'[1] It is natural that some commentators see in this
development the operation of the inherent ambition of bureaucracy to grab more power. Similarly, the apologists of bureaucracy
maintain that it was only an unwanted burden imposed upon them
by the 'truant' politicians.

The unusual task undertaken by the government in Pakistan
also lends support to the cession of additional authority to the
civil servant. The development work envisioned by the State
embraces all aspects of the citizen's life. It aims at a leap from
an agricultural-rural phase of society to the industrial-urban phase
in the lifetime of one generation. The enormity of this task and
the shortage of time place heavy responsibilities upon the government and upon its agent, the civil servant.

The role of leadership also gravitates towards the civil servant
because the majority of the people in this country lack enlightenment or resources to order their affairs by voluntary effort.
Traditions of self-government, as noted earlier, are weak.

The civil servant is in a paradoxical position. Whereas on the
one hand he disclaims the intention of playing the politician's
role of leadership, on the other hand, that is exactly what he is
doing in practice. The mental crisis of the public servants is evident in their public speeches. Generally they start with the premise
that all power vests in the political sovereign, but finish with the

[1] Khalid Bin Sayeed, *Pakistan: The Formative Phase*, Karachi, 1960, p. 383.

conclusion that the mantle of leadership falls on the civil servant. May be this is an *ad hoc* solution for the present phase of Pakistan's history. May be it is an unconscious endeavour to give a doctrinaire clothing to a polity wherein the bureaucrat is the boss.

By way of illustration, we can examine here the views of a senior civil servant, who is incidentally the director of a training academy which is established in order to orient civil servants in the principles of welfare in administration. In the paper, which he contributed to the seminar already referred to above, he maintained that the civil servant has always been the leader of the people 'in spite of himself'. His argument is that the conditions in the country are such that the people themselves expect leadership from him. To quote him, 'They (the civil servants) are not only the leaders and motivators of the particular agency in which they are working; they are and will continue to be, for some time to come, the leaders of thought and action in all spheres of life. Here, our conditions differ from the conditions in more progressive countries. There the general level of education is much higher and therefore the administrators do not stand out as personalities endowed with out-of-the-ordinary qualities. Here they are looked up to, not only because they have power and authority but because of genuine respect for their greater knowledge.'[1] It is difficult not to see in these remarks the patronizing tenor of the patriarch.

The task which the civil servant is being called upon to accomplish has been described by Professor Paul H. Appleby, in these words, 'Not independence and popular self-government alone are the objectives, but such a government dedicated to achievement of mass welfare at a tempo never attained anywhere at the same stage of economic development. History provides no near precedent for what is being undertaken here.'[2] This description refers to the Indian situation, but it is equally applicable to

[1] Raja Muhammad Afzal, 'The New Role of the Public Servant: Expansion or Rediscovery', a paper in the *Report on the Seminar*, op. cit., p. 18.
[2] Paul H. Appleby, *Public Administration in India: Report of a Survey*, New Delhi, 1956, p. 1.

Pakistan. The serious question to which this description gives rise is whether bureaucracy is qualified to effect such a fundamental change. Did anyone ever hear of a revolutionary bureaucrat? Is it not a search for the impossible?

The civil servant suffers from inherent limitations which diminish his chances of playing the role of a leader. He is a creature of habit and routine. He is obliged 'to administer the laws which do not permit him to supply what he personally likes'. He is by nature cautious and slow in the acceptance of change as well as in the implementation of operations. These characteristics inhibit his enterprise. The more perfect bureaucracy becomes the more it grows impersonal, remote and in the words of Max Weber 'de-humanized'. According to the prevailing concept of the 'neutrality' of bureaucracy it is considered to be a special virtue if the civil servant himself is not involved in the policies which he is entrusted to execute.

Professor Marshal Edward Dimock tells us that the characteristics of bureaucracy make it patently suitable 'for consolidating the initial gains',[1] rather than in the development processes. Can it therefore be a useful instrument for the promotion of rapid change which is the primary need of the developing societies? The question is a serious one. Can the bureaucrat really replace the political workers?

According to one view the political worker is indispensable. This view has been expressed in these words, '. . . in Asia chronologically the first necessity for development is the right politician. Others, economists, savers, entrepreneurs, officials, workers, all have their part to play; but they are only instrumentalists, the politician is at once composer and conductor in a concert which has the whole electorate for audience.'[2]

It may be asked where is the 'right politician?' Besides it may be argued that the responsibility of the civil servant to provide leadership to the people is not of his own seeking. He will undertake this onerous duty 'till such time when people get ready to

[1] Marshal Edward Dimock, *Administrative Vitality*, New York, 1960.
[2] Maurice Zinkin, *Development for Free Asia*, London, 1956, p. 63.

accept responsibility'. In other words, it is maintained that like the White Man's Burden, there is also something which may be called the 'Bureaucrat's Burden'. It is said that many of them dislike the responsibility of leadership considering it an imposition. To them the advice of a senior colleague is that 'they will have to expedite the process of developing constructive leadership among the people so that the length of their ordeal is shortened!'

The absence of the 'right politician' from the political scene, even for an interim period, does not lead to the conclusion that it is possible to do without him. Moreover, the evolution of the politician under the tutelage of the civil servant is a phenomenon which might produce results contrary to those desired. It is a process in the reverse direction. Once the layman is instructed in the habit of dependence upon the civil servant it will be difficult for him to attain independent thought and action. How can the people be expected to take their proper position as masters when they are treated as wards. Also how can the civil servant be expected to behave as a servant of the people when he is their educator and tutor.

This situation does not countenance any ready-made solution. Nor does this study attempt to suggest one. The endeavour it makes is to present different aspects of the question at issue in order to facilitate a decision as to the position of the civil servant in society which is in keeping with the ultimate objectives of the community.

CHAPTER 2

METHODOLOGY

The Origin of the Study

As in other developing countries, the social scene is changing rapidly in Pakistan. This change is being brought about by a number of active elements in society. It is of obvious interest to the student of society and of government to identify these active elements, to understand their nature and to assess their contribution to the process of change. The knowledge of this type should enable the planners of the country to determine the direction of this process of change which is giving new form to all sections of society.

The Social Sciences Research Centre of the University of the Panjab, taking note of this need, decided to undertake, as one of its main projects, the study of important groups in the Pakistani society which were playing an influential role in this process of transformation. Within the first two years of its establishment the Centre initiated several studies of special groups. One such special group is the foreign-trained Pakistanis. These nationals of Pakistan, by virtue of their advanced training in foreign countries, have the potential to contribute considerably to the development of the country. They occupy a place of great significance among the agents of change in the developing society of Pakistan. One study in this area which deals with the Pakistanis who had received training in Germany has been published.[1] Another parallel study has also been completed which deals with Pakistanis who had gone abroad for higher training under the auspicies of the Government of the United States of America.[2]

The second area of investigation deals with the Business Community in Pakistan. A pilot study has been undertaken in this area to develop an understanding of the entrepreneurial class, including the business executives, which has sprung up after Independence.[3]

The inquiry concerning the background and the attitudes of the civil servants in Pakistan is a link in the chain of studies mentioned above. It is possible to see these three sections of Pakistani society as pieces in a mosaic. They are performing different functions which are, however, so interrelated that taken together they form a uniform pattern. The foreign-trained expert, the business executive and the public servant are the representatives of the rising middle class. Their education, predominantly Western in concept, in the midst of mass illiteracy, places them in a position of great influence. Furthermore, it gives them a homogeneity which transcends their functional diversity.

The emergence of the middle class in Europe is closely associated with the beginning of the Industrial Revolution. The emergence of the three representatives of that class in Pakistan is perhaps a repetition of history. There is, however, one major difference. Whereas Europe experienced the transformation of this type in a state of half-awake consciousness, in Pakistan it is

[1] Karl Heinz Pfeffer, *Foreign Training for Pakistanis*, (*A Study of Pakistanis Returned from Training in Germany*), Social Sciences Research Centre, University of the Panjab, 1961.
[2] Abdur Rehman Rizwani, *Foreign Training for Pakistanis* (*A Study of Pakistanis Returned from Training Abroad under the ICA Sponsorship*), under preparation for publishing.
[3] *A Study in Entrepreneurship — The Lahore Business Community*, under preparation.

being consciously promoted and speeded up. In view of this undertaking a deeper knowledge of the agents who are leading the process of change becomes imperative.

Of the several agents promoting a change in the Pakistani *milieu* the public servant is in a position of great influence. Note has already been taken of the fact that bureaucracy is playing a far more pronounced role in Pakistan than theory essentially assigns to it and that it is going to play this role for some time to come. These circumstances make it extremely important to examine the complexion and the role of bureaucracy in Pakistan.

It is not a mere coincidence that when this subject was attracting attention in the Social Sciences Research Centre, the Government of West Pakistan was giving some thought to the redefinition of the role of its public servants with special reference to their attitudes towards the public. This fact rendered the atmosphere favourable in which to initiate the study. The Bureau of National Reconstruction of the Government of West Pakistan welcomed the suggestion that the Social Sciences Research Centre should conduct an investigation about the position of the public servants in Pakistan. The Bureau did not promise any financial aid but did offer full support in obtaining permission from the government to undertake this study.

The Seminar on the Expanding Role of the Public Servant

To set the tone for the study, the Bureau of National Reconstruction and the Social Sciences Research Centre joined hands in organizing a seminar on the expanding role of the public servant in the evolving democratic structure of Pakistan. The seminar was held in the Assembly Chambers, Lahore, on 11 and 12 April 1960. The purpose of the seminar was to provide an opportunity for a select gathering of public servants from the various government departments and representatives of the public to discuss the position of the public servants with special reference to their relations with the public.

It was hoped that this discussion would serve three important objectives. Firstly, it would inaugurate a process of heart-searching on the part of the public servants about their role in society.

Secondly, the seminar would yield certain specific recommendations for the revision and modification of training programmes for the public servants of all ranks. A third objective of the seminar, which was specifically mentioned in the cyclostyled invitations issued to the various government departments by the Bureau of National Reconstruction, was 'to get pointers from the seminar for a more intensive inquiry to be undertaken by the Social Sciences Research Centre of the University of the Panjab'.

The total number of participants was between 250 and 300. They were drawn both from the ranks of public servants and from private circles active in public life. The Chief Secretary to the Government of West Pakistan, Mr. M. Khurshid, had given his blessing to the seminar and had directed all government departments to send a senior and a junior officer as their representatives. Also present in the seminar were persons associated with educational institutions imparting instruction in Public Administration and allied subjects, such as the University of the Panjab, the Pakistan Civil Service Academy, the Finance Services Academy, and the West Pakistan Academy for Village Development. Prominent among the private associations represented in the seminar were the Lahore Chamber of Commerce and Industry and the Provincial Civil Service Association. Some women, mainly from the educational institutions, also attended the seminar.

The proceedings of the seminar were inaugurated with an address by the Governor of West Pakistan. The method of discussion was as follows. In the morning sessions, subjects were introduced by a number of speakers in an assembly of all the participants. After the main speeches, the participants were invited to raise questions, which were answered by the speakers. In the evening discussion was continued in groups. For this purpose the participants had been divided into six groups of approximately equal size with an equal distribution of various interests. A recorder, who also acted as the chairman of the group, and a stenographer were appointed for each group.

Each group was given ten questions to discuss. The groups

were asked to examine them and to make definite recommendations regarding the points raised in each question. Although all the groups had the freedom to expand their frame of reference none did so. The questions mainly concerned subjects such as the relationship between the public servant and the public, the improvement of the training of the public servant, and the inter-relationship among the public servants themselves. It will be useful to reproduce here some of the questions verbatim in order to emphasize the importance of the issues which later were represented in our questionnaire.

One question asked: 'What specific change need be brought about in the attitude of the public servants in order to meet the needs of today?' Another inquired: 'In what respects should the public change its own attitude so that the public servants are able to perform their tasks smoothly and effectively?' Still another asked: 'Does status-consciousness exist in the Civil Service and how can it be removed?'

It is a vast and complicated subject to which the seminar had addressed itself. The large number of participants enlarged it further in size but not in depth. However, the seminar proved to be very helpful in many ways. In the first instance it provided a unique precedent of self-analysis by the public servants. This example has been followed by the Police Department of West Pakistan, which helped the Bureau of National Reconstruction in organizing a three-day seminar on 'The Police and the Citizen' in October 1961. It appears that a public discussion on this pattern is fairly useful in providing a medium of communication between the public servant and the people.

In the second place the seminar helped to create a favourable atmosphere in which to begin this study. It introduced the main theme to the public servants, many of whom or many of whose colleagues were later to be our respondents. Also it prepared them psychologically to face the 'grand inquisition' which an interview might otherwise have meant to many.

In the third place the seminar disclosed certain areas of public administration which had not yet received sufficient attention.

One such area was human relations within the public service. Another was the importance of involving the junior officers in the processes of decision-making and in those of implementation relating to new projects. Thirdly, it was pointed out that not only the public servant but the public also should be asked to change its attitude. The participants disapproved of the attitude of extreme obsequiousness on the part of the public towards officers. The people were asked to develop a responsible sense of public mastership. One participant touched upon the class composition of bureaucracy. He demanded that the middle class should be strengthened in the public service of Pakistan. He further explained his meaning by saying that recruitment to the public service should be on a broad basis so that it does not become the preserve of one single class. The writer received great encouragement from the active interest shown by the public servants in discussing their own affairs. The foreign observers made a special note of the spirit of self-analysis among the public servants. It was an occasion of great satisfaction for the writer to find that the public servants were conscious of the need of a reappraisal of their role and that they were willing to discuss this subject in a gathering of officials and non-officials. The seminar in this way gave a promising start to this investigation.

Sample Design

On the completion of the report on the seminar, which the Centre prepared for the Bureau of National Reconstruction, the writer set about determining the type and the number of public servants whose attitudes we would like to study. The writer was mainly interested in the attitudes of the higher public servants who were engaged essentially in the performance of administrative and executive functions, therefore, it was decided to draw a sample from the gazetted officers, as they are called officially, who were serving with the Government of West Pakistan and who were posted in Lahore.

Definition of the Universe

Ordinarily it is not easy to distinguish administrative from non-administrative functions. However, for the purposes of this study

judges, magistrates, lecturers, professors and research officers
have been considered as non-administrative public servants. The
heads of educational and training institutions which are run by
the government have been counted in the class of administrators.
The reason for this decision is that the functions performed by
these officials, in addition to or to the complete exclusion of
teaching, are predominantly administrative in nature.

In order to find the total number of gazetted officers in Lahore
use was made of the *West Pakistan Civil List*, published by the
Government of West Pakistan, in January 1961. After eliminating
the non-administrative officers, the total number of gazetted
officers who were working with the Government of West Pakistan
and who were, at the time of choosing the sample, posted in
Lahore, came to 924.

Method of Sampling
The 924 officers lent themselves to a convenient stratification
into four groups on the basis of the nature of the functions they
performed. Moreover, each group could be further stratified on
the basis of the rank, i.e. the position of each public servant in
the chain of command. Therefore, in order to choose the sample
it was decided to adopt the method of stratified random sampling.
The basic consideration was to give due recognition to the familiar broad sub-divisions into which the universe appeared to be
naturally divided. Next, it was decided to take 40·0 per cent.
of the total number of public servants in each stratum as the
sample.

Categories of Strata
The four categories into which the public servants had been
divided were as follows. Firstly, those who were working in the
Civil Secretariat of the Government of West Pakistan. Secondly,
those who were serving in the Attached Departments. The Attached Departments, since then, have been abolished. Thirdly,
the officers belonging to the Civil Service of Pakistan. Fourthly,
those officers who did not fall in either of the first three categories.

Theoretically the business of government in Pakistan is divided
into two major categories. Firstly, the formulation of policies

and secondly the execution of policies. The public servants who work in the Secretariat are essentially and primarily concerned with the former. These officers are mainly desk workers. They are not assigned any field duties. Their dealings with the public are of a different nature and the extent of direct contact with the public is limited. In the day-to-day work they predominantly deal with the files. These characteristics give these public servants a distinct personality and a peculiar mode of working. Accordingly, the Secretariat officials were constituted into the first subdivision of the universe.

The former Attached Departments derived their name from the fact that they were attached to the corresponding Secretariat Departments. They were field departments. In the terminology of public administration the Secretariat Departments taken together could be described as a staff agency and the Attached Departments as a line agency. The latter were supposed to execute the policies laid down by the former. As executants of policies the officers in the Attached Departments were frequently drawn out from their offices into the field. They came into contact with the public far more frequently than the Secretariat officials. These conditions left an abiding effect on the mode of working of these officials and gave them an identity clearly distinct from that of the Secretariat officers. As a result it was decided to take the public servants working in the then Attached Departments as the second subdivision of the universe.

The officers belonging to the Civil Service of Pakistan (CSP) occupy a special position within the public service. These officers are eligible for appointment to posts in the Secretariat as well as to those which previously formed part of the former Attached Departments. In addition, they are also appointed as district officers. This last appointment predominantly involves work in the field and requires the maximum amount of dealing with the public. Special rules have been framed to regulate the recruitment and the training of the members of the Civil Service of Pakistan. It is generally claimed that the uniformity of their conditions of service develops in the CSP officers a corporate personality and a common outlook. In general the topmost administrative positions are filled by this cadre of public servants. It is possible for a candidate to join this cadre only once in his life-time through a competitive examination. The upper age-limit is twenty-five years for the fresh candidates and twenty-eight for those candidates who are already in government service. Entry of public servants from other cadres into the fold of the CSP is rare. For these reasons it was decided to single out these officers as a separate group within the universe of public servants.

After identifying the public servants who belonged to the Secretariat, the former Attached Departments and the Civil Service of Pakistan, it was discovered that a certain number of officers did not fall into any of the above-mentioned categories. It was noted that these officers constituted a functionally homogeneous group among themselves, as all of them were working at the district level and were attached to the office of the Deputy Commissioner of Lahore including the latter himself. It was decided to take these officers as a separate unit for the purposes of stratification.

Choosing the Sample

Before starting the final enumeration of officers in the Secretariat, the Department of the Board of Revenue, which was originally placed in the category of Attached Departments in the *West Pakistan Civil List*, was transferred to the list of Secretariat Departments. It was felt that functionally the Board of Revenue had more affinity with the Secretariat Departments than with the former Attached Departments. After eliminating the CSP officers who were serving in the Secretariat Departments and adding the officers from the Board of Revenue, the total number of Secretariat officials obtained was 236.

On the basis of the position in the chain of command, these 236 officers were divided into six categories. After counting separately the total number in all the categories the sample number was drawn by taking 40.0 per cent. from each. Meanwhile an up-to-date list of the names of the officers of the Secretariat was obtained from the Services and General Administration Department of the Government of West Pakistan. This was done in order to avoid the inclusion in the sample of the names of such officers who had either been transferred or retired. Subsequently, the sample was chosen at random with the help of *Tables for Statisticians* prepared by Herbert Arkin and Raymond Colton published in New York in 1951. The following table describes the actual number and the sample number in each category of the officers of the Secretariat.

Table 1

THE SAMPLE OF PUBLIC SERVANTS IN THE CIVIL SECRETARIAT

Categories	Actual number	Sample number
Secretaries (non-CSP)	5	2
Additional Secretary, Joint Secretary (non-CSP)	2	1
Deputy Secretaries, Director of Bureau of Statistics (non-CSP)	35	14
Officers on Special Duty, Assistant Director (non-CSP)	8	3
Section Officers, Accounts Officers, Establishment Officers, Statistical Officers (non-CSP)	174	70
Officers of the Board of Revenue (non-CSP)	12	5
Total	236	95

The total number of government departments listed as Attached Departments in the *West Pakistan Civil List*, was twenty-eight. Of these, the offices of the Advocate-General and the Solicitor to the Government were eliminated on the ground that the nature of the functions performed by these departments was mainly judicial. The Board of Revenue had already been transferred to the category of Secretariat Departments, for reasons stated above.

After this screening process, twenty-five Attached Departments were left which comprised 642 public servants who were posted in Lahore and were performing executive functions. These 642 officials were not stratified on the basis of their ranks as had been done in the case of the Secretariat officials. In the Secretariat it is the rank and not the department which distinguishes one type of officer from the other. The kind of work performed by the officers of the same rank in all Secretariat Departments is more or less identical in its essentials. The kind of work undergoes a change with the change of rank, and not with the change of department. On the contrary, department counted more than rank in the case of the former Attached Departments. Moreover, if the officers of the Attached Departments were stratified on the basis of rank and the method of simple random sample were to be applied, it would become impossible to study any department as a whole.

In view of these considerations it was decided to take 40.0 per cent. of the departments (and not the 40.0 per cent. of the total number of public servants) and to interview all the public servants in each department.

The use of different sampling fractions for different strata has the support of social scientists. For example, Leslie Kish writes in an article entitled, 'Selection of the Sample',[1] that on occasions it may be thought convenient or necessary to use different sampling methods or procedures in different strata of the population. In such situations, according to him, one may use different sampling fractions because the process of selection in each stratum is carried out separately and independently. As an illustration he took the example of a universe of workers spread over a number of factories. Applying the principle of different sampling fractions he maintained that it was perfectly valid if in one of the factories the sample was selected in individuals and in another the sample was selected in clusters of work sections.

Forty per cent. of twenty-five departments is ten. In order to

[1] Leslie Kish, 'Selection of the Sample' an article published in *Research Methods in Behavioral Sciences*, edited by Leon Festinger and Daniel Katz. New York, 1953.

choose ten departments the following procedure was adopted. A list of all the former Attached Departments was prepared with the total number of public servants in each who were at that time posted in Lahore (see Table 2 below). In order to pick out ten departments the method of random sample with probability of selection of each department proportional to its size was

Table 2

THE SAMPLE OF FORMER ATTACHED DEPARTMENTS

Former Attached Departments	Total no. of higher public servants posted at Lahore	Public servants performing executive functions	Cumulative number
Agriculture	32	22	22
Animal Husbandry*	53	20	42
Anti-Corruption*	16	15	57
Buildings and Roads	101	62	119
Civil Defence	8	8	127
Co-operative Societies*	17	14	141
Education	112	55	196
Electricity*	79	79	275
Excise and Taxation	9	9	284
Food and Fisheries	11	11	295
Forest	12	11	306
Games	2	2	308
Health*	159	78	386
Industries	67	56	442
Irrigation*	157	60	502
Jails*	6	6	508
Labour Welfare	11	8	516
Local Fund Audit*	14	14	530
Police and West Pakistan Rangers*	59	50	580
Public Relations*	28	25	605
Reclamation and Probation	1	1	606
Bureau of National Reconstruction	14	8	614
Rehabilitation	10	10	624
Stationery and Printing	5	5	629
Village-AID	14	13	642

adopted. Utilizing the numbers given in *Tables for Statisticians*
the ten departments marked by an asterisk in the table below
were chosen. The sample number on adding the public servants
in the ten selected departments comes to 361. It is more than
55·0 per cent. of the actual number which was 642.

The total number of officers belonging to the Civil Service of
Pakistan who at the time of choosing the sample were serving
with the Government of West Pakistan and were posted in
Lahore was 39. In view of the small number of these officers
it was meaningless to stratify them on the basis of rank and to
take 40·0 per cent. of them as the sample. Accordingly, it was
decided to include all of these officers in the sample. An up-
to-date list of the names of the officers of the Civil Service of
Pakistan was obtained from the *Gradation List of the Civil
Service of Pakistan*, corrected up to the first of January 1961,
issued by the Establishment Division of the President's Secretariat
in the Government of Pakistan.

A method similar to that adopted in the case of the CSP
officers had to be used for the fourth category of public servants
in the universe. The officers directly connected with the office
of the Deputy Commissioner of Lahore numbered 25 in all.
Eighteen of these were performing magisterial duties which are
essentially judicial. Only 7 could be classified as executive officers.

Table 3
THE FINAL SAMPLE

| | Officers of the Secretariat | Attached Departments | | CSP Officers | Officers attached with the D.C.'s office | Total |
		No. of Departments	No. of officers in the Departments			
Actual number	236	25	642	39	7	924
Sample number	95	10	361	39	7	502
Percentages	40%	40%	56·2%	100%	100%	54·3%

Due to the extremely small number of these officers there was no alternative but to take a sample of 100·00 per cent.

Summing up, it is now possible to have an overall view of the entire 'universe' and of the sample. The table below gives the total number and the sample number of public servants in each category. Out of a grand total of 924 public servants the sample consists of 502, which is slightly more than 54·00 per cent. of the total.

Preparation of the Questionnaire

When the sample had been drawn, attention was directed to the preparation of a questionnaire. The questionnaire was framed with a view to administering it in a face to face interview. In the terminology of sociologists it may be called 'an interviewing schedule'.

The scope of the questionnaire was delimited by the primary objective to understand the thinking of the public servant. In order to do that, it was also necessary to know the personal background of the public servant himself. Note has already been taken of the anxiety of certain people about the class composition of bureaucracy in Pakistan. Accordingly, it was decided to include in this study, as one of the important areas of inquiry, the question whether or not Pakistani bureaucracy was dominated by a single class. [1]

There is a general feeling among people that the superior services in Pakistan are monopolized by the wealthier classes. This outlook is an inheritance from the nationalist agitators of the time before Independence. There was a suspicion in the minds of the nationalists that the British Government in India followed the policy of associating with the government people of means, who, by virtue of their well-to-do conditions, were inherently interested in preserving the *status quo*. It might be an exaggerated fear, but it is not an utterly wild accusation either. Precedents are available in history, for example Prussia during

[1] Such ideas are prevalent in other countries also. For example, Professor Finer has noted that certain writers in Britain believe that the British Civil Service is a 'class' and not a representative Civil Service. (Herman Finer, *The Theory and Practice of Modern Government*, London, 1956, p. 784.)

the years from 1815 to 1871, where the rulers made it a point
to recruit their officers from the conservative elements in society,
that is the nobility and the 'bourgeois patriciate', so that the
values which were dear to the ruling class could be preserved.[1]

Fears have often been expressed about the tendency of bureaucracy to transgress its defined jurisdiction. It is apprehended that
bureaucracy seeks to promote its own policies in its capacity as
an adviser to its political masters. Also, it is feared that bureaucracy uses its position as the executer of decisions to obstruct
policies which are unfavourable to it. These presumptions are
based on the supposition that bureaucracy develops a homogeneous personality and a group mind as a result of its common
functions and common conditions of work. This supposition may
be doubted, but it does assume more significance if among the
things common between the bureaucrats is also their social origin.

Max Weber has quoted a few instances which illustrate the
operation of the group mind of bureaucracy resisting the introduction of policies which adversely affect its position. In
one case he states: 'all the scornful decrees of Frederick the
Great, of Prussia, concerning the "abolition of serfdom", were
derailed, as it were, in the course of their realization because the
official mechanism simply ignored them as the occasional ideas
of a dilettante.' In France, on the fall of the Second Empire,
the bureaucracy, which had anti-republican sympathies, tried to
obstruct the inauguration of the Third Republic. These instances
show that the class character of bureaucracy is a crucial matter.

The other important questions which could be raised were: 'Is
Pakistani bureaucracy representative of the small, Western-
oriented, educated, urban class? Or is it a replica, on a small
scale, of tradition-bound rural Pakistan? How much is it infused
with young blood so as to meet the challenge of a period of
swift transition? Does it look to the West for inspiration? Or
does it turn to the values of the East for ideas?' This part of
the inquiry tries to find an answer to the question 'Who is the
public servant?' The remaining portion attempts to understand

[1] Ibid., p. 740.

the nature of the relations which exist between the public servant and the public on the one hand, between the public servant and his superiors, subordinates and colleagues, on the other hand.

In constructing the questions two special techniques were adopted. Firstly, most of the questions were formulated in a structured form. Alternative responses were read out to the respondent only when he was at a loss for an answer or when he offered vague or evasive replies. In this way the benefits of both the open-ended and the structured formations were obtained.

The second technique was to put the question in the shape of a hypothetical situation. These situations were drawn from the everyday experience of the public servant in order to refresh his memory about the typical position in which he might often find himself in his work-a-day world. It was also found useful in blunting the edge of questions of a sensitive nature.

This indirect method of putting the questions has been found useful by some other research workers. Two of them wrote in their research report: 'we discovered that an indirect approach and oblique questions reduced the likelihood of evoking one-dimensional discussion and of centring the informant's verbal hostilities on a simple target.'[1] This technique was borrowed from Professor Morroe Berger who had used it in a similar study of civil servants of Egypt.[2] These 'short stories' proved to be quite interesting to the respondents. In most cases the real intent behind the hypothetical question was easily discerned by them.

Another important feature of the questionnaire is the inclusion of two indexes. One seeks to measure the extent of Westernization of public servants. The other indicates the socio-economic status of the public servants. The methods adopted for the construction of the indexes and for their evaluation have been explained in Appendixes III and IV. These indexes should not be taken as precision instruments. They are not 'scales'. They are only crude tools which enable us to determine, in a general way, certain

[1] John Useem and Ruth Hill Useem, *The Western Educated Man in India, A Study of his Social Roles and Influence*, New York, 1955, p. 20.

[2] Morroe Berger, *Bureaucracy and Society in Modern Egypt, A Study of the Higher Civil Service*, Princeton, 1957.

characteristics of the people of this study.

Letter of Authority

The sample being drawn and the questionnaire ready, certain government officials were asked if they would grant an interview for the sake of pre-testing the questionnaire. The officials said that they were not allowed to answer any question without the permission of the government. Accordingly the Government of West Pakistan was requested to issue a letter of authority to the research worker of the Centre enabling him to approach the employees of the government and to solicit the required information from them.

The Chief Secretary to the Government of West Pakistan very kindly granted an interview in which the nature, the scope and the purpose of the proposed study were explained to him. This was followed by a further examination of this matter by the Secretaries to the Government of West Pakistan in one of their meetings.

The Secretaries present in the meeting were provided with the background information about the origin of the study. They were given certain assurances. Firstly, that the study would be financed and conducted by the Social Sciences Research Centre of the University of the Panjab. Secondly, that the answers to the questionnaire given by the officers would be treated as strictly confidential. Thirdly, that anonymity of the interviewee would be ensured in that the views expressed by an officer would not be identified with his name nor would his identity be disclosed to any person, organization or to the government.

The letter of authority was, at last, issued in February 1961, in the form of an official circular addressed to all the Administrative Secretaries and the Heads of all the Attached Departments (see Appendix II). Equipped with this authorization, the pre-testing of two questions was dropped, three questions were expanded and four questions were rephrased. The final form of the questionnaire is reproduced in Appendix I.

Interviewing

Actual interviewing was started on 11 March 1961. The officers were contacted in their offices by a personal visit. They could either grant the interview right away or fix an appointment for some other day. In 94·2 per cent. of the cases the officers agreed to be interviewed in their offices, and 64 per cent. of the cases on the very first visit. Only 5 per cent. of the officers were interviewed at their residences. Three officers were kind enough to visit the Centre for the purpose of being interviewed.

Thirty-six per cent. of the officers insisted on fixing an appointment for the interview. Of these, about one-third, or twelve per cent., of the total did not keep one or more than one appointment. The attitude towards keeping an appointment turned out to be a fairly reliable indicator of the rank of the officer. The middle-grade officers displayed some carelessness in this regard. It was interesting to observe that while some officers took the appointments seriously and noted down the date and time in their diaries, others appeared to be taken by surprise when visited on the appointed day.

Personal visits were found to be ineffective in contacting the top-ranking public servants, because in this case the interviewer had to negotiate with the most formidable of the intermediaries, namely the personal assistant and the peon. In some cases the telephone had to be used to break this stubborn resistance. But in many instances the personal assistant was found holding the telephone line also. What a perfect insulation! In some such cases communication was obtained by correspondence.

In a few cases none of the 'tricks' proved effective and the interviewer had to come back without so much as snatching a fleeting glimpse of the officer who was the centre of his attention. It will be interesting to share with the readers the experience of one of the interviewers with a public-shy official, who certainly does not represent the average public servant, but who presents a good example of impersonality carried too far.

The interviewer visited the office of the official one fine morning. As the official was a very senior officer he enjoyed the services of a personal assistant. The personal assistant seems to be a status symbol in the bureaucracy. His main function is to keep the

'laity' at bay so that they do not disturb the peace of his master.
When contacted, the personal assistant suggested that the interviewer should tell him the purpose of his visit which he would
communicate to his boss, and that on getting the reply of the
boss, he would inform the interviewer. The interviewer explained
to the P.A. that it was necessary for him to visit the officer personally because the nature of his assignment required him to
establish personal contact with the officer and also because he
could explain his purpose better himself than through an inter-
mediary who was not familiar with the nature of the work. This
argument appealed to the reason of the P.A. He went to the
adjacent chamber of his superior to announce the visit of the
'intruder'. He came out in a short while to inform the interviewer
that the boss insisted that the purpose of his visit be communi-
cated to him through his P.A. The interviewer had no alternative
but to do so. After all this haggling the officer sent the reply
that the interviewer should call on him on some other day.

Two more visits yielded a similar result. At last the interviewer decided to contact the officer on the telephone so that he
might dispel any doubts there might have been in the mind of
the officer. The call was received by the P.A. He conveyed the
name of the caller to the boss and asked if he would speak to
him. The boss demanded through his P.A. that he should be
informed of the purpose of the call. The bewildered interviewer
asked how he could do so as long as the boss would not listen
to him. The boss replied once again through his P.A., that the
interviewer should explain the purpose of his call to the P.A.
who would then inform his boss, and thereafter the boss would
tell the P.A. to tell the interviewer whether or not he would speak
to him on the telephone!

Another stumbling block in meeting the senior public servants
turned out to be the peon. Some of the bureaucrats have the
typical disposition of the oriental beauty to conceal herself from
the gaze of the 'vulgar' and the 'riff-raff'. They sit behind closed
doors. As if this were not enough, blinds are also pulled over
the windows to give complete seclusion. This situation permits

a good deal of 'discretion' on the part of the peon in regard to admitting or not admitting a petitioner to the presence of the 'sarkar'. As is well known the peon is a shrewd reader of character. He recognizes instantly, mainly from the dress of the visitor, whether he is 'somebody' or 'small fry'. One's fate depends in many cases on the judgement of this all-mighty watchdog of the 'sahibs'.

The 'sahibs' also have their own ways of judging a man. A few experiments were tried and it was discovered that the combination of a business suit, visiting cards and the use of the English language in conversation is the most effective formula for obtaining an audience. Otherwise the common reply is that the 'sahib' is in conference. What type of a 'conference' this normally is, may be judged from the experience of one of the interviewers. Some of the respondents instructed their peons in the presence of the interviewer to tell the visitors that they were in 'conference' when, in fact, they were answering the interviewer's questions over a cup of coffee.

Each interview took from forty-five to ninety minutes. Most of the interviewees were able to spare time within working hours. In 91·0 per cent. of the cases the interview was completed in a single sitting. Nineteen respondents took more than one sitting. Four of these were interviewed at their homes. The maximum number of sittings did not exceed three in any case.

At first it was intended that a single person should interview all the officers. The idea was that it would ensure uniformity in administering the questions. It was hoped, furthermore, that this procedure would enable the interviewer to gain a first-hand impression of the general climate in each department which would be useful in writing the report.

After one month's single-handed work it was realized that the amount of work was too much for one man to finish in the time available. Besides it was felt that a few interviews in one department were enough to give the principal interviewer the 'feel' of that department. As a consequence two more interviewers were employed. They were given a thorough briefing about the nature,

Table 4

Department-wise Total Sample Number and the Total Number of Public Servants Interviewed

Department	Actual no. in Sample	New additions	Post abolished	Cancelled	Final sample number	Non-cooperative	Inaccessible	On long leave or transferred	Total interviewed	Percentage of persons interviewed
Animal Husbandry	20	—	—	—	20	—	1	—	19	95.0
Anti-corruption	9	—	6	—	3	—	—	—	3	100.0
Co-operative Societies	13	—	—	—	13	—	—	—	13	100.0
Electricity	79	1	—	11	69	1	12	1	55	79.9
Health	78	4	—	4	78	2	—	3	73	93.6
Irrigation	61	—	2	—	59	1	5	1	52	88.1
Jails	6	—	—	—	6	—	—	—	6	100.0
Local Fund Audit	14	—	1	—	13	—	—	2	11	84.8
Police	56	—	—	—	56	3	6	1	46	82.1
Public Relations	25	—	1	—	24	—	—	—	24	100.0
Secretariat	95	—	—	—	95	1	1	—	93	97.9
D. C.'s Office	7	—	—	—	7	—	1	—	6	85.7
Civil Service of Pakistan	39	1	—	—	40	7	1	1	31	77.5
Total	502	6	10	15	483	15	27	9	432	89.5

scope and purpose of the study. They were sent into the 'field' only when it was felt that they had acquired a thorough knowledge of the questionnaire and when they had been tested in a few experimental interviews. Their interviews were subject to vigilant daily checking. In addition, they were asked to write their personal impressions about the interviewees on the back of the questionnaires. In the daily conferences of the interviewers, field experiences were compared and an effort was made to standardize their observations. As a result each filled-in questionnaire developed into a pen-portrait of the officer interviewed. It is interesting to find that this practice is in keeping with the Government Servants' Conduct Rules. Paragraph (a) of sub-Rule 2 of Rule 4 in the Civil Service Rules, 1955, Part II, p. 149, specifically provides that 'a Government servant may at the request of any public body sit for portrait, bust or statue not intended for presentation to him'.

On the whole the interviewing was quite successful. The number of non-co-operative respondents was extremely small. The fact that 25 per cent. of the respondents offered the interviewers some refreshment shows that their visits were not so unwelcome. In all 432 officers were interviewed from the final sample number of 483 in less than six months. The reason for the inability to interview the remaining 53 officers is given department-wise in the table on page 34.

CHAPTER 3

BACKGROUND OF THE PUBLIC SERVANT

Before examining the attitude of the public servants, it may be helpful to become familiar with certain aspects of their personal backgrounds. This information will facilitate comparison of the attitudes of the public servants to their backgrounds in an attempt to discover some of the reasons for a particular type of attitude.

Ordinarily, the term personal background refers to such social characteristics as age, education, rural or urban origin and the like. Additional background features have, however, been included which are peculiar to the Pakistani social setting and which may help in explaining the differences in attitudes among the public servants.

One background feature peculiar to Pakistan is whether the public servant is a local or a refugee. These two terms are the products of the large-scale migration of population which followed the partition of the Indo-Pakistan sub-continent in 1947. A refugee, in Pakistan, is a person who migrated to this country from India after Independence.

Another social characteristic which is peculiarly applicable to

Pakistani conditions and which is important for the understanding of the background of Pakistani public servants is the geographical and cultural area of their origin within the country. This study covers only those public servants who are serving with the Government of West Pakistan, therefore, the geographical and cultural sub-divisions of the western wing only have been taken into account. These areas conform, more or less, to the areas of the administrative units into which the province of West Pakistan was previously divided.

Departments Represented in the Sample

To begin with, the different governmental agencies which are represented in this inquiry can be detailed. The names of the departments and the number of public servants interviewed in each department are given in Table 4. In broad terms the sample covers almost all of the major areas of activity which fall within the jurisdiction of the Government of West Pakistan. These areas are engineering, law and order, information and guidance, medical relief, routine file work, including planning and work relating to the agricultural sector of the economy of the province.

Classes of Public Servants

The public servants in Pakistan are divided into a number of classes, which very broadly indicate their position in the official hierarchy. There are four major classes, namely Class I, II, III and IV. The main basis of distinction between these classes is the method of recruitment, the rate of remuneration and the opportunity for advancement. The officers of Class I are recruited by an independent Public Service Commission. They are assigned to posts of the highest responsibility which are the most highly paid. Sometimes this class of officers is subdivided into Senior Class I and Junior Class I. Since the number of Junior Class I officers in the sample was too small it was decided to combine Junior Class I and Senior Class I officers and to treat them as one unit under the common category of Class I officers.

The officers of Class II likewise are recruited by the Public Service Commission. Their pay scale, however, is lower than that of the Class I officers. Furthermore, the officers of Class II are entrusted with posts of slightly lesser responsibility.

Taken together, the Class I and Class II officers are also described as gazetted officers. This designation is derived from the fact that the names of these officers are notified in the official Gazette published by the provincial government. In view of the more responsible nature of their work and higher rate of salary the gazetted officers constitute the higher public servants in the official bureaucracy of Pakistan.

In general, the public servants of Class III perform clerical duties and they are charged with less responsibility than are the officers of Class I and Class II. Ordinarily they are not recruited by the Public Service Commission. Their pay scales are far lower than those of the Class I and Class II officers.

The public servants of Class IV perform the functions of messengers, janitors and the like. The rate of remuneration for this class is extremely low. The members of the Pakistan Pay Commission, 1949, in describing the public servants of this Class as the proletariat of the public service, expressed the feeling that 'they were recruited on the principles on which one would hire beasts of burden'. [1]

The public servants of Class III and Class IV are known as non-gazetted officials as their names do not appear in the official Gazette. This study concentrates on the higher public servants, which in terms of the prevalent ranks in Pakistan has been taken to mean only the gazetted government officers. The members of Class III and Class IV are, therefore, excluded from its scope.

The sample includes certain public servants which have not been mentioned so far, namely the unclassified public servants. At the time of writing these officers had not been assigned to any particular class because almost all of them belonged to a cadre which was newly created. The classification of these officials, at the time of making up the sample was under the consideration of the government. Their names, however, were listed in the Gazette. Most of these officials were employed in the Secretariat

---

[1] Government of Pakistan, *Report of the Pakistan Pay Commission*, Karachi, 1949, pp. 4 and 27.

of the provincial government and they held positions which ranked a little lower than that of the Deputy Secretary. On the basis of similar indications which were available and on the basis of the opinion of the unclassified officers themselves, it was assumed that the position of the unclassified officers was approximately equivalent to that of Class II officers.

Public servants of three classes are represented in the sample. They are drawn from Class I, Class II and from those who have not yet been classified. Class I officials constitute 49·8 per cent. of the sample, Class II officers 34·7 per cent. and unclassified officers 15·5 per cent. If the Class II and the unclassified officers are combined, together they form 50·2 per cent. of the sample. In other words the sample is almost equally divided between Class I and Class II public servants.

Ordinarily in the Public Service of Pakistan Class II officers outnumber considerably the Class I officers. The high proportion of Class I officers in the sample may be accounted for by the fact that the sample is drawn from the higher public servants who are posted to senior positions in Lahore which is the headquarters of the provincial government.

Length of Service

About two-thirds, or 65·7 per cent., of the officers in the sample were already in government employment when Pakistan came into being. The remaining 34·3 per cent. joined government service in the years following Independence.

Two interpretations are possible from these figures. Firstly, that a majority of the public servants who occupy senior government appointments possess a fairly long experience in their work. Secondly, that at the time of Independence the shortage of trained and experienced public servants was not as acute as is often made out.

The public servants with whom we are dealing are senior officers working at the seat of the provincial government. Many of them occupy the highest posts available in their respective departments. As seniority in service has been the main consideration for promotion the number of senior public servants is high. In other words the first interpretation concerning the senior public servants made above may be accepted as true.

In view of the reasons stated above the second interpretation also needs to be qualified. Examination of the situation in different governmental departments reveals that, whereas the shortage of experienced officers was acute in some departments, it was not so in others. 64·5 per cent. of the officers of the Civil Service of Pakistan in the sample had joined government service after Independence. Similarly 61·6 per cent. of the public servants in the Department of Health were recruited after Independence. As against these 86·0 per cent. of the Secretariat officers and 82·6 per cent. of the police officers had been in government service long before Independence. The fact that one-third of the respondents who had joined government service after Independence were recruited within the first four years of Independence demonstrates that some shortage of experienced public servants was faced by Pakistan on her creation.

Geographical and Cultural Area of Origin

The single, unified province of West Pakistan was established in October 1955. Prior to that the western wing of Pakistan had been divided into about a dozen administrative units. These units varied in the size of their areas, in population and in resources. As a result, they had attained widely different levels of development. These disparities often engendered mutual jealousies and rivalries among these units in matters in which the units had to compete with one another. One such matter was the equitable representation of different units in the public service.

The nature of the rivalry among the administrative units concerning public service is demonstrable in the area of recruitment. Recruitment to the higher public service in Pakistan is carried out by open competition through written examinations, combined with other tests. The examinations and the tests are organized by independent Public Service Commissions, which are appointed separately by the central government and the provincial governments. In principle, this is a fair and a just method, but in practice, it works to the disadvantage of the candidates from the less-developed areas. In some of these areas the number of educated persons is small and the quality of academic attainment is relatively low. If recruitment for the public service were to be made without any safeguards for the less-developed areas an inevitable consequence would be the domination of the public services by the residents of the more-developed areas.

Such a possibility is likely to exist in those categories of the public services which are open for competition to the eligible candidates of all the administrative units. Before the integration of West Pakistan this danger was present in two of the three main categories of public service, namely the Central Services and the All-Pakistan Services. The Central Services are composed of public servants who are recruited by the central government to administer the areas of governmental activity which fall exclusively within its jurisdiction. The All-Pakistan Services are composed of public servants, who, being recruited by the central government, are liable to appointment anywhere in the country. Most of the positions of the highest responsibility, both in the central government and in the provincial governments, are assigned to this category of public servants.

Because of the extraordinary importance attached to the membership in the All-Pakistan Services the attempts to gain representation, on the part of all the administrative units were mainly concentrated on this category of public service. In order to satisfy all of the competing units a certain percentage of seats in the All-Pakistan Services was fixed for each unit in advance of the actual competition.

The integration of the western wing of Pakistan into a single province created a similar problem on the provincial level. Before the integration each previous administrative unit was empowered to recruit its own public servants in order to deal with the matters which fell exclusively within its own jurisdiction. The cadres recruited in this manner were entitled Provincial Services. The public servants of this category were recruited mainly from the educated residents in each unit. As a result, the question of equitable representation of different administrative units on the

Provincial Services did not arise.

Following the integration, new cadres for West Pakistan had to be created. Recruitment to these cadres is made through open competition to which candidates from all over West Pakistan are eligible. This situation compels the candidates from relatively less-developed areas to compete with those of the more-developed areas. In other words, it raises the question of the equitable representation of the people from areas of varying stages of development on the All-West Pakistan Services.

In order to meet this situation, certain safeguards have been provided to candidates from the less-developed areas. Keeping this background in mind it is of obvious interest to determine the proportion of public servants from the different areas in the sample. It is possible to classify the previous administrative units of West Pakistan into four major cultural areas on the basis of linguistic affinity. The distribution of the public servants in each was as follows.

An overwhelming majority, 75·9 per cent., of them were residents in the Punjabi-speaking areas of the former Punjab and Bahawalpur, 11·3 per cent. in the Sindhi-speaking areas of former Sind and Karachi, 8·6 per cent. in the Pushto-speaking areas of the former North-West Frontier Province and Swat and 0·7 per cent. in the Baluchi-speaking areas of former Baluchistan. A statistically insignificant minority of the officers in the sample, namely 2·3 per cent., stated that they had not settled anywhere permanently. Residents of East Pakistan formed 1·1 per cent. of the total number of the respondents.

As about one-third of the public servants in the sample had migrated, after Independence, from a number of diverse areas which now form parts of India, the above figures may not be reliable indicators of the representation of different cultural regions. In order to eliminate the factor of refugee population in determining the representation of different areas the public servants who were locally resident even before Independence were separated from those who had settled after Independence and then the proportions of each area were calculated. This process revealed that out of the 283 officers who were settled before Independence in the areas now constituting Pakistan, 72·7 per cent. were Punjabis, 13·4 per cent. were Sindhis, 12·7 per cent. were from the North-West Frontier Province, 0·4 per cent. were Baluchis and 0·7 per cent. were Bengalis. Comparing these figures with the corresponding overall percentages recorded above it is noticed that Punjabis still constitute the largest proportion. The Sindhis and the Pathans have a little higher representation than appears from the overall percentages. Baluchis and Bengalis, on the other hand, have a far smaller representation than the over-all figures indicate. For example, three of the five Bengalis and two of the three Baluchi respondents were not original residents respectively of Bengal and of Baluchistan.

The public servants drawn from the refugee population tend to represent the cultural variations of the areas from which they have come. In general, these areas are culturally different from the four major areas of West Pakistan which have been men-tioned. However, it is notable that a vast majority of the refugees came from Punjabi-speaking areas which now form part of India. This statement receives support from the fact that 82·6 per cent. of the refugee respondents had settled in the former province of the Punjab after Independence and that 37·5 per cent. of the respondents resident in the Punjab were refugees.

The reasons for the preponderant proportion of Punjabis in the sample appears to be firstly, that Lahore was the capital of the former province of the Punjab, secondly, that Punjabi-speak-ing persons form the largest language group in West Pakistan and thirdly, that the area covered by the former province of the Punjab happens to be relatively more developed than the other areas.

Refugees and Locals Among the Public Servants

At the time of the creation of Pakistan, about one-third, or 34·5 per cent., of the public servants in our sample were not residents of the areas which now form Pakistan. These public servants introduced a new element in the population of Pakistan in terms of numbers and to some extent in terms of cultural patterns.

Of these public servants 82·6 per cent. had settled in the former Punjab and Bahawalpur, 7·4 per cent. in the former Sind and Karachi, 1·7 per cent. in the former North-West Frontier Province and Swat, 1·3 per cent. in Baluchistan and 2·0 per cent. in East Pakistan. Six per cent. of the refugee officers stated that they had not as yet been able to establish a permanent residence in Pakistan.

The proportion of refugee officers residing in different cultural areas was as follows: 37·5 per cent. of the officers in the former Punjab and Bahawalpur, 22·4 per cent. of the officers in the former Sind and Karachi, 2·7 per cent. of the officers in the former North-West Frontier Province and Swat. Two out of the three respondents from Baluchistan and three out of the five respondents from East Pakistan were refugees.

About three-fifths of the refugee officers, or 62·4 per cent., were already in government service at the time of Independence. This information indicates that the refugee public servants contributed to the consolidation of Pakistan not only in numbers but in experience as well.

In answer to a question put by a member of the first Constituent Assembly of Pakistan, the Government of Pakistan prepared a statement showing the total number of refugee public servants employed by the central government. Although the figures are not representative of the refugee public servants in all parts of Pakistan yet they do give some idea of the cultural background of a major portion of the refugee public servants. These figures, also give an inkling as to the status of these refugee officials in the bureaucracy before Independence.

Out of a total of 3,121 refugee public servants, 2,125 had migrated from the provinces of India. The others had come over from the Indian princely states. Muslims from the United Provinces and from the Indian side of the Punjab, including Delhi, numbered 1,764 and thus formed a vast majority of the refugee public servants from the Indian provinces. Only 97 of the 3,121 refugee public servants had held higher administrative positions in the past. Almost all the others had held subordinate positions such as those of a clerk or a peon.[1]

Religion of the Respondents

Religion-wise the distribution of public servants in the sample was as follows: Muslims, 97·3 per cent., Christian 2·4 per cent., Hindus 0·3 per cent. With one exception all of the non-Muslims were men. Most of the non-Muslim respondents were employed in the Police Department and in the Secretariat. As an overwhelming majority of the public servants in the sample was drawn from the same religion it was not considered necessary to compare this factor with any other. It is interesting to note that the proportions of Muslim, Christian and Hindu public servants roughly correspond to the overall proportions of these religious communities in the population of West Pakistan. According to population census of 1961, Muslims form 97·2 per cent. of the total population of West Pakistan, Hindus, including Scheduled Castes form 1·5 per cent. and Christians constitute 1·4 per cent.[2]

Rural or Urban Background of the Public Servants

The majority, or 81·2 per cent., of the public servants in the sample had been brought up in an urban area during the formative years of their lives. Only 18·8 per cent. had lived in a rural setting during that period. In a predominantly rural area such as West Pakistan where the rural community is 77·5 per cent. of the population, these figures are extremely significant. One possible reason appears to be the universal tendency of townspeople to seek employment in public service. Another reason may be that the educational facilities in Pakistan are concentrated in urban areas.

In certain government departments the proportion of public servants with a rural background was even smaller than that for the whole sample. For example, only one of the 31 CSP officers had lived in a village up to the age of fifteen. The percentage of such officers was 17·8 in the Health Department. Recruitment

---

[1] Calculated from figures given in *Statement showing the Total Number of Persons, employed under the Government of Pakistan, Belonging to Different Provinces, States, etc., of India*, Karachi, 1950.

[2] Government of Pakistan, Ministry of Home Affairs, *Population Census of Pakistan, 1961, Census Bulletin No. 2, Sex, Urban-Rural, Religion, Non-Pakistanis*, Karachi, 1961, p. 19.

to the Civil Service of Pakistan is made through a stiff competition on an all-Pakistan basis. The preponderance in this service of persons with an urban background is, perhaps, an indicator that urban candidates stand a better chance of selection than do candidates from the rural areas.

In the Police Department the percentage of public servants from the rural areas was 30.4. The relatively higher proportion of villagers in the Police Department, as compared to the others, appears to be due to the reason that in the recruitment of the police officers a good deal of emphasis is laid on the physique of the candidates in which respect the villagers tend to have an advantage over their compatriots from the towns.

Age of the Public Servants

The officers in our sample ranged from twenty-three to sixty-two years of age. The minimum age for joining government service in the case of gazetted officers is twenty-one. The retirement age, which was previously fixed at fifty-five for the employees of the provincial government, has since been raised to sixty years. There were only two officers who had exceeded this age limit. They had been allowed to continue in service after reaching the age for retirement, at their own request, on the basic pay scale of the posts they were holding immediately before retirement.

More than 90.0 per cent. of the officers were between twenty-eight and fifty-seven years of age. The average age was forty-two years. The respondents were more or less evenly divided between those who were below and those who were above the average age.

One important reason for a large proportion of public servants in relatively higher age-groups is perhaps that the sample is drawn from the higher public servants who are posted to senior positions at the headquarters of the provincial government to which a public servant becomes eligible generally at a ripe age. At the same time it is significant that about one-third of the officers, or 31.0 per cent., were in the relatively younger age span of twenty-three to thirty-seven.

The position is significant in the case of the following categories of public servants. In the Civil Service of Pakistan 40.9 per cent.

of the officers fall in the age-group of twenty-three to thirty-two. The percentage of officers of the Health Department in the same age-group is 47·9. Forty-six per cent. of the police officers and 59·2 per cent. of the Secretariat officers fall in the age interval of forty-three to fifty-two. These figures support the findings made earlier in the analysis of the length of service of the public servants. That is to say, the Civil Service of Pakistan and the Health Department contain a relatively higher proportion of younger officers with fewer years of experience. The situation is just the reverse in the Police Department and the Civil Secretariat.

Table 5

AGE OF THE PUBLIC SERVANTS

Age group	Number	Percentage
23—27	28	6·5
28—32	60	13·9
33—37	46	10·6
38—42	78	18·1
43—47	76	17·6
48—52	91	21·1
53—57	50	11·5
58—62	3	0·7
Total	432	100·0

Graphically, if a line were to be drawn at the forty-second year of age of the public servants they are evenly divided between the officers of twenty-three to forty-two years of age on the one hand and the officers of forty-two to sixty-two years of age on the other hand. If the first group may be considered as comprising the younger public servants, the proportion of the younger and the older public servants is almost equal in the sample.

Educational Background of the Respondents

Table 6 demonstrates that a vast majority of the public servants possessed degrees of higher education. There appear to be two major reasons for such a large percentage of highly educated public servants. Firstly, the possession of a Bachelor's degree is the minimum academic qualification for joining the upper tiers

Table 6

EDUCATIONAL BACKGROUND OF THE PUBLIC SERVANTS FROM DIFFERENT DEPARTMENTS

Department	Undergraduates and below	Percentage	Up to Bachelor's degree	Percentage	Up to Master's or equivalent degree or above	Percentage	Total	Foreign trained officers	Percentage
Animal Husbandry	6	31.6	3	15.8	10	52.6	19	12	63.2
Anti-Corruption	1	33.3	1	33.3	1	33.3	3	—	—
Co-operative Societies	1	7.7	11	84.6	1	7.7	13		
Electricity	13	23.6	27	49.1	15	27.3	55	15	27.3
Health	3	41.0	4	5.4	66	90.4	73	14	19.2
Irrigation	5	9.6	28	53.8	19	36.5	52	15	28.8
Jails	2	33.3	1	16.3	3	50.0	6	—	—
Local Fund Audit	1	9.1	9	81.8	1	9.1	11	2	4.3
Police	15	32.6	18	39.1	13	28.3	46	2	4.3
Public Relations	5	20.8	12	50.0	7	29.2	24	3	12.5
Secretariat	24	25.8	36	38.7	33	35.5	93	6	6.5
Deputy Commissioner's office	—	—	5	83.3	1	16.7	6	—	—
C.S.P. officers	—	—	7	22.6	24	77.4	31	14	45.2
Total	76	17.7	162	34.5	194	44.9	432	81	18.7

of Public Service in Pakistan, and, secondly, most of the public servants in the sample are drawn from the senior officials who are stationed at the seat of the provincial government. In most cases their work involves the planning, the co-ordination and the direction of the activities of the entire province which requires an educational background of an advanced level.

There is a difference in the educational background of the personnel of the various departments. Further examination of Table 6 reveals that a significant proportion of the officers in the Departments of Jails, Police, Animal Husbandry and the Civil Secretariat had not studied beyond the undergraduate level. There appear to be two main reasons for this state of affairs. Firstly, many positions of higher responsibility in these government agencies have been filled by promoting subordinate personnel to higher positions. The educational requirements for subordinate public servants are generally fixed at a relatively low level at the time of appointment. Secondly, in the recruitment of public servants for these departments, the emphasis in general, was not placed on a higher level of education. In the case of the Police Department, for instance, a sound physique is generally considered to be so important that it is no wonder if, for the sake of fulfilling this requirement, educational requirements were fixed at a lower level or were relaxed.

Table 6 shows that a very high percentage of officers in the Health Department and in the Civil Service of Pakistan have received higher education. After the establishment of Pakistan special attention was given to the development and the expansion of the medical service. As there was a scarcity of trained doctors in the country, new institutions for the training of men and women were opened and young people were encouraged to enter the profession of medicine.

The Civil Service of Pakistan is the most coveted service in the country. Competition for positions in this service is intense. Moreover, the minimum age limit for entry into this service is twenty-one which coincides with the age at which students normally complete work for the Master's degree. Probably, for these two reasons, candidates for the Civil Service of Pakistan appear in the competition after receiving a Master's degree rather than after receiving a Bachelor's degree which is the minimum educational qualification.

A further analysis of Table 6 shows that the number of postgraduates is significant in some technical departments, namely Animal Husbandry, Irrigation, and Electricity. In view of the shortage of technically qualified persons in Pakistan and in view of the growing industrial bias in the economy, technical education was especially promoted by the Government of Pakistan. The existing institutions in technical fields were reinforced and new ones were started. In addition, a large number of public servants from the technical departments were sent for training to institutions of higher learning in foreign countries. Most of the public servants who possess degrees of advanced learning from foreign universities are drawn from technical departments. In this respect the Department of Animal Husbandry leads all other departments which are included in the sample even though it also includes a relatively high percentage of people who had no degrees.

Among the non-technical public servants, the members of the Civil Service of Pakistan have been accorded special facilities for advanced training in other countries. As a part of their training until 1960 the successful candidates in the competition for the Civil Service of Pakistan were required to take special courses at the universities of Cambridge or Oxford. Furthermore, in order to meet the scarcity of trained general administrators, a very small number of whom had fallen to the share of Pakistan following the partition of the sub-continent, further recruitment was undertaken and a large number of new officers and public servants from the higher and middle grades were sent to foreign countries for special training in Public Administration. Advantage was taken of the Technical Assistance Scheme of the Colombo Plan for the training of government officers in the Commonwealth countries. Officers were sent under this scheme to the United Kingdom, Canada, Australia and New Zealand. Some CSP officers were also sent, under the auspices of the International

Co-operation Administration, now called the Agency for International Development, of the Government of the United States of America, to the School of Public Administration at the University of California for training in general and developmental administration. These officers were also offered the facilities of in-service experience in government offices and in public concerns, and of study tours to various important projects. A small number of officers went to the Institute of Social Studies at the Hague on scholarships offered by the Government of the Netherlands. During the first nine years after the establishment of Pakistan over 240 officers of the Civil Service of Pakistan and of other services were sent abroad for training under the various aid schemes.[1]

The Social Origin of the Public Servants

One's father's occupation and income are commonly considered to be significant indicators of social origin. In this study three more indicators have been used, namely the education of the father, the mother and the wife of the respondents. The original plan of the writer had been to develop an index of socio-economic status of the respondents' fathers. This, however, proved to be impossible, mainly because of the difficulty in ranking the various indicators.

The years in which the respondents had joined public service varied from 1929 to 1962. In this long span of years the socio-economic conditions were not uniform which meant that it was difficult to apply uniform ranking standards to the various indicators of the status of the respondents. For example, income which was considered to be high in 1929 was not so in 1961. The same is true about educational attainment and other similar factors affecting status. In such a situation, the best thing would have been to demarcate periods of time in which socio-economic conditions might have been more or less uniform and then to rank each indicator separately in each period. This procedure required taking too many decisions retrospectively. Furthermore,

---

[1] Government of Pakistan, *Pakistan 1957-58*, Karachi, 1958 and *Sixth Year*, *Pakistan*, 1953, Karachi.

in ranking income it might have been necessary to find out the cost of living index for different periods which was not available. So the idea of constructing an index of the socio-economic status of the respondents' fathers was abandoned. Instead each indicator has been discussed separately.

Fathers' Occupations

On the basis of the occupations of the fathers of the respondents the findings are as follows. As is shown in Table 7 the fathers of two-thirds, or 66·4 per cent., of the public servants were salaried employees. Except for an insignificant proportion of these, namely 3·1 per cent., who were employed in private enterprise, all the others were in government employment. The land-owning class was represented by 15·0 per cent. of the officers in the sample, business was represented by 10·7 per cent. and independent professions were represented by 5·1 per cent. only.

Occupational Status

Occupational status is a characteristic which does not lend itself easily to precise evaluation. The classification of the respondents' fathers which has been attempted in Table 7 is to a large extent based upon personal judgement. The classification was facilitated a great deal by the fact that about two-thirds of the fathers of the respondents were salaried employees whose rank in the hierarchy was, in most cases, a fairly reliable indicator of their occupational status. The procedure which was adopted for assessing the occupational status is described below.

The respondents' fathers were considered to have occupied a high occupational status if they had held a gazetted appointment in the public service, a commissioned appointment in the army, or a managerial or equivalent position in the railways, in a semi-government agency, in the employment of a princely state or in the employment of a private enterprise. The respondents' fathers whose occupation was farming or business were assigned to a high or low occupational status on the basis of a reasonable monthly income which was determined by the judgement of the writer.

In this manner it was discovered that 46·0 per cent. of the

Table 7

SOCIAL ORIGIN OF THE PUBLIC SERVANTS BASED ON THE OCCUPATIONS OF THE FATHERS

Fathers' occupations	Number	Per cent.
Salaried Employment		
Government service (non-gazetted)	97	22·5
Government service (gazetted)	125	28·9
Army (non-commissioned)	11	2·5
Army (commissioned)	3	0·6
Railways (manual or clerical)	13	3·1
Railways (managerial or equivalent)	8	1·9
Employment in a semi-government agency (manual or clerical)	4	0·9
Employment in a semi-government agency (managerial or equivalent)	3	0·6
Employment by a Princely State (manual or clerical)	6	1·4
Employment by a Princely State (managerial or equivalent)	8	1·9
Employment in a private firm (manual or clerical)	4	0·9
Employment in a private firm (managerial or equivalent)	5	1·2
Sub total	287	66·4
Independent Occupations		
Small land owners	37	8·6
Large land owners	28	6·3
Small businessmen	27	6·4
Big businessmen	19	4·4
Legal practitioners	14	3·2
Medical practitioners	8	1·9
Priest, Maulvi, Pir, politician	6	1·4
No response	6	1·4
Sub total	145	33·6
Total	432	100·0

OCCUPATIONAL S

| | High Occupational Status | | | | | | | |
	Government Service (gazetted)	Army (commissioned)	Railway (managerial)	Semi-government (managerial)	Princely State (managerial)	Private firm (managerial)	Land owners	Big business men
Animal Husbandry	1	—	—	—	—	—	2	—
Anti-corruption	—	—	—	—	—	—	—	—
Co-operative Societies	5	1	—	—	—	—	1	—
Electricity	16	—	1	1	1	—	2	1
Health	30	—	1	1	2	1	2	2
Irrigation	15	—	—	1	1	1	3	2
Jails	2	—	—	—	—	—	—	—
Local Fund Audit	1	—	—	—	—	—	—	—
Police	12	—	1	—	—	1	3	—
Public Relations	5	1	2	—	2	—	—	—
Secretariat	18	—	3	—	1	1	12	14
D.C.'s Officers	2	1	—	—	1	—	—	—
C.S.P. Officers	18	—	—	—	—	1	3	—
Total	125	3	8	3	8	5	28	19

THE RESPONDENTS

| | Low Occupational Status | | | | | | | | Indeterminate Occupational Status | | | |
	Army (non-commissioned)	Railway (manual or clerical)	Semi-government (clerical)	Princely State (clerical)	Private firm (clerical)	Small land owners	Small business men	Sub total	Professions	Miscellaneous	No response	Total
	1	—	2	1	—	1	1	16	—	—	—	19
	—	—	—	—	—	2	—	3	—	—	—	3
	—	—	—	—	—	1	2	6	—	—	—	13
	—	3	—	1	1	4	5	27	4	2	—	55
	2	6	—	—	1	5	2	31	—	1	2	73
	—	1	—	2	—	8	5	26	2	—	1	52
	1	—	—	—	—	2	—	4	—	—	—	6
	2	—	1	1	1	2	1	9	1	—	—	11
	1	1	1	1	—	5	3	28	—	—	1	46
	1	—	—	—	—	4	3	12	2	—	—	24
	3	2	—	—	—	1	5	32	8	2	2	93
	—	—	—	—	—	—	—	—	—	1	1	6
	—	—	—	—	1	1	—	4	4	—	1	31
	11	13	4	6	4	36	27	198	21	6	8	432

respondents' fathers occupied a low occupational status and that an equal proportion possessed a high occupational status. It was not found possible to ascertain the occupational status of the remaining 8·0 per cent. of the respondents.

In consideration of the occupational status of the respondents' fathers in different departments, as shown in Table 8, it was noted that a preponderance of the public servants in the departments of Animal Husbandry, Anti-corruption, Jails, Local Fund Audit and Police were the sons of fathers who occupied a low occupational status. Except for the Police Department, all the other departments are generally not considered to provide as attractive prospects of pay and promotion as do some other government departments. As compared to this group of departments most of the public servants in the Civil Service of Pakistan, Deputy Commissioner's Office and the Civil Secretariat were the sons of fathers who enjoyed a high occupational status.

Fathers' incomes

In one of the questions the respondents had been asked to state the monthly incomes of their fathers at the time when the respondents were fifteen years of age. A quarter of the respondents did not supply the required information. Some of them said that their fathers had died when they themselves were very young and that, therefore, they had no information as to their fathers' incomes. Some said that it was not possible for them to say precisely what was the income of their fathers.

Among the remaining 324 respondents the income of fathers was distributed as shown in Table 9.

Table 9 indicates that the monthly income of 63·6 per cent. of the respondents' fathers was below the mean. A comparison of the arithmetic mean with the two other averages given above indicates that the mean is far higher than the median and the mode.

It also indicates that a small proportion of the respondents' fathers possessed a very high income and that the average income of the majority of the respondents' fathers was far lower than the arithmetic mean.

Table 9

MONTHLY INCOMES OF THE FATHERS OF THE RESPONDENTS

Income in rupees	Number	Per cent.
Up to 50	17	4·0
51—100	30	6·9
101—200	69	16·0
201—300	53	12·2
301—450	37	8·6
451—600	30	6·9
601—800	22	5·1
801—1000	23	5·3
1001—2000	28	6·5
2001—and above	15	3·5
No response	108	25·0
Total	432	100·0

Mean: 532·5	Median: 289·1	Mode: 197·7

Fathers' Education

The educational level of the fathers of the respondents is given in Table 10 below.

Table 10

EDUCATIONAL LEVEL OF THE FATHERS OF THE RESPONDENTS

Fathers' education	Number	Per cent.
Illiterate	28	6·5
Up to middle school level	137	31·7
Up to high school level	115	26·6
Up to undergraduate level	25	5·9
Up to the level of a Bachelor's degree	61	14·1
Up to the level of a Master's or equivalent degree	60	13·9
No response	6	1·3
Total	432	100·0

It will be observed that a little less than two-thirds, or 64·1 per cent., of the fathers had not studied beyond school level. One-fifth, or 20·0 per cent., had studied up to the level of a Bachelor's degree, while only 13·9 per cent. had received education up to the level of a Master's or an equivalent degree. In the period to which the generation of the respondents' fathers belonged a Bachelor's degree was generally considered to be a high level of education. If this standard is accepted it is found that a majority of the respondents' fathers had received a relatively low level of education.

It was noted that the fathers of those respondents who belonged to a higher class had attained a relatively higher educational level. Four-fifths, or 80·0 per cent., of the unclassified officers were the sons of fathers who had not studied beyond school level. More than two-thirds of their fathers were either illiterate or barely literate. The percentage of Class II officers whose fathers had not studied beyond school level was 69·3 per cent., which is lower than that of the unclassified officers. Over one half of them were either illiterate or barely literate. The fathers of 59·5 per cent. of the public servants of Class I had not studied beyond school level. About three-fifths of them were either illiterate or barely literate.

Mothers' Education

Education for women has been generally looked upon with disfavour in this sub-continent. Its value has been recognized only recently. The figures given in Table 11 and in Table 12 which categorize the education of the mothers and the wives of the respondents substantiate this verdict.

Bearing this consideration in mind, the level of education which is described as low for the fathers of the respondents may not be considered low in the case of the mothers of the respondents. Therefore, instead of taking education up to the high school level as an indicator of low education, education up to the primary school level may be considered as low education for the mothers of the respondents. The next two categories, namely the middle and high school levels may be combined to indicate a middle level of education and the remaining categories combined may indicate a high education. On this basis, it is revealed that the mothers of 85·4 per cent. of the respondents had studied up to the primary school level which is a fairly low educational attainment. The mothers of 12·3 per cent. of the officers had received education up to the high school level and the mothers of only 1·9 per cent. of the officers had received education up to undergraduate level or above.

Table 11

THE EDUCATIONAL LEVEL OF THE MOTHERS OF THE RESPONDENTS

Mothers' education	Number	Per cent.
Illiterate	260	61·5
Literate	62	14·4
Up to primary school level	40	9·5
Up to middle school level	35	8·1
Up to high school level	18	4·2
Up to undergraduate level	3	0·7
Up to the level of a Bachelor's degree	4	0·9
Up to the level of a Master's or equivalent degree	1	0·3
No response	3	0·7
Total	432	100·0

Wives' Education

The wives of the respondents belong to a generation which is very different from that of their mothers. In recent years education for women has gained more acceptance. This tendency is indicated by the figures in Table 12.

Taking this factor into consideration, education up to high school level may be regarded as low, up to undergraduate level may be considered as middle and education up to a Bachelor's degree and above may be taken as high. In accordance with this rating the wives of about three-fourths, or 74·3 per cent., of the officers possess a low educational level, the wives of 12·9 per cent·

of the officers possess a middle level education and the wives of 13·2 per cent. of the officers have studied up to a higher level.

Comparing the educational levels of the fathers, mothers and the wives of the respondents shows that the educational level of women is lower than that of men and the educational level of mothers is lower than that of wives.

Table 12

EDUCATIONAL LEVEL OF THE WIVES OF THE RESPONDENTS

Wives' education	Number	Per cent.
Illiterate	51	14·0
Literate	43	11·8
Up to primary school level	35	9·6
Up to middle school level	66	18·1
Up to high school level	76	20·8
Up to undergraduate level	47	12·9
Up to the level of a Bachelor's degree	30	7·4
Up to the level of Master's or equivalent degree	18	5·8
Total	*365	100.0

*18 women public servants and 45 unmarried male public servants are excluded from this table.

Combining the findings about the income and education of the respondents' fathers and the education of their mothers and wives, it appears that a majority of the respondents are drawn from the lower middle classes. The rest of them originate in the upper middle and the upper classes. The proportion of public servants who may be categorized as having middle class status based upon the indicators of income and education is larger than that of the upper class public servants.

Colleges attended by the Higher Public Servants

There appears to be a common belief among the people that students of certain colleges stand better chances for selection in the higher public service. There is nothing peculiar about the

Pakistani civil service in this respect. Such correlations have been found to exist in other countries as well. As an example, we may mention the chapter on the schools and universities of high civil servants in Professor R. K. Kelsall's book, *Higher Civil Servants in Britain*, London, 1961. Professor Kelsall has classified the educational institutions according to the general public esteem and has calculated the proportion of successful candidates from each class on the basis of the last school or university attended.

In this study also the colleges attended by the respondents and the cadres of the public service were classified according to the general public esteem in which they were held. However, a public servant was considered to have belonged to a college which he had attended for the longest period and not the one which he had attended last.

The cadres which have been classified as having a high public esteem are the Civil Service of Pakistan, the Police Service of Pakistan, the Provincial Civil Service, the Health Service and the Engineering Service. The cadres with a relatively low public esteem are the Provincial Police Service, the Secretariat Service, the Co-operative Service, the Prison Service, Animal Husbandry Service and employment in the Public Relations Department. The classification of the colleges we made as follows: the colleges which have been classified as enjoying high public esteem are, Government College and Forman Christian College in Lahore, Islamia College in Peshawar, Gordon College in Rawalpindi, Aligarh University in India, St. Stephens College in Delhi, and European universities in general. The colleges which have been classified as possessing neither high nor low public esteem are Murray College in Sialkot, Edwards College in Peshawar, and D. J. Sind College in Karachi. The colleges which were supposed to be held in relatively low public esteem are M.A.O. College, Dyal Singh College and Islamia College in Lahore and other colleges in West Pakistan. The professional colleges were classified separately.

The findings seem to support the assumption that candidates from the educational institutions which enjoy a relatively high

T

COLLEGES ATTENDED BY THE PU

Colleges attended by the Respondents	Cadres with high public esteem					S t
	CSP	PSP	PCS	Health Service	Engineering Service	
Colleges with high public esteem	22	8	17	3	30	80
	71·0	61·5	65·4	4·3	33·7	34
Colleges with neither high nor low public esteem	1	—	—	1	1	3
	3·2			1·4	1·1	1
Colleges with low public esteem	1	3	4	2	11	21
	3·2	23·1	15·4	2·9	12·4	9
Professional colleges	—	—	3	57	30	90
			11·5	81·4	33·7	39
Indian or East Pakistani colleges	7	2	2	7	17	35
	22·6	15·7	7·7	10·0	19·1	15
Total	31	13	26	70	89	229
	100·0	100·0	100·0	100·0	100·0	100

ANTS IN **DIFFERENT CADRES**

lleges attended he Respondents	Cadres with low public esteem						Total
	Provincial Police Service	Secretariat Service	Animal Husbandry Service	Co-op. Societies Jail & Public Relations Depts.	Miscellaneous	Sub total	
ges with high blic esteem	6	12	4	18	4	44	124
	17·6	17·4	20·0	25·0	50·0	21·7	
ges with neither h nor low pub- esteem	1	11	—	6	—	18	21
	2·9	15·9		8·3		8·9	
ges with low blic esteem	17	40	1	35	3	96	117
	50·0	58·0	5·0	48·6	37·5	47·3	
essional colleges	3	—	14	3	—	20	110
	8·8		70·0	4·2		9·9	
un or East Pak- ani colleges	7	6	1	10	1	25	60
	20·6	8·7	5·0	13·9	12·5	12·3	
l	34	69	20	12	8	203	432
	100·0	100·0	100·0	100·0	100·0	100·0	

public esteem stand better chances of selection for the coveted cadres of public service. For example, 71·0 per cent. of the CSP officers, 61·5 per cent. of the officers in the Police Service of Pakistan and 65·4 per cent. of the officers in the Provincial Civil Service belonged to educational instituions which enjoy high public esteem. Only 3·2 per cent. of the CSP officers, 23·1 per cent. of the PSP officers and 15·4 per cent. of the PCS officers were drawn from colleges which are not highly rated.

A very small proportion of the officers in the departments which are generally rated as low were drawn from colleges of high public esteem. For example, 17·6 per cent. of the officers in the Provincial Police Service, 17·4 per cent. of the officers in the Secretariat Service and 25·0 per cent. of the officers in the Departments of Public Relations, Co-operative Societies and the Jails were drawn from colleges of a higher public esteem. Fifty per cent. of the Provincial Police Officers, 58·0 per cent. of the officers from the Departments of Public Relations, Co-operative Societies and the Jails belonged to the colleges which enjoyed a relatively lower public esteem.

Westernization of the Public Servants

The Concise Oxford Dictionary defines Westernization as making an oriental people or country Western in ideas and institutions, etc. This definition leaves out the explanation of the all important term Western. Although, in the popular mind in the East, every white man coming from any part of Europe or of the Americas represents the West, more specifically, the major source of Western influence has been the civilization of Western Europe and North America.

Rudyard Kipling's celebrated remark 'East is East and West is West and never the twain shall meet' is no longer applicable to the modern world with its growing association and assimilation of people from East and West. Kipling's remark, though exaggerated, does contain a certain amount of truth. There are many characteristics which distinguish sharply the civilization of the West from that of the East. Some of the permanent differences are to be found in religion, in race and in the general way of life. There are other features which mark the West from the East but they are temporary in nature rather than permanent. The most important feature in this category is the predominantly industrial character of the economy of the Western countries. Most of the Eastern countries are still rural and agricultural in character. This basic difference lies often at the root of many of the dissimilarities which a tourist notices in the superstructure of the customs, values and usages of the Eastern and the Western people. Since the general state of the economy of a country is liable to change with the passage of time, and since many of the Eastern countries are making intense efforts to bring about a change in their underdeveloped economies, there is every likelihood that many of the current differences between the West and the East will be eliminated. Family relations, the status of women, the role of government and other aspects of life will evolve along similar lines as they did, decades ago, in Western Europe.

The Western influence was brought to the East partly by the Western people themselves and partly by the Eastern people who personally visited the West. Most of the transmission, especially in its earliest phase, took place in the former manner. The exchange of cultural values between East and West was, however, not on an equal level. Since, in most cases, the West was represented by some imperial or colonial power, the Western influence in Eastern lands was always in a dominant position. Besides, due to the early industrialization of Western Europe, its values, representing the then most advanced stage of the evolution of human society, were superior to those of the predominantly feudal cultures of the East. As a result, the West was on the transmitting end while the East was on the receiving end.

In the sub-continent of India and Pakistan, Western institutions and ideas were introduced by the British, who not only represented the foremost colonial power, but the most highly industrialized society of the time. The character of the Indo-British relations was determined, for the most part, by the fact that the British had established their political domination over India by military conquest. For these reasons, Western values, as represented by the British, acquired the prestige and respect which is usually associated with the customs and manners of a dominant group of people. Impressed by the technological advances of the British society, a group of Indians was sincerely convinced of the superiority of the British culture over the Indian. The status-seeking Indians, however, were eager to emulate British dress, language and manners primarily to associate themselves with the ruling elite.

The process of the Westernization of the Indian people was considerably accelerated as a result of the policies adopted by the British Government in India. The outstanding example of such a policy is the prescription of English as the medium of education in India along with the introduction of the works of liberal European thinkers in the curricula of Indian schools and colleges. In a similar manner Indian standards of official and social life were determined or influenced by the standards of contemporary British society. Once British customs and manners were recognized as the yardstick of the cultural refinement of a person, Indians of substance began to adopt them assiduously. In order to be acceptable in high society one had to appear as much like an English gentleman as possible. In short, Western values, as represented by the contemporary British, became status symbols for many Indians.

The process of the Westernization of Indians was not entirely smooth. Its protagonists, especially among the Muslims, had to face great resistance. Syed Ahmad Khan, the foremost leader of the Indian Muslims in the nineteenth century, played an active role in persuading his compatriots to learn Western arts and sciences. Inspired by the age of reason through which European society was passing in the nineteenth century, he worked out new interpretations of some of the important principles of Islam.

In all fairness, it may be stated that in his admiration of Western ideas and institutions he was not unmindful of the virtues which were present in the indigenous culture of India. On the one hand, he founded the well-known Aligarh College in which the medium of instruction was English, while, on the other hand, he started an Urdu journal in the tradition of *The Spectator* and *The Tatler*[1] whose main purpose was to simplify the Urdu language.

The conservative elements were displeased with any deviation from traditional beliefs and practices. Syed Ahmad Khan's attempt to interpret the injunctions of Islam on the basis of reason rather than faith earned him the disapprobation of his fellow Muslims. The novel *Ibn Ul Waqt*, or *The Opportunist*, written by Nazir Ahmad, a senior public servant and a prominent literary figure demonstrates the general reaction of the conservative Muslims against Westernization in the nineteenth century. Khalid Bin Sayeed thinks that this novel presents a caricature of Syed Ahmad Khan. The novel characterizes a Westernized Indian Muslim who adopts the English language, English dress, English food and English ideas only to earn the displeasure of his own people and the contempt of Englishmen. The Muslims consider him to be a heathen while the Englishmen think that he is aping them. Apart from describing the overt resistance which was offered to Westernization, the novel portrays the inner conflicts to which the Indian Muslim who was inclined towards Western ideas became a prey.

This was the situation in the nineteenth century. For the following generations the adoption of Western ideas and manners was not as difficult. The resistance to Western ideas and practices had weakened, furthermore, the qualms of conscience were less disturbing for the younger generation because they received moral support from the example of their elders who had passed through the same transformation years earlier. In this period the number of Indians going to Europe for higher studies showed a significant rise; many of them returned with European wives. In this way, the younger people not only followed the example of their elders, but went a step further, making the process of Westernization complete.

This period, however, must not be considered as the high-water mark of the tide of Westernization in the sub-continent. The

---

[1] These periodicals were edited by the well-known English essayists of the early eighteenth century, Joseph Addison and Richard Steele, who were very popular for their simplicity of language and light humour.

wave of Western ideas has spread more widely after the achievement of independence. More recently, Western manners, as represented by English society, have given way to Western manners as represented by the contemporary society of the United States of America. This trend is the subject of criticism from two different and opposed sections of the Pakistani people. One section represents the orthodox, religious-minded people who sneer at any departure from the ways with which they are familiar. The other section is comprised of people who may or may not be orthodox Muslims but who are inspired primarily by a spirit of nationalism. The 'nationalists' have shown concern as to whether Westernization might not alienate further the already exclusive elite group of the educated urban class from the mass of the illiterate, rural people of Pakistan.

The implications of such a danger are serious in the case of the higher public servants in Pakistan. It is important to know how and to what extent this danger is real. In order to study the influence of Westernization upon the attitudes of the public servants a rough index was constructed to measure their 'Westernization'. The methods adopted in constructing and evaluating the index are discussed in Appendix III. At this point the simple distribution of the respondents on the Westernization index is given. The relationship of the degree of Westernization with attitudes is discussed under different headings in the chapters to follow.

Out of the total number of public servants only 39, or 9·0 per cent., were highly Westernized in their day-to-day life, 142, or 33·0 per cent., were semi-Westernized and 251, or 58·0 per cent., were not Westernized at all. These figures indicate that most of the public servants are not Westernized. In the sub-group of public servants who are Westernized most are only partly Westernized.

The degree of Westernization was much higher than average in the cases of the public servants of certain categories. For example, out of the 31 officers of the Civil Service of Pakistan 8, 25·8 per cent., were highly Westernized, 16, or 51·6 per cent., were semi-Westenized and only 7, or 22·6 per cent., could be termed not Westernized. In this characteristic, the officers of the Civil Service of Pakistan were closely followed by the officers in the Public Relations Department, Health Department and the Department of Electricity and Irrigation. Westernization was extremely low in the Departments of Local Fund Audit, Co-operative Societies and Jails. The percentages of the non-Westernized officers in these three departments were as high as 100·0, 92·3 and 83·3 respectively.

The officers of Class I were more Westernized than were the officers of Class II and the unclassified officers. Out of the 215 officers of Class I, 25, or 11·6 per cent., were highly Westernized, 89, or 41·4 per cent., were semi-Westernized and 101, or 47·0 per cent., were not Westernized. Among the 150 officers of Class II, 8, or 4·7 per cent., were highly Westernized, 38, or 26·0 per cent., were semi-Westernized and 104, or 69·8 per cent., were not Westernized. No significant variation was observed in the degree of Westernization between the officers of Class II and the unclassified officers.

Out of the 212 officers whose ages ranged from 23 to 42 years, 21, or 9·9 per cent., were highly Westernized, 82, or 38·7 per cent., were semi-Westernized and 109, or 51·4 per cent., were not Westernized. In the group of 220 officers who ranged in age from 43 to 62 years, 18, or 8·2 per cent., were highly Westernized, 60, or 27·3 per cent., were semi-Westernized and 142, or 64·5 per cent., were not Westernized at all. It appears that the younger officers are relatively more receptive to Western influences than are their older colleagues.

The remark made by the authors of *The Western-Educated Man in India*, that 'upward mobility has meant moving into social circles in which Western modes of behaviour were expected if one were to be considered respectable'[1] receives support from the fact that the public servants whose income or socio-economic status was high were also high on the Westernization index. For out of 270 officers whose total monthly income ranged from 300

[1] John Useem and Ruth Hill Useem, op. cit., p. 37.

to 1,000 rupees, 34·8 per cent. were Westernized, one-fifth of whom were highly Westernized. Among the 89 officers whose total monthly income ranged between 1,001 to 1,700 rupees, 45·0 per cent. were Westernized, one half of whom were highly Westernized. In the group of officers numbering 73, whose income varied from 1,701 to 3,000 rupees, 64·4 per cent. were Westernized, of whom one-third were highly Westernized.

Similarly, the officers of upper class status were more Westernized than those of the lower class. Table 14 shows that among the 31 officers of upper class status 87·1 per cent. were Westernized, and that one-third of this group were highly Westernized. As to the officers of low class status, only 19·1 per cent. were Westernized, of whom only one-eighth were highly Westernized.

Table 14

WESTERNIZATION COMPARED WITH THE SOCIO-ECONOMIC STATUS OF THE RESPONDENTS

Socio-economic Status	Least Westernized	Semi-Westernized	Highly Westernized	Total
Low	169 80·9	35 16·7	5 2·4	209 100·9
Lower middle	51 40·5	63 50·0	12 9·5	126 100·0
Upper middle	27 40·9	27 40·9	12 18·2	66 100·0
Upper	4 12·9	17 54·8	10 32·3	31 100·0

Westernization displayed a significant relationship with higher education. Out of 39 officers who had studied up to high school, eight, or 20·5 per cent., were Westernized. Only two of these eight officers were highly Westernized. Among the 37 officers who had spent one to two years in college, 14, or 37·8 per cent., were Westernized. Eight of these fourteen officers were highly Westernized. Among the officers who had studied up to a Bachelor's degree, 70 out of 184, or 38·0 per cent., were Westernized. Of these 70 officers, 10 were highly Westernized. In the group of officers numbering 17, who had studied up to a Master's degree, M.B.B.S., Law or a Ph.D. degree, 89, or 51·7 per cent., were Westernized. Nineteen of the 89 officers in this group were highly Westernized.

Those public servants who occupied a higher position in the chain of command were also high on the Westernization index. For example, 21 out of 34, or 61·8 per cent., of the officers of the first position were Westernized, 5 of the 21 being highly Westernized. As compared to them only 75 out of 229, or 32·7 per cent. of the officers of the last position, were highly Westernized, and a mere 14 of the 75 were highly Westernized.

Not all or even a majority of the higher public servants are Westernized. Nevertheless, those officers who occupy a higher position in the heirarchy, who are highly educated and who have a higher income generally tend to be Westernized. These three factors combined may explain why the officers of the Civil Service of Pakistan are more highly Westernized than the others. It appears that the risk of the cultural alienation of the top-ranking public servants from the ordinary people is greater than that of the low-ranking public servants.

The Socio-economic Status of the Public Servants

One of the important questions was to discover to what degree the socio-economic status of a superior officer influenced his attitude towards his subordinates. An index for the socio-economic status of the public servant was developed. The methods of constructing and evaluating the index have been described in Appendix IV. In the text the overall proportions of the respondents belonging to different socio-economic classes are given. The relationship between his status and the attitude of a public servant towards his subordinates will be discussed under that title.

The survey shows that 209, or 48·4 per cent. of the respondents, held a lower class status in society at large. The lower middle class was represented by 126, or 29·1 per cent. of the officers, the middle class by 66, or 15·3 per cent., and the upper class by only 31, or 7·1 per cent. of the officers. In other words more than three-quarters of the respondents belonged to the low and the lower middle class and a less than a quarter belonged to the upper middle and the upper class.

In the majority of the departments most of the public servants belonged to the lower and the lower middle class. The majority was as high as 100.0 per cent. in the Departments of Co-operative Societies and Local Fund Audit. It was more than three-quarters in the Departments of Animal Husbandry, Electricity, Irrigation, the Jails, Police, Public Relations, Secretariat and the Deputy Commissioner's office. A majority of the officers in the Health Department and in the Civil Service of Pakistan to the extent of 63.1 and 67.7 per cent. respectively belonged to the middle class. Among the 46 doctors who belonged to the middle class 28 belonged to the lower middle class. Among the 21 CSP officers belonging to the middle class only 9 belonged to the lower middle class. Not a single person of lower class was represented in the Civil Service of Pakistan, while about one-third of the officers in this cadre enjoyed upper class status which is by far the highest proportion as compared to any other category of public servants.

Out of the 67 unclassified officers 58, or 86.6 percent., possessed lower class status. Only one had upper middle class status while none had upper class status. In the group of 150 officers of Class II, 97, or 64.7 per cent., had lower class status. Only one officer of Class II enjoyed upper class status. Among the 215 officers belonging to Class I only 54, or 25.1 per cent., possessed lower class status, 131, or 61.0 per cent., possessed middle class status and as may as 30, or 14.0 per cent., enjoyed upper class status. It appears that socio-economic status corresponds to rank in the hierarchy.

This conclusion is supported by an examination of the status of officers occupying different positions in the chain of command. For example, out of 34 officers occupying the first position in the chain of command 12 enjoyed upper class status, 21 belonged to the middle class and only one to the lower class. Out of the 229 officers occupying the last position in the chain of command only two enjoyed upper class status, 68 belonged to the middle class and as many as 159 belonged to the lower class.

Women Public Servants

Eighteen of the public servants, or 4·2 per cent. of the sample, were women. In view of the special position which women, in general, occupy in Pakistani society, we feel that the matters relating to women public servants merit separate treatment.

Legally, Pakistani women are eligible to all types of public employment in government except in a few areas which by their nature are not suitable for women. However, in practice the percentage of women public servants is very small. In fact, the number of working women, in general, is very small. A number of reasons account for this situation. Firstly, women are by tradition not supposed to seek employment to earn a living. That is thought to be man's work. Woman's place, it is generally maintained, is in the home. Secondly, a limited number of Pakistani women are educated. This position is the direct result of the first reason. The opponents of education for women argue that women do not have to find a job for themselves, therefore, they do not need to receive education, not higher education in any case. Thirdly, there is a sharp segregation of sexes on the social plane. This factor reduces the possibilities of men and women working side by side.

Since the advent of Independence, women have made considerable gains in attaining independent status. Education for women is finding favour among more and more people. Attitudes towards the position of women in society are undergoing a change. As a result women have gained admittance to many areas which earlier were barred to them.

In public service, women have shown special interest in and aptitude for the teaching and medical professions. For example, in the sample fifteen of the eighteen women public servants were drawn from the Health Department. None of the women respondents was employed as an educator because the Department of Education did not fall in our sample. Although women have shown an aptitude equal to that of men for clerical jobs yet very few have shown equal interest in such appointments. The few who have done so are employed mainly in private enterprise. There seems to be considerable social prejudice against the employment of women in clerical jobs. Educated girls and their families do not consider it 'respectable' to work in clerical positions. An equally important reason which militates against the employment of women is that job opportunities are inadequate even for the qualified men. A man being the principal and in most cases the only wage-earner for his family receives preference in securing employment over a woman.

A little less than half of the women public servants in our sample had joined government service before Independence which indicates that the idea of public employment of women had gained acceptance far earlier. The period in which most of the women entered government service after Independence illustrates that the movement gained momentum rather recently. Out of the ten women public servants who had accepted government service after Independence, that is to say after 1947, eight had done so after 1956. Of the remaining two, one had joined the service in 1950 and the other in 1952. This indicates that during the first seven years of Pakistan's existence the inflow of women into public service was rather slow.

Geographically speaking all of the women public servants in our sample were settled in the area which formerly constituted the province of the Punjab. A little less than half of them were the original residents of the former Punjab. Most of the others had settled here after Independence on migration mainly from areas which now form part of the Indian side of the Punjab.

As might be expected, almost all of the women public servants were brought up in an urban setting. In regard to their age, one half of them belonged to a relatively high age group, that is from 38 to 47 years of age. The other half were drawn from a much younger age group, namely 23 to 37 years of age. Compared to men, women public servants are far younger.

Almost all the women were highly educated. Only one of them was an undergraduate, five had Bachelor's degrees and twelve held degrees of Bachelor of Medicine and Surgery. Two women had received advanced training in some European country.

All of the women public servants were the daughters of public servants. One third of them were the daughters of public servants who occupied a high rank in the hierarchy, another one-third were the daughters of those who occupied a middle-rank position and another one-third of them were the daughters of low-ranking public servants.

The father's income in the case of eight of the women public servants was less than 300 rupees per month, in the case of seven of them it ranged between 300 and 1,000 rupees and in the case of three it was more than 1,000 rupees.

The educational level of the women public servants' fathers varied as follows. Three had studied upto the high school level or below, five had studied upto the undergraduate level or below and ten had studied upto the graduate level or above.

The mothers of two-thirds of the women public servants had had no schooling. The mothers of the remaining one-third of them had studied between the middle and the high school level.

As the values of the above indicators of social origin were expected to have varied over a period of time it was not possible to rank them for the purpose of developing an index of socio-economic status of the women public servants' fathers. However, since it is important sociologically to know from which strata of society women are drawn into public service, it was decided to rank the four indicators mentioned above according to the judgement of the writer in order to gain a full view of the social origin of the women public servants. This ranking is arbitrary and should not be assigned any greater significance than is intended here.

A monthly income of less than 300 rupees was considered as low income, from 300 to 1,000 rupees as middle-level income, and an income above 1,000 rupees per month as high income. The educational attainment of the fathers upto the high school level or below was considered low, upto the undergraduate level and below as middle, and upto graduate level and above as high. Educational attainment of mothers upto the primary level or below was ranked as low, between the middle school and high school level as middle and upto the undergraduate level and above as high. Since the fathers of the all women public servants belonged to public service their position in the chain of command was utilized roughly to determine the occupational status.

On the basis of this ranking procedure it was revealed that nine of the women public servants scored low, six of them clustered in the middle and the remaining three of them gravitated towards the category of higher social origin. The number of women is too small to draw a significant conclusion from the ranking made above. If the numbers falling in the low and middle scores are added together then 83·3 per cent. of the women public servants in this sample came from lower and middle class families.

An examination of the occupations of the husbands of the women public servants seems to support the statement made above that middle class families contribute a larger proportion of women public servants than do upper class families. Out of the twelve married women public servants seven were married to persons who themselves were public servants. Two of the husbands held positions of high rank while the remaining five held positions of the middle rank. Two women public servants were married to business executives. The husbands of two other women public servants were engaged in independent professions, and the husband of one was running his own business.

A third factor which also indicates that in general women public servants belong to middle class families, is the high educational level of their husbands. The husbands of four women public servants held Bachelor's degrees. The remaining eight held post-graduate degrees. Four of the husbands had the opportunity to study at a European university. It appears that the concept of remunerative employment for women finds relatively easier acceptance among highly educated men. There is still a great dislike for the idea of public employment of women. Contact with Western ideas through higher education within the country or abroad tends to create an intellectual frame of mind which is capable of withstanding social disapprobation of the public employment of women.

CHAPTER 4

EMPLOYMENT OPPORTUNITIES
FOR EDUCATED PAKISTANIS

A set of questions was included in the questionnaire in order to discover what attracted educated people in Pakistan to government service. The findings confirm more or less the general impression among people that in Pakistan employment opportunities for educated persons in agencies other than those run by the government are severely limited.

To the first question in this area, 'Why did you decide to accept government service instead of some other kind of job?', the respondents offered ten different types of reasons. Many of them offered more than one reason. However, in no case did the number exceed three. Table 15 gives the gross number of frequencies of each reason offered. It may be noted that a little over one-third of the reasons are negative in nature. Among the negative reasons the most frequent was lack of employment opportunities in other fields.

Among the positive reasons for choosing government service as a career the most frequently offered consideration was that it gave a certain amount of prestige to the incumbent of an office under government. The nature of this argument may become more understandable if it is kept in mind that before Independence the tenor of government by foreigners was basically authoritarian. Association with it created an aura of authority around its agent, the civil servant, in official as well as in social life. This feeling was reinforced by the fact that opportunities for joining government service were restricted. One of the respondents stated that the eagerness to associate oneself with the government was so great that if a young man was recruited as a police constable the modest appointment was celebrated with great rejoicings. It is significant to note that this consideration in preferring government service over other occupations was relatively more frequently offered by the officers serving in the Civil Service of Pakistan.

The other positive reason which was more often responsible for choosing government service was the security of tenure guaranteed in government service. The third important reason was the prospect of receiving a pension on retirement. These two arguments, in a certain measure and indirectly, reflect upon the conditions of service in private enterprises which do not appear to guarantee security of tenure to the same degree as does the government. In a large majority of private enterprises no pensions are provided.

Family tradition was given by 14·6 per cent. of the respondents as the reason for joining public service. Since this reason cannot be classified as negative or positive it has been listed separately. It demonstrates an interesting sociological phenomenon, namely the extent to which a tendency exists to follow the occupation of one's father. This tendency is, however, notable in a broad sense only, for instance, the son follows the father's example in accepting salaried employment with the government but does not necessarily enter the particular profession of his father such as engineering or medicine. The percentage of public servants whose athers were also public servants is very high, but the percentage of government doctors whose fathers were also doctors or the percentage of engineers whose fathers were also engineers is statistically insignificant.

Adopting government service as a family tradition has another significance which has its roots in the history of the sub-continent. The British Government in India attached great importance to the applicant's family connexions with government servants while making recruitment. Such connexions were supposed to indicate the loyalty of the candidate and his family to the government. Government service had, as a consequence, become a symbol of distinction and prestige, so much so that some people prided themselves in belonging to a family of government servants.

Sometimes the nationalists alleged that the British policy of recruitment of Indians into the public services was influenced by the consideration of creating a class of conservative loyalists who could be utilized as a stabilizing element for the empire. Traces of evidence are found, here and there, which support the above assertion. For instance, Sir Bampfylde Fuller listed 'the Indian staff of our public services' with other conservative elements, such as the Indian Princes, that were disposed actively to assist the British in sustaining their hold on the country. He wrote: 'it is difficult to over-rate the influence of our public services if they remain confident in their loyalty. They include thousands of employees whose relationships ramify throughout every class in the population. They are proud of their position. To an oriental enrolled in a club, a service or a regiment, *esprit de corps* is a sentiment possessing the strength of a patriotic, even a religious fervour. When supported by the government, they exhibit, as a rule, courageous independence of the feelings that may be agitating the country around them, and, in spite of every kind of social pressure, will manfully enforce the law against their countrymen and caste fellows.'[1]

The frequency of the negative reasons was relatively higher in the Departments of Animal Husbandry, Co-operative Societies, Police and Public Relations. The frequency of negative and positive reasons was more or less equal in the Departments of

[1] Sir Bampfylde Fuller, *Studies of Indian Life and Sentiment*, London, 1910.

Electricity, Health, Irrigation, Jails and in the Civil Secretariat.
The considerations offered by the respondents in the Civil Service
of Pakistan, by those in the Deputy Commissioner's Office and
in the Local Audit Department showed a far higher frequency of

Table 15

REASONS OFFERED BY THE RESPONDENTS
FOR JOINING GOVERNMENT SERVICE

Reasons	Frequency
No alternative employment was available	189
Due to economic depression in the 20's	22
Just by chance or did not think much	20
No possibility of employment for a particular profession in a non-government enterprise	10
Temperamentally not inclined towards private practice	9
Sub-total	250
For prestige and status or for power to influence the lives of many	133
For the security of tenure	128
For the benefit of pension	49
Miscellaneous	19
Government service provides better opportunities for national service	10
Sub-total	339
Government service is a family tradition	101
Total	690

positive reasons. One explanation for this pattern of responses
may be that the relative glamour attached to the first group of
cadres, with the exception of the Police Service, is generally
supposed to be low, the glamour attached to the second group
of cadres, excepting the Jails Department, is generally believed

to be higher and the public esteem associated with the third set of cadres, with the exception of the Department of Local Fund Audit, is supposed to be still higher. In other words the responses very roughly indicate that the higher the rating of a cadre the higher is the frequency of positive reasons for joining it.

In order to find out what range of choice in alternative occupations was available to the respondents they were asked to state what other occupation they would have taken up if they had not been able to enter government service. About a quarter of the respondents stated that no alternative choice had been available. If to this category of public servants may be added those who offered service in the army or teaching as their second choice, which occupations are mainly under the control of the government, the percentage of respondents who had no alternative but to seek employment in one agency of the government or another rises to 37·2 per cent. Further, if to this group of officers may be added the 15·5 per cent. of those public servants who would have to seek employment in some private concern if they had failed to join government service, it is discovered that 52·7 per cent. of the respondents had no opportunities of entering an independent profession or business. In most cases these public servants did not possess the necessary educational qualifications to start an independent profession such as medicine or law nor did they have the required resources to undertake independent business. They had no choice but to serve as salaried, professional servants of the State or of some private concern. A survey of the occupational status of the alumni of Delhi University showed similar trends. It was reported in this study that figures supported the thesis 'that university education is primarily regarded as a passport to salaried employment'.[1]

The proportion of the public servants who would have taken up a business career as an alternative means of livelihood was 12·0 per cent. of the total, of those who would have taken up legal practice 11·8 per cent. and of those adopting agriculture

[1] V.K.R.V. Rao, *University Education and Employment, A Case Study of Delhi Graduates*, New Delhi, 1961, p. 9.

as an occupation 11·1 per cent. Private practice in medicine accounted for 9·9 per cent., journalism for 0·9 per cent. and politics for 0·4 per cent. of the officers.

A study of the occupations of the brothers of our respondents reveals that 79·3 per cent. of the brothers were engaged in a salaried employment. Only 8·9 per cent. of them were employed in some non-governmental enterprise. The rest were working in some government department or in a semi-government agency.

Table 16 gives the occupations of the 730 brothers of 342 respondents. In ninety cases the respondents had no brother or no brother was employed as yet. The order of brothers as first, second, third in the Table is not based on the order of primogeniture but on an arithmetical order devised for convenience.

It is significant that 61·6 per cent. of the brothers of the public servants are public servants. It has been noted earlier that a majority of the respondents were the sons or daughters of public servants. It will be remembered that in case of failure to join public service, more than one-half of the respondents would have taken up a salaried job and that more than half of these would have preferred a government job. This evidence reinforces the opinion generally held that job opportunities for educated persons in agencies other than government are extremely limited.

It appears that salaried employment was the primary objective of most of the young men. In this regard government service largely monopolized the market. Not being so well developed, private industry and commerce, which were still in the early stages of development, offered few opportunities for employment. The professions, agriculture or business figured in the calculations of a young man only when he had exhausted all opportunities of finding salaried employment.

An analysis of the responses of the public servants from different departments reveals that about a third of the officers in the Departments of Animal Husbandry, Local Fund Audit and Police stated that they had no alternative but to join government service in one form or another. Nearly a quarter of the officers in the Departments of Electricity, Health, Irrigation and in the

Table 16

OCCUPATIONS OF THE BROTHERS OF THE RESPONDENTS

Occupation of brother	First	Second	Third	Fourth	Fifth	Sixth	Total
No brother or none is employed	90						90
Government service	243	119	59	22	4	3	450
Service of a semi-governmental or local body	30	18	11	9	2	—	70
Service of a Princely State	3	2	1	1	—	—	7
Employed in a foreign private firm	5	7	6	2	3	—	23
Employed in a local private firm	12	10	3	3	—	1	29
Agriculture	12	13	8	6	3	6	48
Business	17	22	17	8	6	2	72
Independent profession	13	3	5	4	3	—	28
Miscellaneous	1	1	1	—	—	—	3
Total							730

Civil Secretariat made a similar statement. The proportion of officers in the Jails Department who gave the same response was 50·0 per cent. while in the Civil Service of Pakistan it was only 9·7 per cent.

As to the choice of alternative occupations, engineers who were respondents in the Electricity and in the Irrigation Departments showed a relatively greater inclination for employment in a private concern. This is indicative of the growing demand for technical personnel in view of the increasing industrialization in Pakistan. Another reason for this tendency among the technical specialists may be, as noted by *The Second Five Year Plan*, that 'status and salaries offered by the government to the technicians is well below their market value'.[1] The major second choices of the CSP officers were teaching or legal practice. This choice reflects the fact that a majority of the CSP officers were graduates in liberal arts. The doctors in most cases, quite naturally, relied on the possibility of starting private practice in medicine. A significant percentage of public servants employed in the Departments of Co-operative Societies, Police and the Secretariat showed inclinations towards business and agriculture as an alternative source of livelihood.

It was observed, as may be seen in Table 17, that the second choice of occupation was, to a considerable extent, determined by the educational qualifications of the respondents. For example, the public servants with a relatively lower educational level exhibited a greater helplessness in offering themselves for a job other than government service. They showed a greater inclination to turn to agriculture or business. Service in some private concern as an alternative finished only as a poor third among the runners-up. A disinclination to accept salaried employment of any kind as an alternative on the part of public servants with lower educational qualification who also occupied a lower position in the hierarchy, seems to be the result of their supposedly unpleasant experiences as subordinates. They had apprehensions that a

[1] Government of Pakistan, Planning Commission, *The Second Five Year Plan*, *(1960-65)*, Karachi, 1960, p. 115.

Table 17
CHOICE OF SECOND OCCUPATION COMPARED WITH THE EDUCATIONAL LEVEL OF THE RESPONDENTS

Education	Cannot think of any	Teaching	Army	Business	Legal practice	Medicine	Agriculture	Service in some private concern	Journalism	Politics	Total
Under-graduates and below	30	—	1	16	—	—	17	10	1	1	76
	39·5%	—	1·3%	21·1%	—	—	22·4%	13·2%	1·3%	1·3%	100·0%
Graduates and above	85	41	4	40	51	43	31	57	3	1	356
	23·9%	11·5%	1·1%	11·2%	14·3%	12·1%	8·7%	16·0%	0·8%	0·3%	100·0%

similarly unpleasant lot would fall to their share even if they accepted employment in some non-governmental enterprise. They inferred that almost any salaried employment, especially as a subordinate, was a bad bargain. They preferred business or agriculture because these occupations guaranteed freedom from being subordinate to any superior. On the other hand the relatively highly educated public servants showed greater resourcefulness in finding an alternative job. Moreover, these officers showed a greater inclination towards independent professions or service in some private concern than towards agriculture or business.

In order to find out how our respondents compared government service with service in a private enterprise a few more questions were put to them. The first question sought to determine the opinion of the public servant about government service as an occupation. The question was put in the following form. 'If you had to recommend to somebody, for example, to your own children, one of the following services, what would be your preference? (a) government service, (b) service in a local private concern, (c) service in a foreign private concern, (d) service in a private concern no matter whether local or foreign.'

The public servants were then asked to give their preference for one of the four employments at the time when they were first seeking employment. The question was designed as an indicator of a state of mind in which a government servant might be imagined to say, 'if I were to be allowed to make a fresh start, I would choose an occupation other than government service.' In other words, this question was aimed at determining the respondents's evaluation of his own decision to join government service in the light of his actual experience in the government service.

The third and the final question in this series was asked to discover what would be the preference of the respondent if he were to choose from among the four alternative occupations at the present time when he had already seen much of government service. The object of the question was to find any public servants who were so dissatisfied with government service as to be willing to change their occupations at this late stage in their careers. Each of these three questions was followed by a supplementary question which asked the respondent to give reasons for his opinion.

Table 18 shows that government service continues to command high preference in all periods. Service in a foreign private concern follows as the second choice. Independent professions and business stand third. It is extremely significant that service in a local private concern emerges as the least attractive choice.

The reasons given for the preference of government service are negative in nature. In most cases the negative reason is that alternative opportunities for jobs are few and far between. This reason is especially more frequently offered in response to the second question by those who had joined government service in the pre-Independence period. In the case of the third question a recurring additional negative consideration for continuing in government service is that 'it is too late to change now'. Most of the respondents are senior public servants who have put in long years of service, have earned many increments in salary and are expecting either promotion or retirement on pension. It is understandable that they are unwilling to leave government service for other employment. However, for the same reason, it is notable that a significant proportion, namely 21·2 per cent. of the officers, are prepared to leave government service, even at this stage, for alternative occupations which they hope will be better than government service. It was discovered that a higher incidence of the desire to leave government service was significantly correlated to a lower income.

On examining Table 18 it will be seen that, starting from the period when the respondents first joined government service to the time of interview when they are calculating the prospects of employment for their children, there is a gradual decline in the higher preference for government service. For example, 88·9 per cent. of the respondents say that their decision made in the past to accept government service was right under the circumstances.

At the time of the interview 78·8 per cent. said that they would continue in government service even if they had the opportunity to take up other occupations. A far smaller proportion, namely 53·3 per cent., recommended government service for their children.

The corresponding percentages for prefering employment in some private concern progress exactly in the reverse direction. Only 9·3 per cent. of the officers would have accepted employment in a private concern in the past, while 18·5 per cent. are willing to consider this as an alternative to government service for themselves even after they have actually been employed as public servants for some time and 38·0 per cent. recommend it as an occupation for their children.

The explanation for this trend is that in the past, private industry and commerce had been established in the sub-continent on a very limited scale. Government possessed the monopoly of the employment market. Most of the people joined government service simply because there was no alternative. After Independence, private industry and commerce have been developed on an enlarged scale. This has created new openings for the mass of job-seeking, educated, young men. In many cases, too, private enterprises offer better remuneration and relatively greater freedom. Human relations between the employer and the employee are reputed to be less impersonal than those in the government departments. The private concerns which are run by foreign managements enjoy the reputation of taking special interest in providing for the conditions of service described above.

As a result educated young men are showing a greater inclination to seek employment in private concerns particularly in those organizations which are owned or run by foreign entrepreneurs. This is indicated by the reasons offered by those respondents who gave preference to employment in a foreign private concern. The major reasons offered were that private firms pay good salaries, recognize the achievements of their employees, provide greater freedom in which to work, encourage easy, personal relations among the staff and always pay for overtime work.

Apart from the negative reason, namely that there is no alter-

Table 18

PREFERENCE OF OCCUPATIONS AT DIFFERENT PERIODS

	Government service	%	Service in a foreign private concern	%	Service in a private concern local or foreign	%	Service in a local private concern	%	Independent profession, business, etc.	%
Preference at time of seeking first employment	384	88·9	27	6·3	12	2·7	1	0·3	8	1·8
Preference at the time of interview	340	78·8	64	14·8	15	3·3	2	0·4	11	2·4
Preference for children at time of interview	230	53·3	128	29·6	31	7·2	5	1·2	38	8·7

native for an educated person but to join government service, there are some powerful positive reasons which are responsible for the sustained inflow of the educated classes into government service. These are the benefits of pension on retirement, a guaranteed security of tenure and the prospects of promotion to positions of higher responsibility which are not available in private enterprise to the same extent. For these reasons government service continues to be the most popular employment. Another important consideration which influenced the decision of the respondents for choosing government service was that government service conferred upon the incumbent a special status in society. A few were attracted to it for the reason that government service demanded less hard work than private enterprise, or private practice in a profession.

If it is assumed that the occupational preferences given by our respondents for their children were influenced by their own experiences in government service, the frequency of responses in favour of or against government service should indicate satisfaction or dissatisfaction with government service. On this basis it has already been pointed out that the frequency of response in favour of government service shows a downward trend as we proceed from the pre-Independence period to modern times. This may be interpreted to mean that the popularity of government service is on the decline.

A comparison of the responses of the respondents from different departments shows that certain categories of public servants are more satisfied with public service as a career than the others. A very small number, 15.8 per cent. of public servants in the Department of Animal Husbandry, recommended government service for their children or for other young men related to them. On the other hand as many as 78.1 per cent. of the officers in the Health Department and 61.3 per cent. in the Civil Service of Pakistan said that they would advise their children to join government service. It may be concluded that officers of the first category are the least satisfied and those of the latter categories are more satisfied with government service.

In most of the other departments the choice was divided by half for or against government service. In general these findings are supported by the occupational preferences offered by the respondents for themselves at the time of interview when they had already put in many years of service in one government department or another. The percentage of officers who would prefer to continue in government service is 47·4 in the Department of Animal Husbandry, 46·2 in the Co-operative Societies, 100·0 per cent. in the Civil Service of Pakistan and 91·3 per cent. in the Police Department. An explanation for this pattern of the responses appears to be that conditions of service, such as the rate of salary and increments, prospects of promotion and the possession of authority are far greater for the latter than for the former categories of public servants.

On comparing the occupational preferences in different periods with the age and class of the respondents the following trends were discovered. Older officers and officers belonging to Class I showed a greater satisfaction in regard to their decision to join government service. Probably the older officers were satisfied with their decision because in the pre-Independence period government service was almost the only source of employment and also because it carried a certain amount of distinction. The Class I officers might derive satisfaction from the fact that in government service they had been able to obtain a progressive rise in the hierarchy including an increased rate of remuneration which usually accompanies the Class I status.

Similarly, more officers among the older age groups and in the category of Class I gave a response in favour of continuing in government service than did the relatively younger and the combined group of Class II and the unclassified officers. This trend may be interpreted to signify that the older and Class I officers are less inclined to risk a change in occupation.

The variations in the choice of occupation for their children in the case of older and younger officers are just the reverse of their occupational preferences in other periods. Relatively fewer officers in the older age-group representing 48·6 per cent. recom-

Table 19

PREFERENCE OF OCCUPATIONS BY THE RESPONDENTS FROM
DIFFERENT DEPARTMENTS FOR THEIR CHILDREN

Department	Govt. service	Employment in a foreign private concern	Employment in any private concern local or foreign	Employment in a local private concern	Independent profession, business, etc.	Total
Animal Husbandry	3 15·8	10 52·6	3 15·8	—	3 15·8	19 100·0
Anti-Corruption	2 66·6	—	—	—	1 33·3	3 100·0
Co-operative Societies	6 46·2	7 53·8				13 100·0
Electricity	28 50·9	19 34·5	5 9·1	1 1·8	2 3·6	55 100·0
Health	57 78·1	11 15·1	3 4·1		2 2·7	73 100·0
Irrigation	21 40·4	25 48·1	3 5·8	—	3 5·8	52 100·0
Jails	3 50·0	2 33·3	1 16·7			6 100·0
Local Fund Audit	5 45·5	4 36·4	2 18·2	—	—	11 100·0
Police	22 47·8	16 34·8	2 4·3	1 2·2	5 10·8	46 100·0
Public Relations	12 50·0	6 25·0	3 12·5	2 8·3	1 4·2	24 100·0
Civil Secretariat	50 53·8	19 20·4	9 9·7	1 1·1	14 15·1	93 100·0
D. C.'s Office	2 33·3	3 50·0	—		1 16·7	6 100·0
CSP Officers	19 61·3	6 19·4	—	—	6 19·4	31 100·0
Total:	230 53·3	128 29·6	31 7·2	5 1·2	38 8·7	432 100·0

mended government service for their children than did younger officers, 58·0 percent. of whom recommended government service for their children or near relatives. This phenomenon may be interpreted to mean that officers with a longer period of service are more inclined to be disillusioned with government service as compared to those whose tenure has not been long.

However, frequencies of preferences in favour of government service among the officers of different classes do not follow the pattern described above. A slightly larger proportion of officers, namely 54·8 per cent., of the Class II and the unclassified categories, recommended government service for their children, while 51·6 per cent. of those belonging to the Class I category advocated government employment for their children.

On separating the Class II and the unclassified officers it was disclosed that the latter were less inclined to recommend government service for their children. The percentage of such responses was the highest in the Class II officers. As a consequence, it is not possible to establish a broad generalization to the effect that the higher the class of public servants the higher is the satisfaction in government service.

Summary

Government service is one of the very few sources of employment available to the educated Pakistani. Apart from this consideration the other major reasons which are responsible for the inflow of educated young men to this career are the guarantee of security of tenure, the benefits of pension on retirement, the prospects of promotion and the possession of authority. The conditions which public servants generally miss in government service are a generous scale of pay, greater recognition of merit and of good performance in the form of quick promotion or salary increments, payment for overtime work, better human relations between the superior and the subordinate and more independence. The public servants are becoming more conscious of the value of these benefits from the experience of the employees of the private concerns, especially those which are under foreign management. The private firms which have sprung up as a result of growing industrialization in the country have been able to create a special attraction for employment with them by providing the more favourable conditions of service mentioned above. *The Second Five Year Plan* also took special note of 'the competing attraction of more remunerative business careers'.[1] However, as private industry is still operating on a small scale, opportunities for employment continue to be restricted. In addition, there is a common feeling reflected by some of the respondents that entry into private employment is governed by patronage. This may act as a damping factor upon the aspirations of prospective candidates. Private enterprise, although it has provided an alternative opening for employment for educated people, is not yet a serious competitor to the government in the employment market.

---

[1] Government of Pakistan, Planning Commission, *The Second Five Year Plan*, *(1960-65)*, 1960, p. 116.

ATTITUDES OF THE CIVIL SERVANT
TOWARDS THE PUBLIC

Attitude towards the Public Representative as a Partner

Bureaucracy is often accused of authoritarianism. A tendency of
this type may exist on two disinct planes, firstly, on the personal
level as manifested by the attitude of the public servant towards
the ordinary citizen, and secondly in the area of authority indicated by a desire, sometimes hidden, sometimes open, and in
extreme cases supported by a definite claim, that the civil service
should not only act as the executor of policies but also as the
legislator. A governmental framework which combines the legislative and the executive functions in a single authority may have
an appeal for the tidy-minded on the basis of the academic argument that it will ensure greater efficiency and speed. The civil
servant, however, may be interested in such a scheme because
it will lead to an extension in his powers. This part of the chapter
mainly deals with the second aspect of authoritarianism. The
object is to find the reaction of the public servant towards the role
of the public representative as his senior partner in government.

Pakistan started her independent political career under the British style of parliamentary government. A distinctive feature of parliamentary government is that the civil servant is expressly prohibited from exercising legislative powers, especially in the area of determining basic national policies. This is considered to be the province of the public representative. In view of the instability which, for the most part, chequered Pakistan's political existence, a feeling developed in Pakistan that the public representatives or, as they are generally called, the politicians, could not be trusted to govern the country. In the short history of Pakistan there were several occasions when constitutional government was suspended. These constitutional break-downs saw the disappearance of the politican from the national scene and the transfer of the substance of power to the public servants.

This situation gives rise to a complex question. Is the civil servant an unwilling beneficiary of the change in the balance of power or is he animated by a conscious desire to create a situation in which he may possess more power?

In seeking an answer to this question the public servants were asked to indicate with which of the following three alternatives they agreed:

(a) The people in Pakistan *are* qualified to run a democratic form of government. Therefore the task of policy-making must be undertaken by the elected representatives of the people and the public servants should confine themselves to the implementation of the policies.

(b) The people in Pakistan are *not yet* ready for a democratic form of government. Therefore, until they are ready for it, they should leave both the task of policy-making and of administration in the hands of the public servants.

(c) The people in Pakistan are *not* qualified, and never will be to run a democratic form of government. Therefore, they should leave the task of policy-making and administration in the hands of the public servants.

The responses to this question were as follows. About one-fifth, or 19.9 per cent., of the public servants said that the people were qualified and ready to run a democratic form of government, while 34.8 per cent. of the public servants said that the people needed more sustained experience and maturity before they would be ready to operate democratic self-government. The percentage of the officers expressing the view that the people were not yet ready and, therefore, that the public servants should meanwhile look after the government was 33·6. Respondents to the extent of 5·2 per cent. of the sample were of the opinion that the people were not ready, nor would they ever be, to practice self-government, 5·5 per cent. of the public servants were reluctant to make any comment on such a 'sensitive' subject and 0·7 per cent. of the public servants were unable to say anything as they had apparently failed to grasp the meaning of the question.

If the percentage of those officers who think that the people are ready for self-government and of those who think that they will be ready in due course, are combined it is revealed that that 88·6 per cent. of the respondents are committed intellectually to a democratic, representative form of government. Only 5·2 per cent. of the officers deemed that some sort of authoritarian system of government would be necessary.

A large majority, or 77·5 per cent., of those public servants who believed in a democratic form of government for Pakistan gave a qualified answer that although it was better to have a representative government the people were not yet fully prepared for it. About half of these officers proposed that the civil servant should be relied upon to train the average citizen for self-government. The other half expressed emphatic scepticism and suspicion of such a scheme. They would prefer a system more or less akin to the Basic Democracies for the interim period. In their view the system of Basic Democracies had the advantages that it did not grant absolute discretion to the civil servant but that it provided a compromise mechanism which might act as a check to bureaucratic excesses. This arrangement retains the public representatives as advisors to officials and does not completely do away with them.

The number of officers who were in favour of increasing the powers of the civil servant was not very high. However, the number of such officers is not without significance. It is notable that

5·2 per cent. of the total are emphatically in favour of an authoritarian system of government and 33·6 per cent. of the total are in its favour for an interim period.

Summing up, it may be said that most of the public servants are committed to the ideal of representative government. They accept the position that overall planning and the formulation of policy is the task of the public representatives and that their primary task is to carry the policies into execution. However, a majority of 68·4 per cent. holds the view that before full authority is handed over to the public representatives the public and their representatives need to be trained in the art of self-government. Irrespective of whether this training process is presided over by the civil servant or by the civil servant and a few selected non-officials, it is common to both the proposed arrangements that the people of Pakistan need a period of schooling in self-government. Some people might like to describe this attitude as authoritarian but perhaps it would be fairer to call it paternalistic.

A majority of the officers in most of the departments were of the view that the people needed more experience to become fully qualified for self-government. The number of such officers was relatively lower in the Departments of Health and Public Relations. Relatively higher proportions of officers in these Departments to the extent of 27·4 and 37·5 per cent. respectively felt that the people were already qualified and ready for self-government.

The officers who were in agreement with the view that the people lacked sufficient experience in self-government were present in a relatively greater proportion among those who belonged to a higher class and a higher position in the hierarchy. Highly educated officers and those of a low educational level were almost evenly divided on this point. Relatively more of the younger officers than the older ones were in agreement with the view that the people of Pakistan as yet lacked sufficient experience in self-government.

Briefly, among the proposals for an alternative to representative government during an interim period, the variations in opinion were as follows. Relatively more officers of a lower class,

Table 20

ATTITUDE OF THE PUBLIC SERVANTS OF DIFFERENT CLASSES, AGES, EDUCATIONAL BACKGROUNDS AND OFFICIAL STATUS TOWARDS A REPRESENTATIVE FORM OF GOVERNMENT

Independent variable		They are ready	They will be ready in due course but in the interim period		They are not ready	Declined to give any answer	Cannot say	Total
			the public servant should not be given the sole authority	the public servant should be given the sole authority				
CLASS	Class I	18·6	42·7	29·8	4·2	4·7	—	215
	Class II and unclassified	21·2	26·7	37·8	6·5	6·5	1·4	217
AGE	Older	22·3	30·0	33·6	7·3	5·5	0·9	220
	Younger	17·5	39·4	34·0	3·3	5·7	0·5	212
EDUCATION	Higher	19·3	35·6	33·1	5·9	5·1	0·8	356
	Lower	22·4	30·2	36·8	2·6	7·9	—	76
POSITION IN CHAIN OF COMMAND	Higher	21·2	40·9	27·3	5·3	4·5	0·8	132
	Lower	19·3	32·0	36·7	5·3	6·0	0·7	300

of a lower educational level, of a lower position in the hierarchy and of a relatively older age were in favour of allowing the public servant to act as the care-taker. On the other hand, more officers of a higher class, of a higher education, of a higher position in hierarchy but of a relatively younger age were hesitant in handing over the entire responsibility to the sole care of the public servant. These officers qualified their statements by saying that during the interim period the public servant should not replace the self-governing institutions but he should educate the people in conducting these institutions in a better manner. The upshot of the matter is that more officers of the first type appear to be authoritarian in the sense that more of them are eager to accept a more powerful role for the public servant. The officers of the second type are less authoritarian. They do not advocate government by the civil servants but government by the civil servants in close association with the people as advisers. The officers of the second type may be described as non-authoritarian paternalists.

Ordinarily, the officers who belong to a higher class and to a higher position in the hierarchy should be expected to be more eager to accept more powers for the public servant. Analysis of the data shows that this is not quite the case. The reason may be that the top executives in Pakistan are also among the highly educated persons in the country. The contact with Western thought through education or through personal visits to the Western seats of learning seems to impart a certain amount of liberalism. In this respect the position of the senior public servant in Pakistan appears to be comparable to that of the Western-educated intellectual who tends to be averse to arbitrary power. This may explain his qualified acceptance of an enlarged role for the public servant. It is worthy of note that the modified arrangement he prefers retains the public servant as the *primus inter pares* and associates the public representatives with him as his advisers only. This feature reflects his limitations as a civil servant in the sense that the solution he offers for the country's leadership problems is administrative and not political in nature.

The claim made, in the above comments, that Westernization

Table 21

ATTITUDE OF THE PUBLIC SERVANTS TOWARDS REPRESENTATIVE GOVERNMENT COMPARED WITH
THE DEGREE OF THEIR WESTERNIZATION

Degree of Westernization	The people are ready for self-government	In the interim period the public servant should not be given the sole authority	In the interim period the public servant should be given the sole authority	The people are not ready for self-government nor will they ever be	Declined to answer	Cannot say
Least Westernized	45 17·9	86 34·2	91 36·3	17 6·8	10 4·0	2 0·8
Semi-Westernized	33 23·2	51 36·0	42 29·6	6 4·2	9 6·3	1 0·7
Highly Westernized	8 20·5	13 33·3	13 33·3	—	5 12·8	—

tends to produce a somewhat liberal outlook is not upheld clearly by Table 21, although the figures in the table do indicate fully a similar tendency.

Relatively more officers among the semi-Westernized and the highly Westernized were of the opinion that the people were already prepared for self-government. A relatively smaller number of officers among the semi-Westernized and the highly Westernized recommended greater authority for the public servant during the interim period. Furthermore, none of the highly Westernized officers expressed the opinion that democracy did not suit the genius of the people of Pakistan.

Attitude towards the Use of Force

Pakistan is engaged in a large-scale effort directed at national development. The main objectives of this effort are to improve the material well-being of the people and to reduce the influence of customs, practices, and beliefs which are not forward-looking. The major part of this effort has fallen to the share of the government so that the public servant has become deeply involved in development work. As is but natural, this national enterprise also demands large-scale participation by the citizens themselves. In the context of this situation it is necessary to determine what should be the relationship between the public servant and the private citizen.

Two major concepts have evolved on this issue. The first concept postulates that due to the paucity of public initiative, the government official should assume leadership and carry the people along with him in the direction which he thinks is best for them. In this enterprise, if necessary the official may even use force, pressure or actual physical compulsion in order to achieve his objective. The protagonists of this concept, in claiming to derive support from the moral purpose of their objective, seem to be favourably inclined towards subordinating the means to the ends. The second concept relies mainly upon persuasion. It is opposed to the use of coercive measures in introducing new values and practices in society, not so much because coercion is opposed to the principles of human dignity, but for the more practical reason that force is not an effective instrument for such a purpose.

The concept of the first type is commonly associated with the extremely authoritarian attitude of some officials while the concept of the second type is usually found in those with a benevolent paternalistic attitude towards the people. There is a common element in both concepts, namely a lack of faith in the ordinary citizen's capacity for self-government. Inherent in both concepts is the claim that the government knows better than the people as to what is good for them. The basic difference between the two lies in the methods suggested in order to obtain the participation of the people in the work undertaken by the government. Whereas those who accept the first concept advocate authoritarian methods and even tolerate tyrannical devices, the adherents to the second concept prefer persuasive techniques. In spirit the concept of the first type resembles dictatorial government. The concept of the second type bears a close resemblance to the *mai baap* or father and mother image of a public servant as glorified by the British colonial government in India.

In the Pakistani social setting a government official quite often finds himself face to face with a situation in which he has to make a choice between these two concepts. As an illustration, an incident reported by a public servant, is reproduced below:[1]

I know a worker (of the Village-Aid Department) who was trying to gain acceptance among people and to give the people, the assurance that what they felt was important. Unfortunately one of the highest dignitaries of the land expressed his intention to tour the area. The district officer told the worker. 'I can't wait for your philosophy to materialize. I want *pohli*[2] to be destroyed before the visit begins.' *Pohli* was destroyed with the help of the Police, the Revenue and the Village Aid staff who made use more of coercion than persuasion. The task of making the people realize that the responsibility for development was their own received a setback. Also there was left behind a legacy of considerable resentment towards the government officials. In due course *pohli* reappeared.

Many more examples of this nature can be given. A similar

[1] Nasim Mahmud, 'The Officer Today', a Paper published in *Seminar on the Expanding Role of the Public Servant in Pakistan's Democratic Structure*, Lahore, 1960, pp. 21-2.

[2] *Pohli* is a parasitic weed.

incident was related to the respondents who were then asked to give their opinions. The hypothetical situation involved a public servant who was entrusted with the task of diverting the course of an inundated *nullah*[1] in order to protect a number of villages from floods. He was authorized to obtain voluntary manual labour from the villagers for the completion of the project. The public servant, having failed to enlist the co-operation of the villagers, used physical force, through the police, to compel them to work on the project. The project was completed. After this situation was presented to the respondents they were asked to indicate whether, in their opinion, the use of force had been justified or not and to give reasons in support of their opinions.

The respondents were almost evenly divided on this point. To be exact, 50·9 per cent. of the total stated that the use of force was justified, 46·9 per cent. said that it was not justified, 1·9 per cent. were undecided and 0·3 per cent. declined to make a statement. Most of those who considered the use of force to be justified offered the reason that the people lacked civic sense and public spirit. In such circumstances, their argument proceeded, the co-operation of the villagers, even if obtained by compulsion, was for the good of the villagers themselves. Those opposed to the use of force offered ten different types of reasons. The most frequently advanced reason was that persuasive methods were better than coercive ones. Use of force, it was feared, created hatred and resentment towards the government. As a result the people would not extend their willing co-operation and the task performed by them would not be satisfactorily done nor would it be of lasting value. As may be seen in Table 22, a relatively small proportion of the respondents disapproved of the use of force on the ground that it was opposed to the principles of human dignity. Quite a few condemned the use of force on the ground that it would discourage the habit of self-help among the people.

One of the arguments advanced against the use of force deserves a slightly more detailed presentation. Not very many of the res-

[1] *Nullah* is an anglicized version of an Urdu word which means a water course, a small branch of a canal used for irrigation purposes.

pondents offered this argument, yet it appears to be based upon a better insight into the social forces which ordinarily discourage self-help among the people. It was said that whenever the government invited the people to volunteer services in some project the practice was to pay them for their services. In this case, the nature of service offered ceased to be voluntary. It was hardly distinguishable from hired labour with the added disadvantage that the volunteers were only untrained workers who lacked the skill of professional labourers. In view of these considerations it was better to use hired labour than rely upon volunteers. It was held that it was not advisable, in any case, to undertake large projects on the basis of voluntary service.

The difficulty with non-paid voluntary service was that not many volunteers were forthcoming. It was maintained that a majority of the villagers were persons of limited means. Most of them had either to attend to their own work in the fields or, in the case of agricultural labourers, they had to earn a daily wage to make both ends meet. In view of these facts a majority of the village population was not in a position to offer voluntary service. Probably their lack of resources in terms of time and money outweighed their spirit of voluntary service.

It was also contended that in the past, especially before Independence, many government officials had behaved in such a manner that they lost the confidence of the people. For example, in certain cases of this kind the official in charge of a project kept for himself all or most of the funds which were placed at his disposal to be distributed among the volunteers as a reward for their voluntary services. On occasions, the official mobilized voluntary services more with a view to win the favour of his superiors than that of the people. The people felt that they had been tricked and cheated. This feeling in turn generated an attitude of distrust towards that official and all officials. Against this background, the use of force, no matter how well intentioned was undesirable as it only tended to reinforce the feeling of distrust.

It is a cause for concern that one-half of the public servants emphatically supported the use of force and that the other half, who opposed the using of force, did so mainly on the basis of the practical difficulties involved and not so much upon the justice or injustice of imposing one's will on others.

Table 22
REASONS OFFERED FOR THE USE OF FORCE

REASON	Frequency
In this particular case the end justifies the means.	203
The people lack civic sense and public spirit.	88
The people should not be allowed to oppose the authority of the government.	6
The rules authorize the public servant to conscript help in emergencies.	2

REASONS OFFERED AGAINST THE USE OF FORCE

REASON	Frequency
Persuasive methods are better than coercive.	71
The use of force creates hatred and resentment towards the government.	61
Officers do not approach the people in the right spirit.	54
The use of force is opposed to the principles of human dignity.	41
The use of force discourages the habit of self-help among the people.	29
The use of force is unlawful.	19
The people do not have resources to volunteer help.	16
The volunteers are generally paid, so in that case, it would be better to hire skilled labourers.	14
Following the use of force the service rendered no longer remains voluntary.	5

A majority of the CSP officers and officers in the Departments of Health, Jails, Local Audit and Public Relations were opposed to the use of force. Officers in the Department of Electricity were more or less evenly divided. In the remaining departments a majority supported the use of force.

It was discovered that relatively more of the Class II officers were inclined to support the use of force. Furthermore, proportionately more officers with a rural background favoured the use of force than those with an urban background.

Family Pressure on the Public Servant

One of the basic virtues of the perfect bureaucracy is that the professional servant of the State is immune to extraneous influences in the discharge of his official duties. The influences which emanate from those who are closely related to the public servant are especially hard to resist.

A hypothetical test situation based upon the every-day experiences of the public servant was designed to determine how well the respondents could withstand the pressure of outside influences in the performance of their duty.

In this case a public servant is assigned the task of issuing permits to the public for the purchase of foreign-made bicycles of which only a limited number is available. One of his relatives asks him to grant him a permit. The public servant has already received a large number of applications. He can favour his relative only at the cost of one of the applicants. This situation was presented to the respondents and they were asked to describe the reaction of the relative if the request was not granted.

Most of the respondents, or 83·8 per cent., feared that the reaction of the relative would be unfavourable. Many of these officers said that the offended relative would speak ill of the civil servant among other members of his family. A few said that the relative would consider the civil servant to be a timid officer.

A very small proportion of the respondents, 5·3 per cent., expected that the reaction would not be unfavourable. About two-thirds of these hoped that the relative would not mind, and one-third felt that the relative might even come to respect the civil servant for being impartial in the performance of his duties.

About 10·9 per cent. of the respondents were uncertain in predicting the reaction of the relative A little over one-third of them said that the reaction depended upon the reputation of the civil servant, meaning thereby that the relative would definitely mind if the civil servant was known to have done similar favours to others in certain circumstances. If he was known to be averse to such requests the relative would accept it with good grace. About two-thirds of this group of respondents stated that the reaction depended upon the temperament and the cultural background of the relative. If the relative was highly educated and of a reasonable frame of mind he would be less inclined to resent the inability of the civil servant to favour him. Otherwise the reaction would be unfavourable.

On comparing the reactions of the public servants of different Classes very little difference was noted except that slightly more of the Class II officers apprehended an unfavourable reaction.

In terms of regions of residence it was revealed that a slightly higher percentage of the officers who had settled in the former Punjab and in Bahawalpur anticipated an unpleasant reaction. These officers were followed by those settled in the former North-West Frontier Province some of whom feared that in their area, the relative might be so annoyed as to take revenge upon the civil servant.

Not much difference in the responses was noted on the basis of the rural or urban background of the public servants except that the percentage of officers fearing an unfavourable reaction was slightly higher among those drawn from a rural background as compared to that of the officers from an urban background.

Influence of Sectarian Considerations upon the Public Servant

It is not uncommon to come across a public servant who has a grievance against his superior. Speaking generally, he might have been transferred to a place or to post which is undesirable to him or have been denied a promotion to which he thinks he is entitled. Occasionally, the public servant may attribute this alleged discrimination to the fact that the superior wanted to favour someone else who was a member of the same religious sect to which the superior officer belonged.

In this context accusations and counter-accusations of favouritism by public servants to members of the same sect are occasionally heard in private circles. The government of the former province of the Punjab had to issue a circular calling upon its servants 'not to propagate their sectarian creed among their subordinates and others'. The circular warned that 'drastic action shall be taken against those who violate these orders'.[1] The circulation of the above order against the background of communal riots in the former Punjab in 1953, brings us face to face with another social factor which may exercise a certain influence upon the performance or behaviour of the public servant.

How influential is this influence? In order to find this out a question was included in this inquiry aimed at this aspect. Since this is a touchy subject, the question was asked in a generalized form. It reads, 'Do sectarian considerations influence the conduct of public servants in the performance of their official duties?' If the respondent replied in the affirmative he was asked to explain how sectarian considerations affected the conduct of the public servant.

Out of the total number of respondents 36·2 per cent. were of the opinion that sectarian considerations did not influence the performance of the public servant, while 28·4 per cent. said that such considerations did have an influence. A qualified response was offered by 19·7 per cent. of the officers who felt that sectarian considerations influenced the conduct of public servants only to a small extent or in a few cases only and by 3·9 per cent. of the public servants who thought that it did not influence the senior public servants. Only 10·6 per cent. of the respondents expressed their inability to say anything on this matter.

The general pattern of replies which describe the ways in which sectarian considerations exercised influence was along the following lines. If the public servants are working in the same office or department, the community of religious beliefs acts as an additional factor in bringing them closer. If they are working in different offices common religious beliefs serve as the basis for

[1] Director Public Relations, Punjab, *The Punjab, 1947-53, A Review of the First Six Years*, Lahore, 1960.

contact between them. Participation in common religious functions provides a stimulus to social contact. Friendly relations
which evolve in this manner on the social plane form the basis
for the operation of this influence on the official performance of
the public servant.

It is significant to note that none of the respondents admitted
that his opinion was based upon his personal experience. Nor
could any one of them give any actual example of the operation
of this influence. Does it mean that favouritism to sect-brethren
is more an imagined situation than a real one?

A majority of the officers in the Department of Public Relations
held the view that sectarian considerations did not influence the
conduct of government officials in the discharge of their official
duties. A little less than half of the officers in the Health Department, in the Secretariat and in the Civil Service of Pakistan expressed the same opinion. A majority of officers in the other
departments felt that sectarian considerations did influence, or at
least had influenced to a limited extent, the conduct of the public
servants.

It was observed that relatively more of the Class II officers,
55.1 per cent., thought that sectarian considerations influenced the
public servant in one way or the other. 49.4 per cent. of the
Class I officers thought that way and 34.4 per cent. of the unclassified officers shared that view.

On comparing the responses to the above question with the
position of the respondent in the chain of command it was discovered that the higher the position the larger was the proportion
of those officers who qualified their statements by saying that
sectarian considerations influenced the public servants to some
extent or that they did not influence the senior public servants.

It was noticed that a slightly greater proportion of the public
servants belonging to the minority sects were inclined to subscribe
to the view that sectarian considerations did carry influence than
did those drawn from the majority sects.

A little less than a quarter of the respondents stated that they
did not belong to any sect. Of this group 41.4 per cent. said that

sectarian considerations did not exercise any influence on the public servants, or not on the higher public servants, in any case.

Influence of Caste Considerations on the Public Servant

It was felt that caste might be another factor which influenced the behaviour of the public servant. In order to test this the public servants were asked to say whether they thought that caste considerations exercised influence upon the conduct of public servants in the discharge of their officials duties. Negative responses were received from 46·0 per cent. of the respondents, while 27·8 per cent. of the respondents answered in the affirmative. As many as 13·7 per cent. of the officers said that the question of caste influenced the public servant to a limited extent only and 3·9 per cent. said that caste considerations did not matter in the case of senior public servants. A sizable proportion of 8·5 per cent. of the officers were unable to say anything in this respect.

It may be observed that the proportion of officers who think caste considerations do not influence the public servants is relatively higher than those who think that sectarian considerations are not influential.

Here again no respondent based his opinion upon personal experience nor did he cite any example.

A majority of the public servants in the Departments of Animal Husbandry, Police and Local Fund Audit thought that caste considerations do influence the public servant. A majority of the officers in the Departments of Co-operative Societies, Health, Irrigation, Jails, Public Relations and in the Civil Service of Pakistan held a view to the contrary. The officers in the Electricity Department and in the Secretariat were more or less evenly divided between the two views.

It was observed that relatively more officers with a rural background were inclined to think that caste considerations exercised influence upon the conduct of public servants.

Influence of Regional Considerations

The public servants in the sample, being drawn from different geographical and cultural areas, were asked to say whether regional considerations influenced the conduct of public servants in the discharge of their official duties. A little less than half of the respondents, or 49.1 per cent., replied in the affirmative. If with them may be combined the 14.4 per cent. of those officers who qualified their affirmative reply by saying that regional considerations influenced the public servant to a limited extent only, the percentage rises to 63.5. Only 22.9 per cent. of the respondents stated definitely that such considerations did not matter.

A slightly larger proportion of officers of a rural background felt that regional considerations influenced the conduct of the public servant. Similarly, a slightly greater proportion of officers who belonged to the former provinces other than the Punjab expressed the same feeling. No material difference was observed in attitude between the refugees and the local officers. Six of the ten officers who had not settled anywhere stated that regional considerations did exercise a good deal of influence.

Table 23 shows that regional considerations appear to be more powerful than the sectarian or caste considerations. Caste considerations turn out to be the least influential out of the three potential factors of influence.

During the interviews the writer gained the impression that, in general, the respondents were inclined to play down the influence which they believed was actually exercised by the sect and caste considerations. A few of the public servants hesitated or flatly refused to disclose their sect affiliation. In many of these cases the writer had personal knowledge that the respondents belonged to a particular minority sect, who betrayed the fear that their connexions with that sect might be used against them.

In the general elections to the National Assembly of Pakistan and to the Provincial Assemblies, held in April 1962, the candidates as well as independent observers had noted that in electoral campaigns appeals were made to caste and sectarian associations. In a symposium on 'Election and Our Responsibility', held in Lahore in April 1962, most of the speakers warned the voters that the country would disintegrate if candidates were chosen on the basis of caste or sect associations.[1]

[1] *The Pakistan Times*, Lahore, 19 April 1962.

Table 23

OPINIONS OF THE RESPONDENTS ABOUT THE INFLUENCE OF SECTARIAN, CASTE AND REGIONAL CONSIDERATIONS

	Exercise influence	To some extent	Not in the case of senior public servants	Do not exercise	Cannot say	Total
Sectarian considerations	126	86	17	157	46	432
	29.1	19.8	3.9	26.2	10.6	100.0
Caste considerations	120	59	17	199	37	432
	27.8	13.7	3.9	46.0	8.6	100.0
Regional considerations	212	62	20	99	39	432
	49.1	14.4	4.6	22.9	9.0	100.0

Analysing the methods adopted to catch votes by the candidates in the elections to the National Assembly of Pakistan a reputable Lahore daily reported, 'The basis of election being the personal merit of the candidate, direct contact with the voters, when their number is limited, is obviously necessary. This approach to the voters is intended to secure firm commitments of support. And for this purpose all the available associations with the voters are being used. *Biradri*[1] affiliations are often being considered important.'[2]

The impression of the writer is that although statements are often made that communal divisions such as sects or castes are foreign to the creed of Islam yet, in practice, few Muslims hesitate to utilize them for personal needs.

Attitude towards Visitors to Government Offices

The attitude of the public servants towards visitors to government offices has two important aspects. The first aspect relates to the general tendency on the part of the official to discourage the prospective visitors. The second relates to the general tendency of the friends and the acquaintances of the public servant to call upon him for social purposes in his office during working hours. The two aspects taken together produce a highly unsatisfactory situation as regards the relations between the official and the people. There is a general feeling that as a result of the prevailing arrangements a visitor who wants to see a public servant for a genuine, urgent reason is either unable to do so or meets considerable difficulty in being admitted. On the other hand, the friends of an official and his fellow public servants find it very easy to visit him quite frequently and in large numbers, for non-official purposes, during working hours. The result is that not only the goodwill of the ordinary citizen is lost but the public servant's time is wasted.

In modern times the public service aspect of bureaucracy has been repeatedly emphasized, yet at the same time direct contact

---

[1] *Biradri* may be defined as a loose association of families belonging to the same caste.

[2] *The Pakistan Times*, Lahore, 22 April 1962.

between the people and the public servant has registered a sharp decline. More and more government work is being done through the written word. In this mode of working the citizen and the public servant seldom come face to face with each other. This situation is supposed to be the direct and inevitable consequence of modern bureaucracy. It is felt that as bureaucracy becomes more perfect, the need for the citizen personally to meet the public servant in order to obtain basic goods and services diminishes. As a result of this type of reasoning the official policy of most of the modern governments is to control and check and not to facilitate the visits of the private citizens to government offices on official business. The impact of such an administrative concept on the bureaucracy of Pakistan is but natural. However, the general inaccessibility of the Pakistani official is also the result of the colonial tradition according to which the government was developed as an entity apart from and withdrawn from the governed.

The foreign origin of the government in itself threw into bold relief the cleavage between the 'official' and the 'non-official'. In general, the appellation of the 'official' came to be identified with all Europeans and that of the 'non-official' with the mass of the Indian population, whom the British chose to call 'the natives'. A strong sense of pride among the foreigners for having established their rule by conquest further reinforced this cleavage. As conquerors, who were also foreigners, the efforts of the British colonialists were naturally directed towards enforcing the complete subjugation of the people. In the period immediately following conquest and annexation, the principles which determined the character of the British administration were not very dissimilar from those generally followed by an army of occupation. It should cause no surprise if the show of force and authority formed an integral part of the British rule in India. Indications are also available to show that this policy received a certain amount of inspiration from a sense of racial superiority.

Racial relations in India present one of the most fascinating areas of investigation. There is no space nor any occasion to dwell upon this subject at length in this study. Only a passing reference may be made to the contribution made by Professor T. G. P. Spear in this field. He informs us that until the middle of the eighteenth century, race relations between the Indians and the English were on terms of equality. However, after the acquisition of power in India, the English attitude registered a sudden change and the long and unpleasant campaign of the British to humiliate the Indian people began. This attitude was characterized by such discriminatory treatment of the Indians as making them stand during their visits to government offices or demanding that they salute in public all Europeans, no matter of what station or circumstance in life.[1]

An attitude of indifference towards the visitors to government offices was a part of this policy. An article written by the late Dr. Maulvi Abdul Haq,[2] the distinguished Urdu scholar, recounts many instances which indicate that the policy of the British officers was intentionally to humilitate Indian visitors. He tells us that an average English officer usually replied to the greetings of an Indian by a mere movement of a finger to show how little he thought of the Indian. The Indian gentlemen who came to see the English officers were expected to get down from their carriages outside the bungalow and walk the rest of the way. Furthermore, they were required to be barefooted when calling upon the 'Sahib' in the visitors' room.

In his autobiography, Gandhi has reported his experience with a British Political Agent on whose orders he was physically pushed out of the office. Gandhi wanted to proceed against the 'Sahib'. He sought the advice of the barrister Sir Phirozeshah Mehta, an outstanding contemporary Indian leader. Mehta sent this advice to Gandhi, 'Tell Gandhi such things are the common experience of many *vakils* (lawyers) and barristers. He is still fresh from England and hot-blooded. He does not know British officers. If he would earn something and have an easy time ... let him pocket the insult. He will gain nothing by proceeding against the

[1] T. G. P. Spear, *The Nabobs, A Study of the Social Life of the English in Eighteenth Century India*, London, 1932, pp. 126-45.

[2] *Daily Bang-i-Haram*, Peshawar, 27 February 1962.

'Sahib' and on the contrary will very likely ruin himself. Tell him he has yet to know life.'[1]

Sir Bampfylde Fuller, himself an I.C.S. officer, admits in his memoirs that 'the English officials in India do not always realize the acuteness with which Indians resent indignities which appear trifling to our robuster judgments.' He deplored the fact that many European clubs did not admit an Indian only because he was an Indian. Furthermore, he regretfully noted that an Indian when travelling by railway met with treatment which was inexpressibly galling to his feelings.[2] The Indians were subjected to similar discrimination in other public places as well. For example, it is a common knowledge in the sub-continent, that the public restaurant 'Gaylords' in New Delhi, refused to serve Indian customers.

The colonial government in India was admittedly built upon concepts of authority. In its more unpleasant manifestations it was inspired by a sense of racial superiority. With conscious effort, the image of the government was developed as remote, stern and all-powerful. This effect was obtained by many devices. Note has already been taken of some of these in the first chapter, such as the high-sounding titles given to the government officials, the large retinue of peons who attended them, and the extraordinary display of pomp and show associated with the inspection tours of government officials. Still another device, which relates to the subject we are now dealing with, was to make the government official customarily almost inaccessible to the public.

There are many practices in the present-day Pakistani administration which are survivals of the pre-Independence period. These practices, on the one hand, stand witness to the inglorious designs of the colonial government to intimidate the Indian people by a show of authority and, on the other hand, they spotlight the diehard qualities of the bureaucracy due to which old practices and usages manage to survive revolutionary changes by the sheer repetition of their usage. Perhaps Kafka had a similar situation

[1] M. K. Gandhi, *The Story of My Experiments with Truth*, Ahmedabad, 1927, p. 234.

[2] Bampfylde Fuller, *Studies of Indian Life and Sentiment*, London, 1910, p. 343-44.

in mind when he wrote that every revolution evaporates and leaves behind the slime of a new bureaucracy. In the course of the visits to the government offices when interviewing the respondents, it was noted that some of them were still guarded by sentries armed with a gun and bayonet. In some instances the entire premises of the departments were declared out of bounds to visitors. Admittance was permitted only during prescribed hours. An elaborate system had been designed to regulate admissions through passes, the procedure for procuring which was, at times, hardly less cumbersome than that which is involved in getting a passport.

The possession of a pass did not in itself settle matters. One had yet to negotiate a few more intermediaries, namely the peon and the personal assistant. It has been noted earlier that this process was by no means easy. The efforts required to meet with a government official, in many cases, were similar to those required to win an obstacle race.

It was very seldom that a department had appointed a receptionist and it was still rarer that a waiting room had been provided. On occasions long queues of people were to be seen spreading out into the middle of the road, unprotected from the sun or rain, clinging to a latticed window, behind which sat a government functionary visible only through a rent in the wire-gauze through which he received applications. While visiting the highest court in the province, the writer was stopped from entering the building through one of its large gates. On inquiry, the guard informed the writer that the large gate was meant only for the judges. Other people who were desirous of entering from that direction should do so from a side-gate which was just large enough to admit one person at a time. This small side-entrance proved to be so close to the large gate that the two had a pillar in common and the two entrances opened on the same road. In one large government department the staircases leading to the first and and the second floors bore the inscription, 'For the use of officers only'. Instances of this kind were not many but they did illuminate the concepts which influenced the attitude of government officials towards the ordinary citizens.

At times it is argued, as noted in the beginning of this section, that it is vain to bewail the lack of personal contact between the official and the people because the more perfect the bureaucracy becomes the more impersonal it grows. It is said that in an efficient administrative set-up the need for the personal intervention of a petitioner should be unnecessary or in any case a rare exception rather than the rule.

Two considerations make the principles mentioned above inapplicable to the conditions which obtain in Pakistan. Firstly, it is generally claimed, that government machinery moves too slowly. It is also common knowledge that personal intervention still plays a significant part in obtaining action in a government department. Some foreign observers consider it to be a peculiar feature of government in the east. The British officials in India often used this argument against the appointment of Indians to positions of higher responsibility, claiming that Indian officials more than the British would be susceptible to personal influence. Although in both cases, the generalizations are too sweeping, it is difficult to deny that personal influence does count. In view of this situation either the government machinery should be made so efficient that a person is able to get redress or information, in time, by pursuing his case through the written word, or equal opportunity should be provided to all for seeing the officials concerned. At present, as is generally believed, not only is the administration slow but often the public official is not easily accessible. The influential person from whose interference the government might be keen to protect the official still manages to break the barriers. It is the man with little influence who is kept from presenting his case before the public servant. It is hard to believe that this arrangement protects the official from extraneous influences or that it does not make an official less responsive to the people.

The second consideration which calls for a re-examination of the usefulness or the justification of imposing restrictions upon the would-be visitors to government departments is that the number of literate people being very small most of them find it difficult to make representations in writing. They find it easier to express their needs verbally. Sometimes all they want is information in which case they must pay a scribe to set their request in writing or to wriggle through check-posts outside the government departments, and locate the right official after a long process of trial and error. In a world where everything is done by the written word, the ordeal for the unlettered is great.

The British officers appreciated the difficulties of such people but they used this situation to sustain some of the feudal practices and institutions of the Moguls. For example, it was maintained that the Indians liked a strong personal rule. In accordance with this policy certain categories of public servants were glorified in the image of Mogul chieftains who held court after the fashion of the Mogul *durbars*. Although the advantages of a face to face interview are realized it is hardly necessary to give the interview the form of a royal audience. This point has been raised because a section of the public service still seems to be devoted to the concepts of personal rule. For example, the officers of the Civil Service of Pakistan are still encouraged to adopt the role of *mai baap* to the people. Similar situations in other countries have not led to such a conclusion. The systems which they have evolved to meet such a situation are more in keeping with the temper of a democratic policy.

Frank Dunnill informs us that in a highly developed country like Britain, the private citizen similarly finds difficulty in communicating his needs to the government official for the same reasons which are applicable to Pakistan. He writes, 'there is a considerable sector of society that is barely literate and whose members find the use of the written word a perpetual stumbling block. For such people the complexities of modern life, and the demands society makes upon them, are almost always on the point of being too much. Every official contact is a burden, every form a mystery, every departure from the simple routine of living a minor crisis.'[1]

In order to meet the needs of such people Frank Dunnill sug-

[1] Frank Dunnill, *The Civil Service: Some Human Aspects*, London, 1956, p. 167.

gests three methods, namely the interview, the use of telephone communication and the simplification of the language used by the government officials in correspondence with the people. Diversity of languages is perhaps the most serious aspect upon which attention should be concentrated in Pakistan. Here, the problem is not so much of simplification, but of replacing English with a local language which people can understand easily. Owing to the shortage of telephones this medium of communication between the public and the official can serve the purpose only to a limited extent. For the majority, therefore, the interview stands out as the most practical medium of communication in the prevailing conditions in Pakistan today.

Professor Paul H. Appleby, who studied the Indian administration on the invitation of the Indian government, has this to say on the same subject, 'an administrative method that permits letters from citizens to go unanswered, poorly answered or long delayed is not properly considerate or responsive. An administrative method that sets high barriers before the entrance of citizens into public offices and occasions many of them to salute leaves much to be desired.'[1]

The creation of an army of guards to obstruct the entrance of citizens to public offices is a waste of manpower. Furthermore, it only increases the number of intermediaries between the two segments of population namely the people and the public servants, contact between whom is necessary, unavoidable and desirable.

The second aspect of the official-public relations to which a reference was made earlier is the custom among the friends of the public servants of visiting them for private purposes in their offices. Usually a friend who drops in to say 'Hello' lingers on for hours. He is followed by another, still another and this goes on. Sometimes, they may drop in all at the same time. The public servant cannot put them off nor can he continue with his work.

The effect of this practice is that work in government departments suffers. The public servant in exasperation contemplates a

[1] Paul H. Appleby, *Public Administration in India: Report of a Survey*, Delhi, 1953, p. 68.

complete ban on all visitors. Sentries, peons and *Jamadars*[1] are posted at the doors. Many other devices, described earlier, are introduced to restrict the inflow of the visitors. The irony of the matter is that the friends and relatives still manage to crowd the public servant's office while a large number of people, with urgent work, many of whom have travelled from distant villages and towns, either fail to reach the office of the public servant or are detained waiting outside for hours. In view of this consideration the multifarious restrictions upon the visitors seem to be invidious and dicriminatory. Instead of banning the admission of all visitors, the need is to stop private visits during working hours. It was difficult for the writer and the interviewers to judge how much time was wasted in the government offices in this manner but it seemed possible to assess roughly the frequency of private visits. The respondents were asked to say if their friends or colleagues visited them in their offices during office hours on private business. Next, they were asked to tell how many of them came in one day on the average. The respondents were also asked to state whether they approved of this practice or not. The findings are presented herewith.

Out of the total number, 34·3 per cent. of the respondents replied that they did not receive private visitors during working hours while 10·1 per cent. of the officers said that only rarely did such visits occur. The statements of 19·5 per cent. indicated that they received one to three such visitors in a day. About one-third of the total, or 31·7 per cent., of the public servants, received such visitors occasionally. Eighteen of the respondents, or 4·0 per cent. received four to ten visitors or more in a day.

It may be observed that more than half of the public servants do receive private visitors during working hours. The proportion is large enough to be significant although it was felt that the respondents were inclined to make modest estimates of the frequency of such visits.

Relatively more officers received private visitors among the lower class of public servants than among the higher. For instance,

[1] Head peons.

the percentages of officers who fell in this category were 68·6 among the unclassified public servants, 55·4 among Class II public servants, and 51·2 among Class I public servants. Almost all of the unclassified officers were drawn from the Secretariat. The high frequency of 'social callers' in this agency of the government is intriguing in view of the fact that this office has established one of the most rigorous machineries for the restrictions of the inflow of visitors. This is an ironical illustration of the fact that the various devices which restrict visits to public offices are not only ineffective but that they work more to the disadvantage of the visitor who has some genuine reason to meet the official than to that of the 'social caller'.

Another department with a relatively higher frequency of visitors was the Police Department in which 54·3 per cent. of the Police officers occasionally received private visitors. The percentage of officers who received private visitors was also relatively high in the Departments of Electricity, Health and Irrigation. Quite understandably, 83·3 per cent. of the officials of the Jails Department did not receive any private visitors.

As to the attitude towards this practice, 70·8 per cent. of the respondents disapproved of it and 7·2 per cent. reserved their opinion in this matter. The remaining ninety-five officers, or 22·0 per cent. of the total, were in favour of this practice with certain reservations. Thirty-one of these officers said that the visits were a welcome relief in that they refreshed the public servant after the drab routine of office work. Eighteen officers stated that they would tolerate a private visitor if he came from outside the town or if his visit was urgent. Five said that they would tolerate it if the visits were occasional. Nine would not mind a private visitor if they were free at the time of the visit. Twenty-four respondents offered no specific reason for being in favour of private visits.

Officers of lower classes were more inclined to give in to private visitors. For example, 74·0 per cent. of the Class I officers disapproved of this practice, 69·3 per cent. of the Class II officer were against this practice and only 64·2 per cent. of the unclassified officers criticized this practice.

CHAPTER 6

THE PUBLIC SERVANT AND THE POLITICIAN

According to the theory of democratic government, administration is the joint responsibility of the public servant and the politician. A British publicist has described the relationship between the two in the following words, 'It is for the electorate to decide in what direction it wishes its country to go; it is for the politician to give words to these desires and to turn them into a policy; it is for the bureaucrat to give the policy form.'[1]

In practice, however, it is not always easy to demarcate the spheres of activity of the public servant and the politician. This has always been a potential source of conflict. Politicians are generally prone to be critical of the public servants for their tendency to transgress their defined jurisdictions and to arrogate more power to themselves. The public servants, on the other hand, seldom miss an occasion to complain about interference by politicians in matters which they consider to be in the realm of pure administration. Relations between the public servant and the politician degenerate to a dangerous extent if interference by either of

[1] Maurice Zinkin, *Development for Free Asia*, London, 1956, p. 78.

the two in the other's sphere becomes wilful and frequent.

Apart from the inherent spirit of competition for more power which animates the relationship between the average public servant and the average politician another factor which produces an imbalancing effect upon this relationship is the personal equation between the two. If a minister is a man of sufficient personal distinction he will make himself master of his department but if he is content simply to endorse the decisions of his permanent advisors he lets the civil servants run the government. Michael Stewart, a member of the British Parliament, informs us that 'the bureaucracy becomes more powerful in proportion to the incompetence of other parts of government. When there are ignorant ministers, careless Parliaments, and overburdened law courts, the civil service does what it can to carry on the government in spite of these drawbacks.'[1]

There are three major factors which must be taken into account in order to appreciate the nature of the relationship between the Pakistani public servant and the politician. The first is the tradition in this respect which Pakistan has inherited from its past. This tradition has two important dimensions firstly, the paramount position which bureaucracy occupied in British India and secondly, the hostility which the politician, and especially the nationalist, harboured towards the civil servant. In the history of the Indo-Pakistan sub-continent the civil servant made his appearance before the politician. During most of the period of British rule in India, the government was predominantly bureaucratic in nature. Constitutionally all power was vested in the civil servants. The few instalments of a share in the power which were doled out to the politician from time to time, were rendered ineffective owing to the instability of political life in India. The civil servant in British India had no sustained experience of working with the politician as an equal partner, letal one of accepting him as a superior.

The public servant and the politician, on the contrary, had usually faced each other as adversaries. The politician's primary

[1] Michael Stewart, *The British Approach to Politics*, London, 1959, p. 61.

objective was to secure independence for his country which, in effect, amounted to breaking the monopoly of the civil servant over governmental power. The civil servant, on the other hand, as the agent of the established authority, often found himself in opposition to the politician. Mutual respect between the politician and the civil servant was not generally established. Professor W. H. Morris-Jones thinks that this lack of mutual trust has been carried over to the post-Independence period. He informs us that 'it is a relic of the past when the civil service was an arm of that foreign administration which put in prison a large number of those who are now the leading politicians.'[1]

The second major factor which influenced the relationship between the public servant and the politician in Pakistan is the relative superiority in personal ability and experience of the average public servant over the average politician. Excepting East Pakistan, most of the areas in Pakistan had come into contact with modern political institutions such as elections, representative assemblies and local self-government, rather late. Furthermore, a preponderant percentage of the population of Pakistan lives in rural areas. Rural people are commonly considered to be conservative by nature and incapable of thinking in terms of abstract principles. This cultural lag has restricted the growth of well-organized political parties based upon well-defined principles. Whatever little political activity exists in the villages centres around personalities. Mass illiteracy has discouraged attempts at spreading the ideas which are essential for the creation of conditions suitable for the operation of democratic political institutions. In such circumstances political activities are dominated by influential personalities whose power is not always matched by enlightenment and altruism. Cabinet ministers chosen from such politicians have failed to win the respect of the permanent civil servants. Except when his personal interests were involved, the politician tacitly succumbed to the superior knowledge of the civil servant in allowing him to take decisions on his behalf on major issues of policy.

[1] W. H. Morris-Jones, *Parliament in India*, London, 1957, p. 152.

Speaking on this issue a member of the first Constituent Assembly (Legislature) of Pakistan said, 'The policy of the British Government was to maintain *status quo*, and as such, it was their duty not to let the officials do anything other than that. It was to keep that steel frame, of which Lloyd George talked about thirty years ago, in a perfect condition, unshaken, fully tight. That is what they were supposed to do. The position has entirely changed now. It is a new born country. We are living in critical times and in a growing age, so to speak, and we want dynamic administration. That is not the job of the officials. It is the job of the cabinet which unfortunately, is following the officials without probably the officials wanting to do it. Our cabinet must be one of the most official-ridden cabinets.'[1]

It is appropriate to quote in full the evaluation of Pakistani politicians by a Pakistani senior public servant. In a published article he writes:

Independence unfortunately did not prove to be an unmixed blessing. The services had to face new difficulties and frustrations. The ministers who assumed office were in many cases amateurish, fond of cheap publicity and harboured unconscious hostility towards the administration. They fraternized with junior officers and indulged in back chat. To make themselves popular, they acted on *safarish*[2] and interfered in promotion and disciplinary cases. They always found reasons for doing so. Their yardstick was different and they were inclined to support those who indulged in flattery and adulation. Some of the ministers were old slogan raisers, immature and naive in the business of government. They were appointed for their services to the party and not on personal merit. They liked to bluster in public and were often rude to officials; they thought that such behaviour was a sign of strength. In the olden days, if an officer went wrong he was called up in private and given a good dressing, but he was never humiliated in public. Even if he had to be got rid of, this was done without washing the dirty linen in public.

The new ministers adopted a different technique; they ruthlessly attacked and criticized in public and thought that they were doing a wonderful thing. When, however, they met the officers whom they had humiliated, in person, they said that their remarks were not meant to be taken seriously and were only intended to

[1] *First Constituent Assembly (Legislature) of Pakistan, Debates, March 22 1950*, Vol. I, No. 8, Karachi, p. 286.
[2] Favouritism.

produce a political effect. They did not realize that they were doing irreparable damage to the administration. When political animosity increased and ministries began to tumble in quick succession, the officers, who were loyal to the outgoing ministry out of a sense of duty, at once became suspect. A stage came, in the Punjab, when some of the worst demonstrations of political animosity and intolerance were made and when with each change of ministry the top officers began to be reshuffled. Loyalty to the regime in power was looked upon as a sin worth avenging. 'The ox and the ass were treated alike. With the demoralization of services, officers were afraid to record honest opinions in personal files. Adverse reports to favourites of ministers lost all meaning. It became difficult to keep the contents of personal files secret. The spoils system, with all its attendant evils, had come to establish itself.[1]

The third major factor which exercised its influence upon the relationship between the public servant and the politician was the instability of the political governments in Pakistan. Owing to this instability, the political governments were superseded by executive authority on a number of occasions. In the case of certain provincial governments and also of the central governments there were rapid changes in ministries. Because of these conditions, the civil service was able to gain, apparently unsought ascendency over the politicians. The following quotation about government and politics in Australia also applied to conditions in Pakistan:

There is no doubt that the influence of higher public servants upon the policy of Australian governments has always been great. It has arisen partly from their permanency, partly from their expertness. Their permanency is important because the Australian political tradition has been one of fairly rapid change of ministries.[2]

All the evidence presented above leads to the inference that the civil service in Pakistan has always occupied a powerful position. A good deal has been said about the helpless innocence of the civil servants and their victimization at the hands of the politicians. However, it is hard to accept this position without reservations. If it were really so how could it be possible for some of the senior

[1] Mian Anwar Ali, 'The Role of the Senior Administrator', an article published in *The Pakistan Times*, Lahore, 5 July 1961.

[2] J. D. B. Miler, *Australian Government and Politics: An Introductory Survey*, London, 1959, p. 162.

civil servants who are supposed to be politically neutral to move into topmost political positions? Furthermore, one hardly ever comes across a civil servant who might have had to sacrifice his career as a result of resistance to political pressure. On the contrary, many instances are often cited of officials who were the beneficiaries of partisan services to politicians.

Mian Anwar Ali, whose comments in a published article on interference by politicians in the work of the civil servants have been quoted earlier, wrote in the same article that on the restoration of a political regime after the withdrawal of Martial Law, the civil servants might once again be faced with situations in which they had either to submit and become a tool of the politician in his sinister designs or resist the pressure and suffer. However, he agreed with a former chief minister and a friend of his, on the point that in a situation like the one described above, the civil servant was not always the righteous martyr. It was often found that, 'pressure was not resisted and that officers were sometimes "willing". We must remember that when servicemen cease to be politicians there will be less of politics in the services.'[1]

Probably the most serious case known publicly in which the civil servants were subjected to the test as to whether they followed their consciences or their political superiors was the period of violent disturbances in the former province of the Punjab in 1953. According to the *Report of the Court of Inquiry constituted to inquire into the Punjab Disturbances of 1953*, the officials were fully aware that the situation of law and order in the province was deteriorating every day and that it called for firm action. It appears, however, that the political leadership was only interested in allowing the things to drift as they did. Therefore, 'whenever there was a reference either they (the officials) were persuaded to change their strong views or official decorum restrained them from protest. Mr. Daultana (the Chief Minister of the Punjab), therefore, says that everybody agreed with whatever decisions we find on the files and the officers concerned have not contradicted him.

[1] Mian Anwar Ali, 'The Role of the Senior Administrator' second instalment of the article published in *The Pakistan Times*, Lahore, July 6 1961.

We ought to hold, therefore, that the responsibility was joint, though we feel differently.'[1]

In the above quotation the first sentence is worthy of note. One possible conclusion which may be derived is that in a clash of conscience and expediency the officials allowed themselves to be prevailed upon to yield to the latter. Mention has already been made of the unending controversy between the public servant and the politician in Pakistan, which relates to the apportionment of blame to each other for the political instability in the country and for the failure of constitutional government resulting in the imposition of Martial Law. For an unbiased observer it is safe to assume that the accusations of both parties have a fair amount of truth. The politician has been under fire for quite some time and the civil servant has managed to look innocent, yet one marvels at the ease with which the politician was able to handle the civil servant for his personal ends. Probably it was so because the civil servant had abandoned political neutrality which was otherwise the basic demand of the ethics of his profession. Interference by politicians in the executive functions and interference by the civil servants in politics are intimately related. One development leads to and promotes the other. It is not possible to say which of the two parties first started the vicious circle nor is it possible to say exactly when and in what circumstances this situation had first arisen.

Seemingly, the real position is that the unhealthy condition of political life and administration was the result of violation of the basic rules and conventions of representative government committed mutually by the public servant and the politician. A Pakistani English language daily described the nature of this state of body politics in the following words:

... Thus every important political *pehlwan*[2] had acquired a brood of official *pathas*[3] who were more interested in advancing the fortunes of their patrons than in the discharge of their public

---

[1] *Report of the Court of Inquiry constituted under Act II of 1954 to inquire into the Punjab Disturbances of 1953*, Lahore, 1954, p. 384.

[2] A wrestler.

[3] An apprentice or a probationer of a wrestler.

functions. Of course each side expected and received some return for services rendered, mainly at the expense of the public.[1]

In most cases, the extreme form of this perverted behaviour was witnessed immediately before or during the elections to the representative bodies. The general pattern was usually as follows.

In order to secure its position the political party in power sought the help of the officials conducting the elections. The officials were asked to harass the opponents of the 'official' candidates or they were asked to give active support to the 'official' candidate in the election campaign. The public servants who refused, or who were considered likely to refuse, were transferred to some other place. Originally, transfer of an official was ordered simply to eliminate him from the main scene of the election battle and to replace him with a more pliable civil servant. Following rapid changes in the ministries the transfer orders were also motivated by the desire to punish a civil servant who had helped and was again likely to help the opposition party. As a consequence, the civil servants who did not toe the line of the political party in power were transferred to posts or places which were personally inconvenient to them. Sometimes they were posted to positions which were lower in status than they were entitled to by seniority and competence.

With the repetition of such developments the civil servants started taking sides in politics, partly in self-defence and partly for considerations of material gain. In order to win the support of the recalcitrant civil servants the politicians resorted to rewards in the form of promotions, prize jobs in the government and the like. In extreme cases certain civil servants succeeded in obtaining such favours from all political parties.

In a Master's thesis on the *Civil Service of Pakistan* which was presented to the University of the Panjab in 1956, the author[2] stated that frequent changes in governments in Pakistan became one of the most serious causes of a sense of insecurity in the public

---

[1] *The Pakistan Times* (Editorial), Lahore, 28, August 1955.

[2] Salim A. Jilani, *The Civil Service of Pakistan*, An M.A. thesis submitted to the Department of Political Science, University of the Panjab, Lahore, 1956, (typescript), pp. 122-3.

services. Every new government made transfers and promotions of public servants to enhance its political position. The most flagrant abuse of the public servant was during the elections. The district officers and the police officials were required by the government in power to harass the opponents of the 'official' candidates and to muster support for the 'official' candidates. The public servants were expected to connive at the illegal and corrupt practices of the supporters of the official candidate. Official denunciations were often made against interference by government officials in elections but no action was taken.

The Master's thesis mentioned above, listed a number of cases of political transfers, promotions and demotions which give a fair idea of the nature of the problem and of its impact on the body politic. These transfers occurred immediately before the assembling of the newly formed Provincial Assembly of West Pakistan on 19 May 1956. On 27 April 1956, two Deputy Inspectors-General of Police, four Superintendents of Police, six Deputy Superintendents of Police and many of the subordinate staff were transferred from the Bahawalpur Division to other divisions and districts. Four days later, Mr. Anwar Ali, Inspector-General of Police, West Pakistan, was transferred to a junior post as Provincial Transport Controller. Mr. Anwar Ali refused to accept the transfer and appealed to the President of Pakistan. In the place of Mr. Anwar Ali, Mr. A. B. Awan, an Inspector-General of Police in the former North-West Frontier Province was appointed as the Inspector-General of Police, West Pakistan. Mr. M. Shariff, Inspector-General of Police in the former province of Sind, made a representation to the Governor of West Pakistan, that since he was senior to Mr. Awan, he should be made the Inspector-General of West Pakistan Police. Mr. Shariff, however, was appointed as the controller of Transport and Mr. Anwar Ali proceeded on leave.

On 6 May 1956, two Deputy Inspectors-General of Police, and seven Superintendents of Police were transferred in Rawalpindi, Lahore and Multan Divisions. Two Deputy Inspectors-General did not accept the transfer and proceeded on leave.

On 10 July 1956, the Additional Chief Secretary to the Government of West Pakistan was transferred to the less attractive post of the officiating member of the Board of Revenue. It is alleged that the transfer was made to get the support of his wife who was a member of the Provincial Assembly of West Pakistan for the political party in power. Within fifteen days the wife of the official concerned joined the ranks of the party in power and the official was reinstated in his original post.[1]

Against such a background of turmoil the public servant often found himself in a difficult situation. On the one hand, he was supposed to obey his superiors, on the other his conscience demanded that he should not do anything against its dictates.[2] The question, in effect, is, 'Should a public servant obey his superior no matter whether the latter is right or wrong, or should he obey his conscience and defy the orders of his superiors, if in his judgement they are unreasonable and illegal?'

In order to find the opinion of the respondents on this issue a hypothetical situation was constructed which was drawn from the past experiences of the public servants in this country. The situation was described to the respondents and their comments were recorded. The question read as follows, 'At a given time, during elections, a minister asks a certain public servant to overlook the illegal practices of the supporters of a certain candidate or to muster support for that candidate or to harass his opponents. What, in your opinion, should the public servant do?' Table 24 shows that 41·0 per cent. of the respondents said that the public servant should refuse to do anyone of these things while 5·3 per cent. of the officers said that the public servant should express his inability to do anything unlawful in a polite and diplomatic manner. A small group of 15 officers, or 3·5 per cent. of the sample, said that the public servant should ask the minister to give the orders in writing or should report the matter to his

[1] Ibid., p. 125.

[2] It is reported that a conflict of the nature described in the text above put such a strain on the public servants that thirty-two of them suffered from nervous break-down. Furthermore, a fair proportion of them were stated to have been confined in mental hospitals. *The Pakistan Times*, Lahore, 1 June 1960.

immediate superiors in the civil service. One hundred public servants, or 23·1 per cent. of the total, said that the public servant might apparently agree to oblige the minister but, in practice, he should perform his duty in an impartial manner.

Eighty-nine officers, forming 20·6 per cent. of the sample, said that the officer should yield to the influence of the minister. Another 3·5 per cent. of the respondents said that the public servant on such an occasion, should apply for sick leave or for long leave or for transfer. Three per cent. of the public servants declined to make any comment.

Combining the first three categories of responses it is found that 49·8 per cent., or about one-half, of the respondents believe in defying an unjust command of a superior. Combining the fifth and the sixth categories of responses it is revealed that 24·1 per cent., or about a quarter, of the respondents believe that the public servant must obey the command of his superior no matter whether it is right or wrong. A quarter of the respondents, or 23·1 per cent., fall somewhere in between the two positions. The last variety of respondents, however, appears to be inclined more towards those who would yield rather than towards the defiant ones. If the above classification is accepted, the respondents are, more or less, evenly divided between the two extreme positions, namely unconditional surrender to political pressure and resistance.

In different cadres or services the responses varied considerably. It may be observed from the above table that officers in the Animal Husbandry Service and those officers who do not belong to any service (such as those from the Department of Public Relations and certain other departments) show less firmness in resisting unlawful political pressure. Officers belonging to the Civil Service of Pakistan and the Police Service of Pakistan, on the other hand, claimed that they would show a greater steadfastness. It is interesting to take note of the fact that within the Police Service, the officers of the Provincial Police Service appear to be relatively less sure of themselves in resisting pressure from the politician. Only 2 of the 13 PSP officers, or 15·4 per cent., are inclined to yield while as many as 12 out of 34, or 35·2 per cent., of the of-

Table 24

REACTION OF THE RESPONDENTS TOWARDS PRESSURE FROM POLITICAL SUPERIORS

Cadre	Declined to answer	Yield	Apply for leave or transfer	Apparently agree but in practice do the right	Express inability to do anything unlawful	Refuse	Insist on orders in writing or report to superiors	Total
Animal Husbandry	—	8 / 42.8	—	5 / 26.3	1 / 5.3	5 / 26.3	—	19 / 100.0
Engineers	2 / 2.2	22 / 24.4	1 / 1.1	26 / 28.9	2 / 2.2	37 / 41.1	—	90 / 100.0
Health	3 / 4.3	11 / 15.7	6 / 8.6	17 / 24.3	—	29 / 41.4	4 / 5.7	70 / 100.0
Police Service of Pakistan	1 / 7.7	—	—	2 / 15.4	—	9 / 69.2	1 / 7.7	13 / 100.0
Provincial Police Service	3 / 8.8	11 / 32.3	1 / 2.9	—	—	18 / 52.6	1 / 2.9	34 / 100.0
Secretariat Service	—	9 / 13.0	3 / 4.3	17 / 24.6	4 / 5.8	33 / 47.8	3 / 4.3	69 / 100.0
Civil Service of Pakistan	2 / 6.5	—	—	8 / 25.8	8 / 25.8	11 / 35.5	2 / 6.4	31 / 100.0
Provincial Civil Service	—	4 / 15.4	—	7 / 26.9	5 / 19.2	8 / 30.8	2 / 7.6	26 / 100.0
Miscellaneous	—	4 / 50.0	1 / 12.5	—	—	3 / 37.5	—	8 / 100.0
No service	2 / 2.8	20 / 27.8	3 / 4.2	18 / 25.0	3 / 4.2	24 / 33.3	2 / 2.8	72 / 100.0
Total	13 / 3.0	89 / 20.6	15 / 3.5	100 / 23.1	23 / 5.3	177 / 41.0	15 / 3.5	432 / 100.0

ficers of the Provincial Police Service displayed the same inclination. Similarly, more of the Provincial Civil Service officers, or
16 out of 26, than the officers of the Civil Service of Pakistan,
16 of whom out of a total of 31 showed an inclination to yield
to political pressure.

The most probable reason for this difference of response lies
in the fact that whereas the appointing authority of the officers
of the CSP and the PSP cadres is the central government, that of
the Provincial Police Service and the Provincial Civil Service is
the provincial government. The powers of the provincial ministers
in regard to the officers of the first two cadres are limited, which
is not the case in regard to the officers of the other two categories.
In disciplinary matters, the officers of the provincial services are
under the full control of the provincial governments. This may
offer an explanation for a greater sense of insecurity among the
provincial civil servants.

Officers of Class II also manifested a relatively greater sense
of insecurity than the officers of Class I. For example, whereas
20·9 per cent. of the Class I officers indicated that they would
yield to the pressure of the politician, 30·0 per cent. of the Class
II officers expressed the same opinion. Similarly, whereas 53·6
per cent. of the Class I officers asserted that they would refuse
to yield, only 42·6 per cent. of the Class II officers said so.

Responses also varied on the basis of the position of the public
servant in the chain of command. Only three out of 34, or 8·8
per cent., of the officers who occupied the first position in the
chain of command indicated that there was no alternative but to
yield to the influence of the minister. Six out of 56, or 10·7 per
cent., of the officers who occupied the second position in the chain
of command, 10 out of 42, or 23·8 per cent., of those who occupied
the third position, 18 out of 65, or 27·7 per cent., of those who
occupied the fourth position, 1 out of 6, or 16·7 per cent., who
occupied the fifth position and 65 out of 229, or 28·8 per cent.,
of those who occupied the last position in the chain of command
offered similar responses. Conversely, as many as 82·3 per cent.
of the officers of the first position in the chain of command

asserted that they would defy the unlawful orders from their political superiors. While only 55·4 per cent. of the second position, 40·5 per cent. of the third position, 43·1 per cent. of the fourth position, 83·4 per cent. of the fifth position and 46·3 per cent. of the last position claimed to resist the political pressure. Except in the case of the officers who occupy the fifth position in the chain of command, the above figures form a pattern on the basis that the lower the rank in the hierarchy the lesser is the self-confidence shown by the public servant in withstanding unlawful political pressure from the top.

It was also observed that public servants with a higher socio-economic status showed relatively greater confidence in resisting political pressure. For example, 30·1 per cent. of the officers with a low status said that the public servant should yield to the pressure of the politician. As compared to them only 12·9 per cent. of the officers of high status replied in like manner. Similarly while 45·0 per cent. of the officers with a low socio-economic status suggested that the public servant should refuse to yield to political influence, 58·1 per cent. of the public servants of a high status recommended that course of action.

Consequences of Resistance to Political Pressure

The respondents were asked an additional question in order to check what circumstances determined their reactions to political pressure. This question asked what treatment the public servant might expect if he refused to yield to political pressure.

Three hundred and forty-nine officers, or 80·7 per cent. of the sample, expected victimization or harassment. Only 45 officers, or 10·5 per cent., of the total were hopeful that nothing untoward would happen. Seventeen of these officers, or 37·7 per cent, were drawn from the Civil Service of Pakistan. A group of 25 officers, or 5·8 per cent., of the respondents stated that the nature of the consequences which might follow resistance to political pressure depended upon the personality of the politician or upon the connexions of the public servant concerned or upon the outcome of the election results. Thirteen, or 3·0 per cent., of the officers, were unable to say anything.

Among the first group of 349 officers certain officers distinguished between victimization and harassment. According to the respondents victimization might take place in one of the following
ways. In the first instance, the political superior might suspend
the public servant from his duties. Secondly, he might demote
him. In an extreme case, the respondents feared, the political
superior might contrive to dismiss the recalcitrant public servant.
Sometimes, victimization might take the form of entering unfavourable remarks in the confidential report of the public servant.
In some cases the public servant might be bypassed at the time
of due promotions. The examples of the harassment given were,
transfer to a place or a post which was inconvenient or unsatisfactory to the public servant, involvement in false disciplinary or
criminal cases and denial of prize jobs.

Out of the 349 officers who expected victimization or harassment or both, 88, or a quarter, feared victimization, 192, or a
little over one-half, anticipated harassment and 69 or less than
one-fifth foresaw both victimization and harassment.

The responses of the public servants to the consequences of
resistance to political pressure were compared with their attitude
towards offering resistance to political pressure. It was revealed
that 96 officers, or $22 \cdot 2$ per cent., of the sample, had decided to
yield to political pressure because they feared victimization or
harassment, 88, or $20 \cdot 3$ per cent., being fearful of similar consequences had stated that in such a situation they would apparently
agree to oblige the political superior but in actual fact would not
carry out his unlawful orders.

Twelve officers, or $3 \cdot 2$ per cent. of the sample, in spite of their
optimism that no victimization would follow, suggested that political pressure should not be resisted. Another six officers, or $1 \cdot 3$
per cent. of the sample, recommended the same course of action
although they had no idea as to the consequences which would
follow resistance to political pressure. These 18 officers, forming $4 \cdot 5$ per cent. of the sample, for all practical purposes may
be bracketed with those respondents who advised not to resist
political pressure for fear of victimization or harassment. It is

likely that these officials were scared of political victimization or harassment so much so that they were not willing to make a statement to that effect lest they might offend the past or the would-be political superior.

Only 31, or 7·1 per cent., of the officers felt absolutely secure. They said that the public servant must offer resistance to political pressure because the political superior could do him no harm.

One hundred and sixty-five officers, or 38·4 per cent. of the sample, advised resistance to political pressure although they were aware that victimization or harassment or both would follow. Nineteen, or 4·4 per cent. of the officers, had given the same reply although they did not know what consequences would follow. Thirteen, or 3·0 per cent. of the officers, had declined to say anything on the ground that they had no practical experience in this matter.

Combining the frequencies of the similar responses, it was learnt, that nearly one-half, or 47·1 per cent., of the respondents were inclined to yield to political pressure for fear of victimization or harassment, while almost an equal proportion, or 49·9 per cent., were inclined to resist political pressure even at the risk of unfavourable consequences. The impression of the writer and of other interviewers is that quite a large number of the public servants advocated resistance to political pressure more as a show of courage than as a result of genuine belief. Many of such officials, it is surmised, would give in if they were actually subjected to political pressure. The two general inferences which may be drawn are firstly, that the image of the politician is far from favourable in the mind of the public servants and secondly, that more of the public servants would give in to political pressure than would stake their career to resist it.

Very large proportions of officers in all departments expected unfavourable consequences as a result of defying political pressure. The proportions ranged from the minimum of 79·1 per cent. to the maximum of 100·0 per cent. The group of officers in the Civil Service of Pakistan was the only exception, of whom just 38·7 per cent. expected unfavourable consequences. More than half, or 54·8 per cent., of the CSP officers believed that the political superior could do no harm to the public servant.

In other words the officers of the Civil Service of Pakistan seem to have a greater sense of security against political victimization. As has been mentioned previously, in matters of discipline the officers of the Civil Service of Pakistan are under the control of the central government and that the provincial governments have a limited jurisdiction in this area. However, the provincial governments exercise full control over all provincial cadres. The influence of this factor may be noted in the variations of reactions between the officers of the Civil Service of Pakistan and those of the Provincial Civil Service.

As compared to the 38·7 per cent. of the CSP officers, 73·1 per cent. of the PCS officers feared victimization or harassment for resisting political pressure. Again, as compared to 54·8 per cent. of the CSP officers who thought that the political superior could not do any harm to them, only 23·0 per cent. of the PCS officers felt that way.

Comparison of the statements of the officers of the Police Service of Pakistan and those of the officers of the Provincial Police Service revealed a similar trend though not in a significant manner. Out of the 34 officers of the Provincial Police Service 27, or 79·4 per cent., feared unfavourable consequences of resisting political pressure. As compared to this group of officers 9 out of 13, or 69·2 per cent., of the officers of Police Service of Pakistan expected unpleasant consequences. Four, or 11·8 per cent., of the officers of the Provincial Police Service and 3, or 23·8 per cent., of the officers of the Police Service of Pakistan had the confidence that the political superior could not harm the public servant.

It was observed that officers of Class II had a relatively greater sense of insecurity against political pressure than the officers of Class I. Out of the 150 Class II officers 134, or 89·3 per cent., feared unpleasant consequences of resistance to political pressure and only 3, or 2·7 per cent., had the confidence that the political superior could do them no harm. Out of 215 Class I officers, 161, or 74·9 per cent., expected unfavourable consequences as a result of resisting political pressure and as many as 38, or 17·7 per cent., had the assurance that no unpleasant consequences would follow.

The officers with a high-ranking position felt relatively less insecure against political pressure than those who occupied a low position. For example, 21 out of 34, or 61·7 per cent., of the officers occupying the first position in the chain of command expected political victimization while 196 out of 229, or 85·7 per cent. of the officers of the last position expected a similar fate. As much as 12 out of 34, or 35·3 per cent., of the officers of the first position in the chain of command believed that no victimization would follow while only 10 only of 229, or 4·4 per cent., of the officers of the last position entertained that hope.

Summary

More of the officers in the superior cadres such as the Civil Service of Pakistan and the Police Service of Pakistan show a spirit of resistance to political pressure than the officers of inferior cadres namely the Provincial Civil Service and the Provincial Police Service. Similarly, more of the high-ranking officers than those of the low rank displayed that spirit.

More of the officers of inferior cadres namely the Provincial Civil Service, Provincial Police Service expected unfavourable consequences as a result of resistance to political pressure than did the officers of the superior cadres such as the Civil Service of Pakistan and the Police Service of Pakistan. More of the low-ranking officers anticipated unpleasant repercussions following resistance to political pressure than did the high-ranking officials.

CHAPTER 7

HUMAN RELATIONS AMONG THE PUBLIC SERVANTS

Human Relations between the Public Servant
and his Superiors inside the Office

Relations between a superior officer and his subordinates, during the pre-Independence period, were as a matter of policy governed by the maxim 'familiarity breeds contempt'. A good officer was supposed to keep a 'safe' distance from his subordinates. Otherwise, it was believed that the subordinates might mistake kindness for weakness and might not work efficiently. Some of the British officers were even wont to believe that the indigenous people responded better to fear than kindness. One way of maintaining the proper distance was to make the subordinates stand when they visited the offices of their superiors.

Although this type of behaviour persisted after Independence, the spirit of revolt against the old order which accompanied Independence has been steadily undermining this tradition. In order to ascertain the strength of this tradition, it was decided to utilize the gesture of offering a chair to subordinates as an indicator of the superior-subordinate relations. The responses were fairly encouraging.

More than three-quarters of our respondents, or 80·8 per cent., stated that they were offered a chair by their superiors when they visited their offices. A small proportion namely, 3·7 per cent. of the public servants, stated that their superiors sometimes did and sometimes did not offer them a chair. According to 7·2 per cent. of the respondents only some of their superiors offered a chair. In the cases of 1·2 per cent. the officers sat down without being asked while 7·2 per cent. stated that they were not offered a chair at all. In other words, in the case of about one-fifth of the public servants the attitude of their superiors towards them was not entirely satisfactory.

The situation in this respect invites special attention to certain departments. For example, in the Department of Animal Husbandry 5 out of 19 officers, or 26·3 per cent., stated that they were not offered a chair when they visited the offices of their superiors, or that this courtesy was offered only occasionally depending upon the sweet will of the superior, or that only some of the officers did so while others did not. Twenty-eight out of 73, or 38·4 per cent., of the officers of the Health Department were denied this courtesy in a similar fashion. Almost all of this group of officers belonged to Class II. In the Civil Secretariat, 27 officers out of a total of 93, or 29·0 per cent., were denied the courtesy of being offered a seat by their superiors. Twenty-three out of this group of 27 officers were drawn from the category of the unclassified and the Class II officers. All the 31 officers of the Civil Service of Pakistan stated that they were never so treated.

It was observed that more officers of the lower class than officers of the higher class were denied this courtesy. For example, 91·2 per cent. of the Class I officers, 71·3 per cent. of Class II officers and 68·7 per cent. of the unclassified officers were offered a chair on visiting their superiors. Just as an officer of Class I stands a better chance of getting a seat than does an officer of Class II, so does the officer holding the first position in the chain of command as compared to those holding inferior positions.

Human Relations between the Public Servant
and his Subordinates inside the Office

In determining the attitude of the respondents towards their subordinates they were asked to say whether or not they offered a chair to their subordinates when the latter visited their offices. Two-thirds of the respondents, or 66·4 per cent., replied in the affirmative. About a quarter, or 24·1 per cent., of the officers stated that ordinarily they offered a chair to their immediate subordinates and that they offered a chair to the others, including the clerks, if they had to stay in their offices for a long time. Only 7·0 per cent. of the public servants offered a chair to their immediate subordinates while 2·5 per cent. of the respondents did not offer a chair at all.

The officers who did not offer a chair to their subordinates were mainly drawn from the Health Department. Most of them were doctors who belonged to Class II. They had, as subordinates, such persons as attendants and the like. According to this group of respondents there was seldom an occasion to offer their subordinates a chair due primarily to the nature of the work.

The Police Department, the Civil Service of Pakistan and the Irrigation Department contained a large proportion of the officers who offered a chair to their junior subordinates only when they had to stay in the office for quite some time.

It was observed that the officers of a higher class were more discriminatory in their treatment towards subordinates. For example, 37·7 per cent. of the Class I officers did not consider it an obligation, social or otherwise, to ask a visiting subordinate to take a seat. Fewer Class II officers, or 32·7 per cent., displayed this type of behaviour. A still smaller proportion, or 22·4 per cent., of the unclassified officers subscribed to this point of view.

The officers who occupied a higher position in the chain of command were relatively more inclined towards the view that, primarily the senior subordinates were entitled to the privilege of receiving a seat on the occasion of a visit to a superior's office. They regarded it as a nice gesture on the part of a superior officer to offer a seat to his subordinates but they asserted that the lesser subordinates had no right, not even a social one, to such treatment and that it was within the absolute discretion of the superior officer to make this gesture. To give actual figures, 44·1 per cent. of the officers occupying the first position in the chain of command upheld this attitude. A slight difference was noted when comparing them with the officers occupying the last position in the chain of command, 30·1 per cent. of whom supported this view.

It was felt that the actual practice of the public servant might not be an adequate source of information concerning his attitude towards his subordinates. In order to know what was his opinion as compared to his practice in this respect an additional question was put to the public servant. It asked, 'Do you think an officer should offer a chair to his subordinates when they visit his office?' In either case, whether the public servant replied in the affirmative or in the negative, he was asked to give reasons for his reply.

A little over three-quarters of the respondents, or 78·7 per cent. recognized the value of this gesture as a matter of principle. About one-sixth of the public servants took the position that ordinarily the senior subordinates alone should be accorded this courtesy. Some of these officers thought that it was advisable to extend this courtesy to junior subordinates as well when they had to remain in the office for a considerable period. Only 3·2 per cent. of the officers were against offering a seat to their subordinates.

The officers who were against offering a seat did so mainly for the reason that due to such courtesy the subordinates developed a familiarity with the superior as a result of which he came to take the superior officer lightly. It was stated that the subordinate might even start taking liberties with the superior officer.

On the other hand, a large number of the respondents felt that this gesture was of signal importance in developing better relations between subordinate and superior. This attitude on the part of the superior officer tended to create greater loyalty and respect on the part of the subordinate towards his superior officer. As a result, the subordinate tended to perform his duties with devotion and a sense of personal interest.

Some of the respondents thought that on grounds of efficiency and better work, it was desirable for the subordinate to be made comfortable otherwise he would work badly.

Quite a few of the respondents took the position that ordinarily subordinates had been treated in such an impersonal and indifferent manner that they had developed a feeling of extreme inferiority which was represented in certain cases by a cringing and sneaking attitude towards a superior. In order to remove this feeling and in order to create a sense of self-respect in the subordinates, it was necessary for the superior officer to treat them with greater dignity.

It is interesting to note in Table 25 that whereas over three-quarters of the public servants hold the view that as a matter of principle the subordinates should be offered a chair, only two-thirds in fact do offer a chair. This may mean that the attitude of the superiors towards the subordinates is still less favourable than the figures indicate. Or does it mean that a principle which is good in spirit does not work so well in practice? In other words, does it mean that the subordinates do in fact begin to take their work and their superiors less seriously than they would otherwise?

Police officers specifically insisted on keeping a 'safe' distance between the superior officer and the lower subordinates. It was maintained that the Police was a para-military organization. Simple considerations of discipline demanded that the superiors should not become too familiar with the subordinates. In the Police Department 39·1 per cent. of the officers subscribed to this view but as many as 71·7 per cent. of the Police officers actually practised it.

Discrepancies between profession and practice are notable in certain other cases as well. For example, 83·9 per cent. of the CSP officers were in favour of offering a seat to subordinates, while only 54·8 per cent. actually did so. Similarly, 82·8 per cent. of the officers in the Secretariat thought it advisable to offer a chair to subordinates but only 69·9 per cent. actually did so.

'Whether an officer offers a seat to his subordinates or not'

Table 25

ATTITUDE AND PRACTICE OF PUBLIC SERVANTS TOWARDS

OFFERING A CHAIR TO SUBORDINATES

	A chair should be offered	Only to senior officers, to others in the discretion of the superior	If I am in the mood	Indif-ferent	No	Total
Attitude	340	72	2	4	14	432
	78·7	16·6	0·5	0·9	3·4	100·0
Practice	287	131	3	—	11	432
	66·4	30·4	0·7		2·5	100·0

would appear to be a trivial matter. In a few cases the superior officers and his subordinates sit in the same room. In other instances the subordinate's visit to his superior's office is so short that there is hardly an occasion to indulge in such courtesies as asking the subordinate to sit down. The fact that an officer does not offer a seat to his subordinate is not necessarily an expression of an authoritarian attitude. It might very well be due to a sense of urgency and pre-occupation with the work at hand.

In most cases, however, this small gesture does provide some guide to the attitude of the officer. If he is not authoritarian he is most likely to be a snob or a pedant. This interpretation has its roots in the history of this country. It has already been noted that the policy of the foreign rulers in this country had been to keep the subordinate at arm's length. The very term 'subordinate' demonstrates a lack of understanding of the team-work necessary in any successful collective enterprise. This policy had been, in extreme cases, developed into the concept that the people of the sub-continent were by nature used to an authoritarian system. An indifferent attitude towards the subordinate was only one manifestation of this carefully developed concept. A long period of practice had hardened this behaviour into a tradition.

This tradition exercises a good deal of influence upon the public servants who occupy a higher position in the hierarchy. It is likely that this phenomenon is simply a projection of the relations which exist between the upper and the lower classes in Pakistani society at large. This question brings us into another dimension of superior-subordinate relationship, namely relations between the two on the social plane, outside of the office.

Human Relations between the Public Servant and his Subordinates outside the Office

Hierarchy is the basic feature of bureaucracy. It is an inevitable consequence of applying the principle of distribution of work in any enterprise. Some people do very important work, others do less important work but no one is self-sufficient. The ultimate output is the result of the collective effort of all. A spirit of fellow-feeling, or *esprit de corps* as it is commonly called, is essential for all collective enterprises.

However, in practice, it is not unusual for the people who are engaged in a common effort to lose sight of the common objective. In such a situation the most immediate aspect of a collective effort which has been placed in the charge of a functionary comes to assume for him primary importance. Also relative positions in the hierarchy tend to acquire more exaggerated significance than was originally intended. A manifestation of this trend is the development of an increased distance between those who occupy a higher place in the hierarchy and those who occupy a lower place. In an extreme case the distance between the high and the low, which initially grows inside the hierarchy, extends into social life as well.

In order to examine this aspect of Pakistani bureaucracy two special questions were designed. Both questions were constructed in the form of hypothetical situations which were read out to the respondents in order to obtain their reactions. In the first situation the public servant was asked to imagine that in a certain department a clerk was transferred or retired and his colleagues had arranged a farewell party in his honour. He was asked to state: 'Should or should not the public servant attend the party if invited?' If the respondent replied in the affirmative, he was asked to indicate whether the public servant should attend the party, as a gesture of his goodwill and leave soon, or should he stay at the party but keep a distance from his subordinates or should he stay on at the party and mix freely with his subordinates?

A person who replied that the public servant should not attend the farewell party organized by the subordinates or who insisted that a distance should be maintained between the superior and his subordinates even in a social gathering may be classified as status-conscious in his attitude towards his subordinates. A person who was in favour of attending such a social gathering and who believed in the free mixing of the superiors and the subordinates may be described as non-status-conscious. A person who subscribed to the view that a superior officer should attend such a function as a gesture of goodwill and leave soon may be termed 'pedantic'.

On the basis of this interpretation the findings are that 54·8 per cent. of the respondents are not status-conscious in social relations with subordinates, 29·9 per cent. are pedantic and 15·3 per cent. are status-conscious.

It was observed that out of the 31 officers of the CSP 17, or 54·8 per cent. fell in the category called pedantic while 7, or 22·6 per cent., displayed a status-conscious attitude towards subordinates and an equal percentage of them were not status-conscious in regard to their subordinates. Out of the 46 public servants in the Police Department 15, or 32·6 per cent., displayed status-consciousness, 11, or 23·9 per cent., belonged to the pedantic category and 20, or 43·5 per cent., were not status-conscious. If the percentages of status-conscious and pedantic responses are combined in the cases of the CSP and the Police officers, it is discovered that the attitude of a majority of 77·4 and 66·5 per cent. of the officers in the two services respectively is highly unfavourable towards subordinates. On a similar basis a majority of 61·5 per cent. of the officers in the Irrigation Department were more inclined towards status-consciousness in respect to their subordinates.

A majority of the officers in the remaining departments did not appear to be status-conscious. The majority of the non-status-conscious officers was as high as three-quarters or more in the Departments of Animal Husbandry, Public Relations and the Local Fund Audit.

An explanation for the above pattern of responses may be that the Civil Service of Pakistan and the Police Service enjoy a reputation of being privileged cadres. The officers of these two services generally hold positions of great authority in the government organization. Their rates of remuneration are also high. These conditions may be responsible for creating an 'inflated' self-concept among the officers of these cadres. The image of these officers in the public mind is not that of the average public servant but that of one who is a servant of the public but who takes the role of a master. An attitude betraying a tinge of status-consciousness on their part towards subordinates may be explained in part as an effort to sustain their own self-concept and to maintain the image in which they think the public views them.

As compared to the CSP and the Police Service, officers in the departments do not exercise as much executive power. As a result, they do not see themselves, nor does the public view them, in the role of a ruler. In many cases, the higher public servants in these departments have themselves previously served in subordinate positions in their own cadres. The cumulative effect of these factors is that the attitude of superior officers in the above-mentioned cadres is free from status-consciousness towards those who work under them. It is notable that among the group of officers who do not hold purely executive posts, those with relatively less executive authority display less status-consciousness in relations with their subordinates. For example, officers who are less status-conscious are present in larger proportions in the Departments of Animal Husbandry, Local Fund Audit and Public Relations than in the Health Department, the Irrigation Department, and among the officers who work with the Deputy Commissioner's Office.

The officers of Class I are more inclined to be status-conscious and pedantic towards subordinates in social relations than are the officers of Class II and the unclassified officers. However, within the latter two categories, the unclassified officers were relatively more status-conscious and pedantic than the officers of Class II. The actual combined percentages of status-conscious and pedantic officers in each Class were 52·6, 36·0 and 41·6 respectively.

With the exaltation of the position of a public servant in the hierarchy his attitude towards his subordinates undergoes a change. Examination of Table 26 shows that, with the exclusion of the category of fifth position in the chain of command which is represented by one respondent and is therefore of no statistical significance, there is a gradual decline in the frequency of status-consciousness in relations with subordinates in a descending order of the position in the chain of command. The same is the case in the pedantic category.

It was observed that officers who were more Westernized were also more status-conscious in their social relations with their subordinates. For example, 55·8 per cent. of the least Westernized officers did not display status-consciousness in social relations with their subordinates and 46·2 per cent. of the highly Westernized officers did not display status-consciousness in social relations with their subordinates and 46·2 per cent. of the highly Westernized officers did not display status-consciousness. Furthermore, 27·1 per cent. of the least Westernized officers displayed a pedantic attitude towards subordinates in social relations. As compared to them 48·7 per cent. of the highly Westernized officers displayed an attitude of this type.

A significant correlation was established between the socio-economic status of a public servant and his attitude towards his subordinates. Table 27 shows that more than half of the officers from the upper classes displayed a pedantic attitude. The attitude of the officers in the upper middle class did not emerge in a clear cut manner. The attitude of a sizable proportion among them was free from status-consciousness. The attitude of almost an equivalent number may be described as pedantic. In the groups of officers of the lower middle and the lower class respectively more than half

Table 26

ATTITUDE OF PUBLIC SERVANTS OF DIFFERENT RANKS
TOWARDS SUBORDINATES IN SOCIAL RELATIONS

Position in the chain of command	Status-conscious	Pedantic	Non-status-conscious	Total
First	7 20·6	17 50·0	10 29·4	34 100·0
Second	11 19·7	21 37·5	24 42·9	56 100·0
Third	5 11·9	15 35·7	22 52·4	42 100·0
Fourth	10 15·3	18 27·7	37 56·9	65 100·0
Fifth	1 16·3	3 50·0	2 33·3	6 100·0
Last	32 14·0	55 24·0	142 62·0	229 100·0

exhibited an attitude which was free from status-consciousness. If the frequencies of responses representing status-conscious and pedantic attitudes were to be combined in the case of officers of different status the proportions of such responses show a gradual decline from the upper status to the lower status.

No significant variations were observed between the younger and the older officers in their social relations towards subordinates. Almost an equal majority of these groups of officers were non-status-conscious.

In order to record their reactions the respondents were confronted with another typical situation in which they might find themselves in regard to their social relations with subordinates. The situation which they were asked to imagine was as follows, supposing that an officer is sitting alone in a restaurant and one of his Class III subordinates, for example, a clerk, walks in. The officer is aware that no other table is free. Should the officer ask

Table 27

THE ATTITUDES OF THE RESPONDENTS OF DIFFERENT SOCIO-ECONOMIC STATUS TOWARDS SUBORDINATES IN SOCIAL RELATIONS

Attitude	Low	Lower middle	Upper middle	Upper
Status-conscious	32	16	14	4
	15·3	12·7	21·2	12·9
Pedantic	49	39	25	16
	23·4	31·0	27·9	51·6
Non-status-conscious	128	71	27	11
	61·2	56·3	40·9	35·5
Total:	209	126	66	31
	100·0	100·0	100·0	100·0

his subordinate to come and sit with him? The respondents were asked to give reasons for their replies.

About two-thirds of the respondents, or 64·4 per cent., replied in the affirmative. A quarter, or 25·2 per cent., of the officers replied in the negative. 4·9 per cent. said that 'there was no harm' if the officer did invite his subordinate. A small number, amounting to 5·5 per cent., stated that the situation had no reality for them. About one half of this group of officers said that Class III subordinates neither have the means nor the inclination to visit those restaurants which are frequented by the higher public servants. The other half said that they themselves did not have the time or money to go to such restaurants.

Those replying in the affirmative may be taken as non-status-conscious, those replying in the negative may be counted as highly status-conscious and those falling in-between as neither highly nor non-status-conscious but pedantic in social relations with subordinates.

Three main reasons were offered by those who were non-status-conscious. In the first place they maintained that common courtesy demanded that the officer should invite his subordinate. Such a gesture, it was hoped, would create goodwill between the superior and the subordinate which would have a favourable influence upon the quality of work in the office and upon its output.

The second argument in favour of inviting the subordinate was that the restaurant is a public place. When outside the office the subordinate is equal to the officer in his rights and privileges of making use of the facilities provided by a public place.

The third argument supporting increased social contact between the superior and the subordinate was that it would create a sense of self-respect in the mind of the subordinate and would help eliminate status-consciousness on his part.

Those who were opposed to developing social contacts between the superior and the subordinate, in the first instance, maintained that familiarity would damage discipline in the office. It was feared that the subordinate might take undue advantage of such casual social relations with his superior with the result that office discipline might be impaired.

In the second place, it was stated that contact between the subordinate and the superior inside the office was so brief and impersonal that social relations on an appreciable scale were impossible. In spite of working in the same office for years the superiors and the lower subordinates tend to remain strangers to each other.

In the third place, it was maintained that in interests there was little in common between the superior and the lower subordinate. The higher public servant is generally highly educated. In his tastes and opinions he is usually a man of finer sensibilities. On the other hand, the lower subordinate is generally a person of lower academic training. His tastes and opinions are basically different from those of his superiors. In such conditions, it is difficult to evolve, even with conscious effort, any fruitful social relations between the two. Rather it might be a torture for the subordinate to sit side by side with his superior over a cup of tea in an elegant restaurant. It was asserted by a few that the subordinate himself would not accept this courtesy even if offered.

Combining the status-conscious and the pedantic responses it is revealed that slightly less than one-third of the public servants are, according to their own opinion, status-conscious. The second and also the third argument advanced by them in support of their position casts a serious reflection upon the state of human relations within government offices. The fact that the superior and the subordinate remain social strangers despite sustained contact in the office implies that the rank in the hierarchy, which was originally intended to be a convenient device for the distribution of work, has degenerated into an unsurmountable barrier in the way of smooth contact between fellow workers.

The situation invites special attention in the Civil Service of Pakistan and in the Police Department where 51·6 per cent. of the officers of the first and 50·0 per cent. of the officers of the second cadre are altogether averse to the establishment of social contacts between superior and subordinate. The percentages of officers who fall in the category of non-status-conscious are 22·6 and 50·0 in the CSP and the Police respectively. It further shows that the superior-subordinate relations are especially unhappy in the Civil Service of Pakistan.

A majority of the officers in all Classes appeared to be non-status-conscious. However, the majority was the largest among the Class II officers. To give the exact figures 78·0 per cent. of Class II, 74·6 per cent. of the unclassified and only 51·6 per cent. of the Class I officers displayed this type of attitude. The percentages of the status-conscious officers in the three classes were 16·7, 14·9 and 34·4 respectively. These figures may be interpreted to mean that the tendency towards status-consciousness is relatively greater among the Class I officers than among the Class II and the unclassified officers.

Of the younger officers 69·9 per cent. did not display status-consciousness in social relations with their subordinates while only 22·2 per cent. were status-conscious. As compared to them 60·0 per cent. of the older officers did not display status-consciousness and 28·2 per cent. did so. Analysis of this data indicates that variation in attitude towards subordinates between officers of different ages is not significant.

That the tendency towards status-consciousness tends to be greater among the high-ranking officers than among the low-ranking ones, was more clearly demonstrated by comparing the attitudes of the officers occupying different positions in the chain of command. Whereas 44·1 per cent. of the officers of the first position showed status-consciousness in their social relations with subordinates, only 17·9 per cent. of the officers of the last position did the same. Conversely, as many as 75·1 per cent. of the officers holding the last position were free from status-consciousness while only 38·2 per cent. of the officers of the first position appeared to be so.

Westernization seems to exercise some though not a significant influence upon the attitude of a public servant in regard to social relations between the superior and his subordinate. Of the least Westernized respondents 68·5 per cent. were not status-conscious, 3·2 per cent. may be described as pedantic and 22·3 per cent. were status-conscious. Among the highly Westernized officers the corresponding figures were 53·8, 15·4 and 23·1. The tendency towards a non-status-conscious behaviour in social relations with subordinates appear to be relatively greater among the officers who are not Westernized.

The socio-economic status of the public servant, as should be expected, exercises significant influence upon his attitude towards the nature of social relations which should exist between his subordinate and himself. Examination of Table 28 shows that the proportion of the non-status-conscious officers is the highest, or 77·0 per cent., among the respondents who have a low status and that this proportion gradually decreases as the status rises. The proportion of the pedantic officials is the highest among the respondents who enjoy an upper-class status. The proportion of the status-conscious officials is the highest, or 43·9 per cent., among the respondents of the upper middle class, while it is the lowest, or 16·3, among the respondents of low status. To sum up, it may be stated that the lower the socio-economic status of the official the more he tends to be free from status-consciousness in social relations with his subordinates.

Table 28

THE ATTITUDES OF THE PUBLIC SERVANTS OF DIFFERENT SOCIO-ECONOMIC STATUS TOWARDS SUBORDINATES IN SOCIAL RELATIONS

Attitude	Low	Lower middle	Upper middle	Upper
Status-conscious	34 16·3	37 29·4	29 43·9	9 29·0
Pedantic	5 2·4	6 4·8	2 3·0	8 25·8
Non-status-conscious	161 77·0	73 57·9	33 50·0	11 35·5
Non-committal	9 4·3	10 7·9	2 3·0	3 9·7
Total	209 100·0	126 100·0	66 100·0	31 100·0

Out of the total respondents as many as 80·8 per cent. were offered a seat on visiting their superior's office while only 7·2 per cent. were not. As compared to this 66·4 per cent. of the respondents offered this courtesy to their subordinates and only 2·5 per cent. did not do so. These figures indicate that not all the respondents accord the same courteous reception to their subordinates as they get from their own superiors. This inconsistency in behaviour might be as a result of the fact that whereas all the respondents are themselves gazetted officers, most of their subordinates are non-gazetted officials such as clerks and peons. The attitude of the public servants seems to have been influenced by the tradition of British India where many a courtesy was extended only if the recipient happened to be a gazetted official. Probably it was this tradition which had found expression in the attitude of the 7·0 per cent. of the respondents who stated that they offered a seat to immediate subordinates only or in the attitude of the 24·1 per cent. of the respondents who said that ordinarily they offered this courtesy to the immediate subordinates but extended it to the other subordinates as well if they remained in the office for a considerable time. Proper human relations on the part of the superior officers need to be established more in the case of non-gazetted officials than in the case of the gazetted officials.

It seems that human relations between the public servant and his subordinates are less satisfactory outside the office than inside. Out of the total respondents only 2·5 per cent. said that they did not offer a seat to their subordinates, while 15·3 per cent. said that a gazetted officer should not attend a social function arranged by his non-gazetted subordinates and 25·2 per cent. said that a gazetted officer should not mix freely with a non-gazetted subordinate in a public restaurant.

CHAPTER 8

ATTITUDES OF THE CIVIL SERVANTS TOWARD ASSOCIATING SUBORDINATES IN THE PROCESS OF DECISION-MAKING

What should be the role of the subordinate in the process of decision-making? Should he be associated in the process, or should he be asked to mind his own business and simply do whatever is decided at the top level? According to modern administrative concepts it is held that if the subordinate is involved in the making of decisions which he is supposed to implement, his performance should improve. If, however, subordinates are not given any part in the making of decisions they are likely to develop an irresponsible attitude represented by a lack of interest in and enthusiasm for the work they are doing.

The director of a Pakistani institution established for the training of public servants once reported that most of the officials who came for training in that institution complained that, in their departments, they were not given any share in the decision-making process. These officials stated, 'a subordinate is not supposed to think and so we have given up the habit of thinking officially, which, of course, we do in private circles and rave in it to our heart's content criticizing everything out of spite.'[1]

A set of four questions was designed in order to ascertain the opinions of the respondents on this subject. The first question seeks to find out how far down below his own rank a public servant is willing to go to associate his subordinates in the process of decision-making with regard to basic policies. The second question aims at finding out how far the public servant thinks it advisable to consult his subordinates when deciding upon the methods for the implementation of policies. The third question seeks to find out to what degree the public servant is willing to associate his subordinates while making decisions about the internal administration of his department. The fourth question is designed to discover what ranks of subordinates would be welcomed by the public servant as participants in the decision-making process which relates to staff welfare.

The responses to the four questions have been analysed in three parts. Firstly, the attitudes of all the respondents towards one question have been compared with their attitudes towards each of the remaining three questions. Secondly, a similar comparison has been made of the attitudes towards the four questions in the cases of each sub-sample of respondents drawn from one distinct background. Thirdly, in each question, the attitudes of the public servants of one particular background have been compared with those of other backgrounds.

PART 1

COMPARISON OF THE ATTITUDES OF THE RESPONDENTS
TOWARDS THE FOUR QUESTIONS
Attitudes of the Respondents as a whole towards associating
Subordinates in Decisions relating to Policy-making
Slightly less than two-thirds of the respondents, or 63·2 per cent.,

----

[1] Raja Muhammad Afzal, 'A Year of Village Development Academy: The New Concept', *The Civil and Military Gazette*, Lahore, 15 October 1950.

were in favour of associating subordinates of all ranks who were directly concerned with a particular policy decision. About a third of the respondents, 31·7 per cent., felt that it was good to involve subordinates with policy-making decisions but that this association should be restricted to the senior subordinates only. Most of these officials thought that the junior public servants could not be expected to make any substantial contribution to the process of determining basic policies, partly because of their lack of maturity and higher academic training and, partly because their subordinates were inclined to agree to whatever their superior officers said. A very small number of officers, forming 4·6 per cent. of the sample, held the view that the superior officer ought to make policy decisions himself. Three respondents, representing 0·7 per cent. of the total, offered no reply.

Attitudes of the Respondents as a whole towards associating Subordinates in Decisions relating to the Implementation of Policy

The attitudes of the public servants towards associating subordinates in decisions relating to the implementation of policy did not show any significant variation from their attitudes towards drawing upon the opinions of subordinates in policy-making decisions. Almost an equal proportion, or 61·1 per cent. of the officers, were in favour of associating subordinates of all ranks. The proportion of officers who held the opinion that only the senior subordinates should be associated was less than in the first question. The proportion of officials who thought that no subordinate need be associated was doubled. The variation in the last case was notable, but since the proportions, as shown in Table 29, between which the variation exists are extremely small, the variation is not of any great importance.

During the interviews it was found that certain public servants were of the opinion that once a policy was decided upon, there was not so much a need for consulting the subordinates about the methods of implementation, as there was for determining the policy. Some of these officers felt that a good officer was one who decided how to implement a decision himself, and not one who went around consulting his subordinates about the best method of implementing a policy decision. They thought that the officer who asked for group advice was likely to impress his subordinates with his lack of ability, imagination, and qualities of leadership.

Attitudes of the Respondents as a whole towards associating Subordinates in Decisions relating to the Internal Administration of a Department

There are many matters relating to the internal administration of an office upon which the officer in charge must make decisions. Examples of some of these matters are the distribution of work among the subordinate staff, the arrangement for the seating of the subordinates and, occasionally, the fixing of the working hours. The manner in which decisions on such matters are taken varies with different officers. It is generally believed that, in most cases, the officer in charge makes such decisions without consulting any subordinates.

Sixty-nine officers, or 15·9 per cent. of the sample, were of the view that it was not necessary to associate subordinates in decisions relating to internal administration. Two-fifths, or 40·1 per cent., of the respondents thought that only the senior subordinates might be associated. A little over a quarter, or 27·4 per cent., of the public servants, were willing to involve officials down to the clerical rank. Only 69 officers, or 15·9 per cent. of the officials, were willing to associate subordinates of all ranks including peons and other officials of the lowest rank. The largest concentration, or 40·1 per cent., of the responses under the category 'only the senior subordinates should be associated', indicates that the prejudice against the association of the lesser subordinates in decisions relating to internal administration of a department is stronger than that against their association in decisions on other matters.

Attitudes of Respondents as a whole towards associating Subordinates in Decisions relating to Staff Welfare

The attitudes of the respondents towards associating subordinates in decisions relating to staff welfare seem to have been influenced by the consideration that such decisions, being a matter of personal interest to the officials of all ranks, should be made in association with all the officials concerned no matter of what rank. As many as 57·9 per cent. of the respondents were in favour of associating subordinates of all ranks including the officials of the lowest rank in decisions about the general welfare of the staff. A quarter, or 25·0 per cent., were willing to include all subordinates except those of the lowest rank. Only 13·9 per cent. of the respondents insisted that only the senior subordinates should be associated with decisions relating to staff welfare, while 2·5 per cent. of the respondents maintained that no subordinates should be associated.

On comparing the attitudes of the respondents towards associating subordinates in the four different types of decisions it was observed that more than half of the public servants were willing to associate subordinates of all ranks in decisions relating to policy-making, the implementation of a policy and staff welfare. The largest majority, or 82·9 per cent., was in favour of associating subordinates of all ranks in decisions regarding staff welfare. The proportion of responses in favour of associating subordinates of all ranks in decisions concerning internal administration, being 43·3 per cent., was the lowest.

So far the attitudes of the respondents towards associating subordinates in the four different types of decisions provided in the questionnaire have been examined irrespective of their background. At this stage it is proposed to compare the attitudes towards associating subordinates in the four different types of decisions in the case of the officials of each department, cadre, rank and age.

PART 2

COMPARISON OF THE ATTITUDES OF THE RESPONDENTS
IN THE SUB-SAMPLE TOWARDS THE FOUR QUESTIONS
Attitudes of the Officials of each Department
The general pattern of responses in each department towards the questions of associating subordinates in the four different types of decisions was the same as in the case of the responses of all the public servants of the sample. Most of the officers in each department were willing to associate subordinates of all ranks in

Table 29

COMPARISON OF THE ATTITUDES OF THE RESPONDENTS TOWARDS ASSOCIATING THE SUBORDINATES IN DIFFERENT TYPES OF DECISIONS

Types of decisions	Associate no subordinate	Associate senior subordinates only	Associate all subordinates	No response	Total
Decisions on policy matters	20 4.6	137 31.6	272 63.1	3 0.7	432 100.0
Decisions on methods of implementing policy [a]	43 9.9	122 28.3	264 61.1	3 0.7	432 100.0
Decisions on internal administration	69 15.9	173 40.1	187 43.3	3 0.7	432 100.0
Decisions on staff welfare	11 2.5	60 13.9	358 82.9	3 0.7	432 100.0

all types of decisions. The largest majority, however, in every department was in favour of associating subordinates of all ranks in decisions relating to staff welfare while the proportion was the smallest in favour of associating subordinates in decisions regarding internal administration.

By way of illustration, the position of the officers of the Department of Animal Husbandry is given in Table 30. Most of the officers in this department were willing to associate the subordinates of all ranks in all types of decisions. However, whereas as many as 16 out of the 19 officers were willing to do this in decisions on staff welfare, only 4 were in favour of following this policy in making decisions regarding internal administration.

Attitudes of the Officials of each Cadre

The attitudes of the respondents in each cadre in the matter of associating subordinates in the four different types of decisions followed the same pattern as did the attitudes of the respondents in each separate department. Most of the officers in each cadre were willing to associate subordinates of all ranks in all types of decisions. The largest majority, however, in each cadre was in favour of associating subordinates in decisions regarding staff welfare while the proportion of officers in support of associating subordinates in decisions on internal administration was the smallest.

For the demonstration of this point the position of the officers of the Civil Service of Pakistan is described. Most of the officers in this cadre were in favour of the association of subordinates of all ranks in decisions of all types. However, out of a total of 31 CSP officers, 24 were in favour of applying the above principle in decisions relating to staff welfare while only 11 were in favour of doing the same in decisions relating to internal administration.

The Attitudes of the Officials of each Class

The attitudes of the officers of each class towards associating subordinates in the decision-making processes in the cases discussed above varied with the type of decision in a similar manner. For example, most of the Class I officials were willing to associate subordinates of all ranks in decisions relating to policy-making,

Table 30

COMPARISON OF THE ATTITUDES OF THE OFFICERS OF THE DEPARTMENT OF ANIMAL HUSBANDRY TOWARDS ASSOCIATING SUBORDINATES IN DIFFERENT TYPES OF DECISIONS

Types of decisions	Associate no subordinate	Associate senior subordinates only	Associate all subordinates	Total
Decisions on policy matters	1 5.3	6 31.6	12 62.2	19 100.0
Decisions on methods of implementing a policy	1 5.3	4 21.1	14 73.7	19 100.0
Decisions on internal administration	7 36.8	8 42.1	4 21.1	19 100.0
Decisions on staff welfare	1 5.3	2 10.5	16 84.2	19 100.0

Table 31

COMPARISON OF THE ATTITUDES OF CLASS I OFFICERS TOWARDS ASSOCIATING SUBORDINATES IN DIFFERENT TYPES OF DECISIONS

Types of decisions	Associate no subordinate	Associate senior subordinates only	Associate all subordinates	No response	Total
Decisions on policy matters	17 7.9	79 36.7	119 53.3	—	215 100.0
Decisions on methods of implementation of policy	30 14.0	68 31.6	116 54.0	1 0.4	215 100.0
Decisions on internal administration	31 14.4	92 42.8	92 42.8	—	215 100.0
Decisions on staff welfare	9 4.2	35 16.3	170 79.1	1 0.4	215 100.0

implementation, internal administration and staff welfare. However, the proportion was the largest, or 79·1 per cent., in favour of following this procedure in the area of staff welfare, and the smallest, or 42·8 per cent., in following the same procedure in the matter of decisions on internal administration.

The Attitudes of Officers of Different Positions in the Chain of Command

The attitudes of the officers of different positions in the chain of command towards associating subordinates in the decision-making process paralleled the findings presented above. For example, 20 out of 34, or 58·8 per cent., of the officers occupying the first position in the chain of command, were in favour of associating subordinates of all ranks in decisions relating to staff welfare while only 9 out of 34, or 26·4 per cent., were willing to do so in decisions concerning internal administration of a department. The general pattern of response was the same in the case of officers of the lowest position in the chain of command.

The Attitudes of the Younger and the Older Officers

In order to compare the attitudes of the respondents on the basis of their age they were divided into two groups representing the younger and the older officers. The officers whose ages ranged from 23 to 42 years were considered as younger and the officers whose ages varied from 43 to 62 years were taken as older officers. Out of the 212 younger officers, 144, or 67·9 per cent., were in favour of associating subordinates of all ranks in decisions relating to policy-making, 133, or 62·7 per cent., were willing to follow the same practice in decisions relating to the implementation of policy, while only 104, or 49·0 per cent., approved of the same policy in decisions relating to internal administration and as many as 185, or 87·2 per cent., supported this procedure in decisions relating to staff welfare. These figures indicate that as in the case of officers of different departments, cadres and ranks, so among the younger officers, more public servants are in favour of associating subordinates of all ranks in decisions of policy-making, of implementation and of staff welfare than in decisions relating to internal administration. The same general observations are true about the officers in the older age groups.

PART 3

COMPARISON OF THE ATTITUDES OF RESPONDENTS OF DIFFERENT BACKGROUNDS TOWARDS EACH QUESTION

The Attitudes towards associating Subordinates in Different Types of Decisions among Officers of Different Departments

The departments in which the largest number of officers favoured the association of all subordinates in decisions relating to policy matters were the Jails Departments, the Department of Health Services and the Department of Public Relations. Five out of 6 of the officers of the Jails Departments, 59 out of the 73 of the officers of the Department of Health Services and 19 out of 24 of the officers of the Department of Public Relations subscribed

Table 32

COMPARISON OF THE ATTITUDES OF THE YOUNGER OFFICERS TOWARDS ASSOCIATING SUBORDINATES IN DIFFERENT TYPES OF DECISIONS

Types of decisions	Associate no subordinate	Associate senior subordinates only	Associate all subordinates	No response	Total
Decisions on policy matters	9 4.2	58 27.4	144 67.9	1 0.5	212 100.0
Decisions on methods of implementing	23 10.8	55 25.9	133 62.7	1 0.5	212 100.0
Decisions on internal administration	32 15.1	75 35.3	104 49.1	1 0.5	212 100.0
Decisions on staff welfare	5 2.4	20 9.4	185 87.2	2 0.9	212 100.0

to this view. The proportion of the CSP officers holding the same opinion was also very large. Twenty-two out of the 31 CSP officers favoured the association of all subordinates in decisions relating to policy matters.

A much larger number of the officers of the Departments of Jails and Health favoured the association of all subordinates in decisions relating to implementation of policy than did the officers of other departments. The proportions of officers supporting this attitude were 83·3 per cent. and 82·2 per cent. respectively. Fourteen out of the 19 officers of the Department of Animal Husbandry were willing to associate all subordinates in decisions relating to the implementation of policy.

It was only in the Department of Health that more than half of the officers supported the association of all subordinates in decisions relating to internal administration. Forty-nine out of 73, or 67·2 per cent., of the officers in the Health Department were willing to associate subordinates of all ranks in decisions on internal administration. The next highest proportion of officers holding the same opinion was just over 44·0 per cent. in the Irrigation Department and in the Civil Secretariat. The proportion of officers holding the same view was as low as 9·1 per cent. in the Department of Local Fund Audit, while 72·7 per cent. of the officers of this department said that association in decisions about internal administration should be restricted to senior subordinates. As many as 61·3 per cent. of the CSP officers held the same opinion.

On the question of associating subordinates of all ranks in decisions relating to staff welfare a very large majority of officers in almost all the departments expressed their agreement. With the exception of the officers attached to the Deputy Commissioner's office, of whom 50·0 per cent. approved of this attitude, the proportion of such officers in all other departments varied from 75·0 per cent. to 100·0 per cent.

The public servants employed in the Department of Health Services supported in very large numbers the association of the subordinates of all ranks in all types of decisions. A large proportion of officers of the Civil Service of Pakistan held the same attitude except in decisions relating to internal administration.

The Attitude towards associating Subordinates in the Various Types of Decisions among Officers of Different Cadres

Twenty-two out of 31, or 71·0 per cent., of the CSP officers, were in favour of associating subordinates of all ranks in decisions relating to policy-making. The numbers and percentages of officers holding the same opinion among the PCS officers were 18 out of 26, or 69·2 per cent., among the Provincial Police Officers, 21 out of 34, or 61·8 per cent., and among the officers of the Police Service of Pakistan 6 out of 13, or 46·2 per cent. On the question of associating subordinates of all ranks in decisions of policy the CSP officers appear to be non-authoritarian in the largest majority, while the officers of the Police Service of Pakistan are non-authoritarian to the least extent.

The position was the same on the question of associating subordinates of all ranks in decisions relating to the implementation of policy. Whereas 67·7 per cent. of the CSP officers accepted the above policy, only 30·8 per cent. of the officers of the Police Service of Pakistan did so.

On the question of association of subordinates of all ranks in decisions relating to internal administration, no significant variation was observed in the attitudes of the officers of the Civil Service of Pakistan, the Provincial Civil Service and the Provincial Police Service except that the proportion of the supporters of the association of the subordinates of all ranks was the largest in the last mentioned cadre. The proportion of such officers was again the lowest in the Police Service of Pakistan.

On the question of associating subordinates of all ranks in decisions relating to staff welfare the proportions of the supporters of this view were, 91·2 per cent. in the Provincial Police Service, 77·5 per cent. in the Civil Service of Pakistan, 73·1 per cent. in the Provincial Civil Service and 53·9 per cent. in the Police Service of Pakistan. Here again, the officers of the Police Service of Pakistan turn out to be non-authoritarian in the smallest proportion. The Provincial Police Service emerges as the cadre in which large proportions of officers hold non-authoritarian views on the question of associating subordinates in all types of decisions.

The Attitudes towards associating Subordinates in the Various Types of Decisions among Officers of Different Classes

One hundred and nineteen out of 215, or 55·3 per cent. of the Class I officers, were in favour of associating all subordinates in policy-making decisions. As compared to them, 107 out of 150, or 71·3 per cent., of the Class II and 49 out of 67, or 70·1 per cent., of the unclassified officers approved of this policy. These figures indicate that more of the Class II and the unclassified officers than the Class I officers are willing to associate subordinates of all ranks in decisions of policy.

A similar trend was witnessed in the responses of the Class II and the unclassified officers, on the one hand, and the Class I officers, on the other, to the question of associating subordinates of all ranks in decisions relating to the implementation of policy.

No significant difference was observed in the attitudes of the public servants of different classes on the question of the association of the subordinates of all ranks in decisions relating to internal administration. Only about two-fifths of the public servants in each class approved of the above position.

No significant difference was observed in the attitudes of the public servants of different classes on the question of associating the subordinates of all ranks in decisions on staff welfare. About four-fifths of the officers in each class approved of the association of all subordinates in these matters.

The Attitudes towards associating Subordinates in the Various Types of Decisions among the Officers occupying Different Positions in the Chain of Command

Seventeen out of 34, or 50·0 per cent., of the officers occupying the first position in the chain of command were in favour of associating subordinates of all ranks in decisions relating to policy matters, while 164 out of 229, or 71·6 per cent., of the officers occupying the last position in the chain of command approved of this practice. It is understandable that more officers of a lower position than those of the higher one should support the association of subordinates in the decision-making process.

A similar association was established in the attitudes of the officers of the first position in the chain of command and of those of the last position respectively in the other types of decisions.

The Attitudes towards associating Subordinates in the Different Types of Decisions among the Younger and the Older Officers

On the question of associating subordinates of all ranks in decisions relating to policy-making, 144 out of 212, or 67·9 per cent., of the younger officers approved of this procedure, while 128 out of 220, or 58·2 per cent., of the older officers did the same. Although a majority of officers in both age groups held the same view, the majority was larger among the younger officers.

· On the question of associating subordinates of all ranks in decisions relating to the implementation of policy 133, or 62·7 per cent., of the younger officers and 130, or 59·1 per cent., of the older officers approved. The variation is not significant.

On the matter of associating subordinates of all ranks in decisions relating to internal administration smaller proportions of both the younger and the older officers indicated their agreement. The percentages for officers of both the categories were 49·0 and 37·8 respectively. Very broadly, the tendency to associate subordinates in decisions on internal administration is greater among the younger officers than that among the older officers.

On the question of associating subordinates of all ranks in decisions concerning staff welfare very large majorities of both the younger and the older officers, 87·2 and 78·7 respectively, expressed their approval. The majority of the responses of this type, as may be noted, is slightly larger among the younger officers.

Summary

Considering the respondents as a whole, more are in favour of associating subordinates of all ranks in decisions relating to staff welfare than in decisions of other types. Furthermore, far fewer of the respondents are willing to adopt the same procedure in decisions relating to the internal administration of a department.

This pattern of attitude is displayed by the public servants of each department, each cadre, each class and each position in the chain of command and also by the younger and the older officers. It was noted that a very large number of the officers of the Health Department supported the association of subordinates of all ranks in decisions of all the four types.

Out of the four cadres of the Civil Service of Pakistan, the Provincial Civil Service, the Police Service of Pakistan and the Provincial Police Service the officers of the last mentioned cadre favoured the association of subordinates of all ranks in decisions of all types in much larger proportion than those of the other cadres. The officers of the Police Service of Pakistan who showed willingness to accept this practice were represented by the smallest proportion.

Relatively more of the Class II and the unclassified officers than the officers of Class I supported the association of subordinates of all ranks in decisions of policy-making and of implementation. No significant variation was noted in the attitudes of the officers of the three classes in the remaining two types of decisions.

The officers who occupied the last position in the chain of command approved of the association of the subordinates of all ranks in all the four types of decision.

In very broad terms more of the younger officers than the older officers supported the association of subordinates of all ranks in all the four types of decision.

CHAPTER 9

ATTITUDE OF THE CIVIL SERVANT TOWARDS HIS OWN ROLE

The Public Image of the Public Servant

What is the image of an officer in the mind of the people? This question, as one or two of the respondents suggested, should more appropriately be directed to the people and not to the officers. However, this could not be done in view of the restricted scope of this study. Yet it was important to know what the officer thought was his image in the mind of the people because this might be one of the important factors which influenced the attitude of the public servant towards the people.

Four different images of the public servant were described to the respondents who were asked to indicate which of them, in their opinion, best conveyed the attitude of the people towards a public servant. The four alternatives were:

(a) The people look upon an officer as a person who is above them and who is there to rule them.

(b) As a person who is a servant of the State and whose main job is to protect the interests of the State.

(c) As a person who is a servant of the public and whose main job is to safeguard the interests of the public.

(d) As a person who is a leader of the people and whose main job is to guide and educate the people.

Out of the total number of 432 respondents 245, or 56·7 per cent., were of the opinion that people looked upon an officer as a ruler. Ninety-three of this group of respondents qualified their statement by saying that mainly the uneducated, the poor and the people from the villages regarded an official as a ruler. The second type of response indicates some of the reasons for the image of the public official being so awesome. It is understandable that the unlettered and the less-informed citizen is dependent upon the public servant, to a far greater degree, than is the educated and the well-informed. In this situation, it is open to the public servant to assume whatever role he will. He may help the less-informed citizen and win his goodwill or he may exploit the citizen's ignorance and earn his distrust and contempt.

It is revealing that only eight officials thought that people looked upon a public servant as a friend and a guide. Four of them belonged to the Health Department, one to the Police Department and three to the Civil Secretariat.

Twenty public servants replied that the type of image of an officer in the mind of the public depended upon the department to which the officer belonged or the position he occupied in the government. It is of interest to test whether the image indicated by the respondents has any relationship with the department from which they are drawn.

The response that officials are looked upon as servants of the public was given by 82 officers. Twenty-three or a little less than one-fourth of these respondents were drawn from the Health Department, 13 were working in the Civil Secretariat and 11 belonged to the Civil Service of Pakistan. It appears that officials whose duties have a welfare bias, such as Health Department officers, are more likely to be regarded as servants of the people.

The reply that people regard public officials as servants of the State was offered by 55 respondents. Seventeen, or a little less than one-third, of this group of officials belonged to the Civil Secretariat. Ordinarily, the officials of the Secretariat perform routine functions, which discourage sustained personal contact between the official and the people. As a result, the image of these public servants in the mind of the people is that of State servants who perform their duties primarily because they are paid for it. This image betrays a certain amount of indifference towards the public servant on the part of the people. To explain it further, the people do not look upon the public servant as a ruler or a leader nor do they regard him a servant of the public. They consider him to be a professional servant whose main concern is to serve his employer, the government, rather than to serve the people.

Twenty-two respondents went beyond the four categories of image provided in the questionnaire to express the opinion that the people looked upon the public servant with contempt. Some said that the businessmen and the influential people displayed that attitude. Some said that the intelligentsia and the middle class thought of them in a derogatory sense. Four of these officers were from Police Department, 4 from the Health Department and 2 from the Civil Service of Pakistan. This type of response shows the other extreme of the image of the public servant as a ruler. The attitude of contempt towards public service is significant, however, in its nature and not in its magnitude.

No significant variation was observed in the responses of the public servants of different classes as to the public image of the public official. More than 50.0 per cent. of the public servants in all classes thought that the people looked upon them as rulers.

The image of the public official is still unfavourable in the minds of the people. Most of the officials are still looked upon as ruling masters or merely as professional servants primarily concerned with doing the job no matter how it affects the people. The image of the official as a servant of the people is not yet well developed.

Service Associations as Self-Protecting Bodies

According to Civil Service Rules public servants are allowed to

organize themselves into service associations whose function is
to protect their conditions of service. The rules specifically provide
that the membership of the association shall be confined to a
distinct class of government servants and shall be open to all government servants of that class. Explicit instructions have been in-
corporated in the rules to safeguard the political neutrality of the
service associations. Paragraph (c) of Rule 23 prescribes that 'the
association shall not be in any way connected with any political
party or organization or engage in any political activity.'[1] Sub-
paragraph (ii) of paragraph (f) of Rule 23 lays down that the
association shall not 'pay or contribute towards the expenses of
any trade union which has constituted a fund under section 16
of the Indian Trade Unions Act, 1926 (XVI of 1926).'[2]

Associations of public servants in Pakistan as in most other
countries are not supposed to play the role of trade unions. They
may be regarded as trade unions 'in the sense, a pet rabbit like
a tiger, is a bona fide quadruped'. The service associations are
primarily considered to be bodies formed for the purpose of pro-
tecting the conditions of service of the members. The conditions
of service differ with different classes of public servants in different cadres. As a result, separate service associations are formed
for different cadres and within each cadre for different classes of
public servants. With the exception of the cadres which comprise
a single class of public servants, for example the Civil Service of
Pakistan and the Provincial Civil Service, in no other cadre does
one single association exist for the cadre as a whole.

In order to obtain the views of the respondents on the formation of service associations and on the role of the existing associations a number of questions were included in the questionnaire.
Firstly, a respondent was asked to state whether or not he was
a member of a service association. Those who were members of
some association were asked to give their opinion about the work-

[1] Government of Punjab, Finance Department, *Civil Service Rules (Punjab)*,
Vol. 1, Part II, (Second Edition) 1955, Lahore, 1956, p. 154. Similar provisions were made in the Notification No. 6/1/48-Ests. (S.E.) of the Establishment Division of the Cabinet Secretariat of the Government of Pakistan.
[2] Ibid. p. 154.

ing of their own association. They were asked to say whether they thought the association was active, inactive, or active only when faced with some specific issue. Those who were not members were asked to give reasons for not enrolling themselves. Exactly one-third, or 33·3 per cent., of the officers in the sample belonged to departments which had not formed any service association or in which the association was so inactive as to be non-existent. These departments were the Civil Secretariat, Public Relations, Co-operative Societies, Local Fund Audit and Jails. Public servants in all other cadres, namely Animal Husbandry, Engineering, Health, Police, Civil Service of Pakistan and the Provincial Civil Service had organized themselves into service associations. In each cadre except the Civil Service of Pakistan and the Provincial Civil Service there were separate associations for Class I and for Class II public servants.

Out of the total, 45·8 per cent. of the respondents were not members of such an association. A little over two-thirds of this group of officers were not members because no service association had been formed. The others who were not members although service associations did exist advanced the following reasons for not joining.

Some of the officers were not enthusiastic because the service association which concerned them was almost inactive. A few maintained that formation of a service association was not necessary because Civil Service Rules provided enough safeguards for the public servant. They also emphasized that if a public servant felt aggrieved an individual representation should procure him the desired redress. Collective action was considered unnecessary and undesirable. A very small proportion were averse to participation in the activities of service associations on the ground that it involved lot of party politics. It was alleged that in general the office-bearers were more eager to promote their personal interests than to protect the collective interests of the entire body of members.

Over half, or 54·2 per cent., of the public servants in the sample were members of the associations of their respective cadres. About a third of these officers felt that their Service Association was not active at all. A little over one-third of other officers thought that their Service Association was largely inactive with sporadic spells of activity. A little less than one-third of the members felt that their Service Associations were fairly active.

Some service associations had failed to excite enough interest to encourage membership. For example, out of the 11 officers in Class II cadre of the Animal Husbandry Service in the sample, 8 were not even members of their service association. The interviews revealed that a larger proportion of the members of subordinate cadres as compared to those of superior cadres of the same service show a lack of interest in membership in their service associations. Two explanations may be offered for this behaviour. Either it is due to the reason that the public servants of subordinate cadres do not appreciate the advantages of collective bargaining or they are disillusioned as to the effectiveness of service associations as instruments of collective bargaining. The second explanation receives support from the fact that relatively smaller proportions of officers in the subordinate cadres think that their service associations are active as compared to the proportions of superior cadres holding that opinion.

A large majority of the public servants, to the extent of 85·1 per cent., supported the idea of the formation of service or staff associations by the public servants. Only 9·7 per cent. did not like the idea. Three per cent. of the respondents did not feel strongly either way. A negligible proportion, or 1·8 per cent., of the officers, most of whom belonged to the Police Service, stated that public servants in the subordinate cadres should not be allowed to form service associations. They felt that public servants in the subordinate cadres did not appreciate the significance of the idea behind the formation of such protective associations. They might misuse this right or might lend themselves to exploitation by outsiders. Some of the Police officers cited the example of a strike of the subordinate staff of the Police Service in the province of the former Punjab, somewhere in the 1950's. They argued that the spreading of such an attitude among subordinate Police officials was particularly dangerous. The proportion of such officers was, however, not very large. Most of the officers of the Police Service discounted the above argument and maintained that the members of subordinate cadres were as much entitled to form protective associations as were the members of superior cadres.

A majority of the public servants who were in favour of the formation of a service association envisioned it as an instrument for collective representation of their demands and as a mouth-piece for the ventilation of their grievances. Many visualized such a body as a medium for exchange of ideas, for social contact and, in certain cases, as a medium of eliciting opinion on important national issues. A very small fraction was of the view that service associations were useful in preventing the domination of one cadre over the other. One public servant assigned a more enlarged role to service associations. He hoped that these bodies could be developed into agencies for self-discipline and for self-help among the public servants.

Those who were opposed to the formation of service associations offered the following arguments. First of all, it was maintained that public servants could not spare time for such activities. In the second place, it was feared that the formation of service associations usually led to activities typical of trade unions such as agitation and strikes, which caused unnecessary restlessness and undermined discipline. Some of the officers also maintained that service associations were undesirable because they were commonly exploited by the more active members or by the office-bearers for personal gains. A few felt that service associations were necessary because Civil Service Rules were sufficient for the protection of their rights. A small number of officers opposed the formation of service associations on the ground that these engendered narrow loyalties which reinforced class-consciousness.

Service associations as they exist in Pakistan are not very active or effective bodies. The general pattern of working of those associations which may be considered to be active is to meet once in a year at a dinner which is usually accompanied by an address of the president of the association. In certain cases, sports are organized on such occasions. On rare occasions the associations make representations to the government in the form of memoranda concerning their conditions of service. The questionnaire concerning the provincial administration circulated by the Pay and Services Commission in 1960 contained a question which sought the opinion of public servants about the introduction of a machinery in the government departments on the lines of the Whitely Councils in the United Kingdom. No such question was included in the questionnaire prepared for this study nor did any respondent, except one, hint at the possibility of using service associations as a base for organizing Whitely Councils.

Some of the respondents thought that service associations failed to excite enough interest on the part of its members primarily because of the apathetic attitude of the government towards associations of this kind. A few alleged that the government was even hostile to the activization of the service associations. It appears that these bodies have yet a long way to go to become effective media of communication between the employer and the employees.

CHAPTER 10

SOME SPECIAL ISSUES IN THE PUBLIC SERVICE OF PAKISTAN

The Generalist and the Specialist in Government

The controversy regarding the role of the generalist as opposed to the role of the specialist in government has vexed most of the modern states. In general, no solution has been found which might be acceptable to all concerned. The nature of this controversy has taken the following form in Pakistan.

The system of government in Pakistan is founded on the principle that policy-making in administration can be sharply differentiated and separated from the execution of policy. Pakistan has also inherited a very strong tradition that the former function can be performed better by the public servants whose 'dominant professional value is classical generalism or guardianship, similar conceptually to Confucian and Platonic canons'.[1]

Under the influence of the administrative tradition described above it is considered to be possible as well as desirable to bifur-

[1] Ralph Braibanti, 'The Civil Service of Pakistan: A Theoretical Analysis', Reprint from the *The South Atlantic Quarterly*, Vol. LVIII, No. 2, Spring 1959, p. 262.

cate each government department into two sections. The section
charged with policy formulation, generally called the administrative department, is supposed to fall in the sphere of the generalist.
The second section described as the executive department or attached department, is supposed to belong to the technical specialist. The direct result of this policy is that administratively the
technical specialist is bound to remain under the control and discipline of the generalist. Furthermore, any possibility of the
technical specialist finding his way up into the top administrative
positions is ruled out once and for all.

Naturally, the technical specialist feels very unhappy about
these restrictions. His constant endeavour has been to gain admittance to the top administrative positions. This subject has received the attention of the government many times, both before
and after Independence. An important policy statement on this
subject was made by Sir Richard Tottenham in 1946 which has
been quoted repeatedly by those who have examined this matter
in the following years. Tottenham maintained that the duties of
the administrative departments corresponded very broadly to
those of the general staff of the army organization. He concluded from this analogy that just as the staff officer in the army
did not conduct operations in the field so the head of the administrative department should not ordinarily be charged with executive duties. [1] This amounts to saying that, just as the field officer
in the army organization does not formulate policies, so the head
of the executive department should not ordinarily be charged with
administrative functions. In other words it means that the technical specialist is not considered qualified to become the administrative head of a government department.

The concept underlying the statements quoted above has for
the most part, remained the official policy of the government. It
was endorsed by the Administrative Inquiry Committee in 1953.
The next important pronouncement on this subject was made in
1955. Taking note of the general desire of the heads of the various

[1] As quoted in the *Report of the Council for Administration of West Pakistan,*
February 1955, Lahore, p. 5.

executive departments, who were in most cases technical specialists, to be made eligible for appointment as administrative heads
of their respective departments, the Council for Administration
of West Pakistan of 1955 recommended that the provincial government should not introduce any system in which a head of an
executive department would have to perform the dual functions
of the administrative head responsible for the framing of government policies and of the executive head, responsible for carrying
out those policies. The Council, however, did not rule out the
possibility of a technical specialist with an undoubted flair for
administrative work and without too departmentalized an outlook,
becoming the administrative head of a government department.

The Provincial Administrative Commission, appointed in 1959,
made similar recommendations. The members of the Commission
observed in the report, 'to saddle an executive head with staff
functions in addition to his normal operational duties will be
either at the expense of efficiency in operations or of the comprehensive study of all aspects of a particular programme or policy
and its repercussions'.[1]

The government policy of prohibiting the appointment of technical specialists as the administrative heads of government departments has often invited violent criticism from the technically
trained public servants. They complain that they are given a
secondary place in the processes of policy-making, are granted a
low rate of pay and are thus condemned to positions carrying a
permanently low status as compared to those positions open to
generalists.

The West Pakistan Engineers Association passed a resolution
in April 1962 in which it appealed to the government to grant a
better place to engineers in the administrative set-up and to mini-
mize the efforts of other services 'in grabbing power' in such a
way as to run down the engineering services unnecessarily. The
Association expressed the view that, as compared to the 'non-
technical' Civil Service of the country, the engineering services

[1] Government of Pakistan, *Report of the Provincial Administration Commission*, Lahore, 1960, p. 91.

were given an unfair deal in the matter of salaries, prospects of promotion, warrant of precedence and prestige.[1]

In a memorandum submitted to the Pay and Services Commission of 1959 the West Pakistan Engineers Association alleged that the government was inclined to give more preferential treatment to non-technical public servants than to engineers and technologists. This discrimination, they asserted, was indicated in the lower salaries prescribed for engineers and by the fact that engineers were denied a reasonable share in the top administrative posts. In support of their claim, the Association stated that the government paid 64 lakhs of rupees annually to 332 officers of the Civil Service of Pakistan, making an average of 1,604 rupees per month for each member. On the other hand, for 1,071 engineers of the Irrigation Department and of the Building and Roads Department the total annual expenditure on salaries was only 78 lakhs of rupees, giving an average of 603 rupees per month for each member.

The Association alleged that prospects of promotion for engineers were also less favourable than were those for non-technical public servants. It was stated that for the 332 officers of the Civil Service of Pakistan, there were 77 posts carrying a monthly salary of 3,000 rupees or more. As against this, for 1,071 engineers, there were only a few posts carrying equivalent remuneration.

The West Pakistan Engineers Association demanded scales of pay higher than those for the non-technical services. The Association also demanded that engineers should be made eligible for appointment to the posts of Chairman of the Planning Commission, Directors of Supplies and Industries, Members of the Economic Commission, Chairman of the Industrial Development Corporations, Chairman of the Water and Power Development Authorities, and engineering advisers to Pakistan's diplomatic missions abroad.

At the time of writing it is not known what recommendations have been made by the Pay and Services Commission in regard to the position of technical specialists *vis-a-vis* the generalists. In

[1] *The Pakistan Times*, Lahore, 8 April 1962.

the meantime, however, the executive departments of the Government of West Pakistan have been reorganized, which development is indicative of the efforts being made to re-examine the positions of the technical specialist and the generalist.

Subsequent to the recommendations of the Provincial Reorganization Commission concerning decentralization of government activity,[1] the Government of Pakistan appointed the Provincial Reorganization Committee, in August 1961, to prepare a detailed scheme for the reorganization of the departments of the provincial government. Among other things the Committee recommended the abolition of the establishment of the executive departments at the provincial headquarters. All the supervisory functions which were performed by the executive departments from the provincial headquarters were transferred to the corresponding administrative departments in the Civil Secretariat. Most of the operational functions of the executive departments which were previously performed by the heads of the executive department from the provincial headquarters were transferred to the corresponding administrative departments in the Civil Secretariat. Most of the operational functions of the executive departments which were previously performed by the heads of the executive departments from the provincial headquarters were delegated to the regional or divisional heads of those departments. The former heads of executive departments were transferred to the Secretariat as advisors to the heads of the administrative departments. In certain cases, for example, in the Department of Health and in the Department of Irrigation, Communication and Works, the executive heads were appointed as the administrative heads of the departments as well.

The purpose of the departmental reorganization appears to be the centralization of planning and the decentralization of operations. The supreme leadership of each department has been unified in a single head of the department in contrast to the previous arrangement in which each department had two heads, one in

---

[1] Government of Pakistan, *Report of the Provincial Administration Commission*, Lahore, 1960, p. 101.

charge of executive and the other in charge of administrative matters. It is difficult to say whether the appointment of technical specialists as the administrative heads of their departments is a matter of policy or merely a temporary arrangement.

Certain press reports have indicated that the appointment of the technical specialists as the administrative heads was an *ad hoc* arrangement. 'Some of the senior officers of the attached departments (executive departments)', it was reported, 'could not possibly get over the feeling that their chances of promotion had been marred, although assurances had been given by the authorities concerned for the legitimate protection of their positions. Originally it was proposed that the (executive) heads of departments would function as advisors to the Secretaries (administrative heads) but it has now been decided that in some cases they would be given Secretariat status commensurate with their present positions.'[1]

Whether temporary or final, the decision reported above is significant. It marks the acceptance of one of the basic demands of the technical specialists. The decision of the Government of West Pakistan to choose the administrative head of the Health Department from among the trained doctors in the employ of the government was hailed by the Provincial Health Service Association as a gain for the specialists. The President of the Provincial Health Service Association expressed his gratitude at the government's decision to appoint, for the first time, a member of the Provincial Health Service as the administrative head of the Provincial Health Department. He expressed regret that the members of the Provincial Health Service had been helpless victims of slander and abuse on the part of those who wanted to cover their own short-comings. He was, however, confident that the Provincial Health Service had sufficient potential to constitute a potent factor in the national development.[2]

In view of the strong feelings of the public servants on this controversy it was decided to seek the opinions of the respondents,

[1] *The Pakistan Times*, Lahore, 15 February 1962.
[2] *The Pakistan Times*, Lahore, 13 May 1962.

which included both technical specialists and generalists, in regard to the role of the specialist and the generalist in government. The form of the question was as follows:

As you know, the policy of the government is to appoint CSP officers to a diverse variety of important posts. Do you not think that in the modern age of specialization either:

(a) the specialist posts should go to a specialist only, no matter whether he is a CSP or a non-CSP officer, or

(b) arrangements should be made so that the CSP officer would receive previous training in the specialized field of the post for which his appointment is being considered.

Most of the officers in most of the cadres were in agreement with the proposal that specialist posts should be held by technical specialists, meaning thereby that a doctor of medicine should be the head of the Department of Health Services, an educationist should be the head of the Education Department. The proportion of officers in the Engineering Service who agreed with this view was the highest, demonstrating near unanimity among them on this issue. Numerically, this opinion was held by the officers of the Police Service, Animal Husbandry Service and Health Service in descending order. It is largely significant that four-fifths of the CSP officers and more than half of the PCS officers were in favour of having a generalist as the head of the administrative department. A little less than half of the PCS officers responded in favour of the idea that, before appointment, a generalist should be enabled to familiarize himself with the technical aspects related to the particular branch of administration to which he might be assigned as chief administrator. One-half of the officers of the Secretariat Service were of the view that technical specialists would figure better as policy-makers for technical government departments. A little less than one-third of them were of the opinion that generalists were more suitable as policy-makers. About one-sixth of them preferred to have generalists as policy-makers, but they qualified their statements by insisting that, as administrative heads of specialized departments, the generalists should preferably be first orientated to the nature of those posts before assuming their responsibilities.

Four officers suggested that a pool of administrators should be created. It was hoped that such a course of action would solve the specialist versus the generalist controversy. One officer proposed that there should be one administrative service, instead of many cadres, among the non-technical personnel. Another public servant put forth the suggestion that there should be an advisory committee for each administrative department instead of having a single officer as the head of the department. These proposals merit special treatment because they came from some of the most experienced men in the public service. In the following paragraphs it is proposed to discuss separately the attitudes of officers of different cadres and to examine separately each individual proposal mentioned above.

The Attitudes of the Officers of the Animal Husbandry
Department towards the Appointment of Generalists
as Administrative Heads of Technical Departments

Sixteen out of 19 of the officers in the Department of Animal Husbandry were opposed to the appointment of a generalist as an administrative head of their department. This feeling was expressed more strongly by top-ranking officers. The main reason offered was that a generalist was usually neither interested in nor well-informed about the technical complexities which were of basic importance in making and evaluating development schemes in technical departments and that, due to lack of technical background, the generalist was not fitted for a well-informed and effective manipulation of the technical skills of the personnel of that department. It was stated by the technical specialists in the Department of Animal Husbandry that they had to spend a good deal of time and energy in educating the generalist head of the department in the technicalities of most of the schemes and projects which were presented to him for his approval. This education had to be repeated every time one generalist was replaced by another. It is easy to imagine that such a situation, particularly when repeated, is intensely annoying to the specialist. This argument was usually accompanied by a feeling of frustration because an executive head of the Department of Animal Husbandry could never become its administrative head, but would be obliged to play second fiddle to a generalist who was less well-informed on matters relating strictly to the specialized aspects of the technical department.

Not all of the officers in the Department of Animal Husbandry were united on this issue. A small minority of 3 officers preferred to have a generalist as the administrative head. Their main argument was that in postings, promotions and disciplinary matters there was a need of having, as the final authority, a person who was impartial and unbiased. A generalist, it was believed, ensured this condition satisfactorily. A specialist, who would naturally be drawn from the executive department, could not maintain an impartial attitude towards his subordinates as he would have, in the course of his career, developed favourable or unfavourable attitudes towards them.

The overall impression formed was that a majority of the officers of the Department of Animal Husbandry would like to have one of the technically qualified officers from among themselves, or promoted from within, as the policy-maker for their department. There appeared to be no insistence on making the executive head of the Department of Animal Husbandry concurrently the administrative head. Most of the officers of the department would be satisfied if the two posts were held by two different persons, provided both of them were sufficiently familiar with the science of Animal Husbandry.

The Attitudes of the Engineers towards the Appointment of Generalists as Administrative Heads of Technical Departments

The engineers seemed to be the most vocal of all technical specialists in demanding the replacement of generalists by specialists as heads of policy-making departments. The fact that 87 out of 90 engineers in the sample supported this demand demonstrates the near unanimity which exists among the engineers on this subject. Their line of argument was similar to that of the officers of the Department of Animal Husbandry. In general, the top-ranking engineers were more insistent than were the junior officials of the group. Most of the engineers demanded that the executive heads of the engineering departments should be granted status equal to that of the administrative head. This demand amounted to combining the policy-making functions with the executive functions. A few of the engineers, however, did not press for a combination of the offices of the administrative head and the executive head; they would be satisfied if the generalist head of the administrative department were to be replaced by an engineer.

Some of the engineers stated that the sharp separation of the policy-making and the executive functions had been introduced only on the integration of West Pakistan. No such separation had existed in the previous administrative units of West Pakistan. They claimed that the combination of the policy-making and the executive functions in a single person would ensure, as it did previously, economy in time and money.

The Attitudes of the Police Officers towards the Appointment of Generalists as Administrative Heads of Technical Departments

The Police officers, unlike the engineers, did not demand that the generalist head of the administrative department should be replaced by a Police Officer. Their criticism was directed against the Civil Service of Pakistan for monopolizing all administrative appointments which carry great prestige and power. A few Police officers in our sample, mainly from the Police Service of Pakistan, as distinct from the Provincial Police Service, expressed a desire that the status of joint secretary, which the Inspector-General of Police had enjoyed previously, should be restored to him. A majority, however, proposed the establishment of a single service of all the non-technical cadres and the provision of opportunities for movement from one 'sub-cadre' of the newly formed non-technical service to another on the basis of aptitude and performance.

Some of the Police officers invited attention to the distinguished performance of a number of Police officers as administrators. The names mentioned were those of Khan Qurban Ali Khan, a former Inspector-General of Police in the government of the former province of the Punjab who rose to be the Agent to the Governor-

General, a position equivalent to the Governor of a Province; Mr. Zakir Hussain, formerly Inspector-General of Police in East Pakistan, who rose to be the Chairman of the Pakistan Public Service Commission, Governor of East Pakistan and later the Minister of Home Affairs in the Government of Pakistan; Mr. G. Ahmad who served as the Chairman of the Planning Commission of the Government of Pakistan; Mr. Anwar Ali, former Inspector-General of Police in West Pakistan, who became the Secretary of Home Affairs in the Government of Pakistan.[1] The respondents maintained that the record of such men furnished sufficient proof that Police officers could be good administrators and that administrative posts, therefore, need not be reserved for a single cadre of the public service. They insisted that the practice of appointing senior Police officers to top administrative posts should be accorded a formal recognition and that it should be more regularly and frequently applied.

This stand was taken more by the officers of the Police Service of Pakistan than by the officers of the Provincial Police Service. The latter appeared to be more concerned with getting a larger percentage of higher posts within the Police hierarchy through promotion from below. They were critical of the rate at which the officers belonging to the Provincial Police Service were promoted to higher Police posts in the cadre of the PSP. Higher administrative posts did not immediately interest the officers of the Provincial Police Service. Only those of them who had already been, or were about to be, promoted into the PSP cadre appeared to show some interest.

The Attitudes of the CSP Officers towards the Appointment of Generalists as Administrative Heads of Technical Departments
The CSP officers occupy the first place among the generalists. As might be expected a good majority of the CSP respondents, 23 out of 31, were in favour of retaining generalists as heads of

---

[1] There are other instances of senior Police officers holding top administrative posts. At the time of writing, the post of the Chief Secretary to the Government of East Pakistan was held by a Police officer. Furthermore, the Chairman of Pakistan Industrial Development Corporation in East Pakistan was a Police officer.

administrative departments. Four officers thought that, before an appointment as the administrative head of a department, the generalist should be orientated to the field of specialization of the department concerned. Three officials said that a pool of administrators should be created. One CSP officer agreed with the proposal that technical specialists should be preferred as the administrative heads of the specialized departments.

The burden of the argument in support of the generalist as the policy-maker was that, being free from the influence of any specialized branch of knowledge or of administration, he was better qualified than was the technical specialist to give due attention to all aspects of a programme or a proposal. The technical specialist, it was stated, was bound by prejudices which were produced by his specialized academic training, and which were increased and reinforced in the course of his long tenure in a single technical department. As a result, it was difficult for the specialist to take a detached view of government plans. He was likely to accord an exaggerated importance to technical aspects and to ignore or neglect other aspects, especially those which have a bearing on the human or the economic side.

The specialist's prejudices were also likely to influence his decisions relating to the personnel working under him. The generalist, being an outsider, suffered from no such prejudices and, therefore, was more likely to make detached decisions on matters relating to personnel.

Another argument offered in favour of the generalist was that he brought to bear upon the proposals of the specialist a freshness of outlook. Whereas the specialist was predominantly influenced by the technical aspects of a scheme, the generalist examined and evaluated that scheme from a far wider point of view. The task of the head of the administrative department, it was stated, was to co-ordinate the activities of different government departments. For such a sanction it was important that the co-ordinator should not belong to any one particular department. The quality of impartiality, it was maintained, was possessed by a generalist and not by a specialist.

A few of the younger officers in the Civil Service of Pakistan seemed to be dissatisfied with the quality of the generalist which was available in the country. Their replies indicated that, in their view, 'generalism' was exaggerated. They emphasized the need of developing a certain amount of specialization on the part of the generalists. It was proposed that after the first appointment the generalist should be asked to seek one particular branch of administration which suits his aptitude and ability. He should be enabled to concentrate upon that particular branch by being allowed to work in a single well-defined area of government activity or in activities which are interrelated. Full weight should be given to the training, experience, aptitude and ability of a generalist with special reference to the department to which he is being considered for appointment. This plan would produce a generalist-specialist who had, not only the broad outlook of a generalist, but the sustained interest and experience of a specialist.

The Attitudes of the PCS Officers towards the Appointment
of Generalists as Administrative Heads of Technical Departments

The officers of the Provincial Civil Service form the second most important category of generalists. Quite naturally, therefore, a majority of the PCS respondents were in favour of retaining the generalists as heads of administrative departments. However, more of the PCS than of the CSP officers considered it necessary and beneficial to orientate the generalists to a specialized programme before assigning to them special departments. One PCS officer suggested that one way of orientating the generalists was to post them in the executive branch of various departments for short periods. More PCS officers than CSP officers agreed with the idea that Pakistan had entered the age of specialization in which the generalist should, with profit, be replaced by the specialist. As compared to 3·2 per cent. of the CSP officers, 34·6 per cent. of the PCS officers subscribed to this view.

The Attitudes of the Officers of the Secretariat Service
towards the Appointment of Generalists as Administrative
Heads of Technical Departments

In general, the officers of the Secretariat Service are recruited to assist the generalists in the co-ordination and the supervision of the activities of the executive departments. The evidence of these officials on the competence of the generalists in running the specialist departments is important. Thirty-five out of 69, or 50·7 per cent., of the officers from the Secretariat Service were of the opinion that it would be better if technical specialists were appointed as the administrative heads of technical departments. Eleven, or one-third of this group of officers, qualified their support for the generalist by demanding that the generalist, who is to be appointed as administrative head of a particular department, must be thoroughly orientated to the department before taking over his duties.

Some of the officers of the Secretariat Service, who themselves were non-technical by training, voluntarily admitted that, due to lack of an understanding of technical aspects, they found it difficult to evaluate many of the plans referred to them for sanction and approval by technical specialists. They said that it was wrong to presume that administration of a technical department could be undertaken effectively without sufficient information about the basic technicalities of a specialized government activity. General administration, by which is commonly meant the approval of development schemes, preparation of new schemes and management of the personnel of a department, was not a function which could be separated from the so-called technical operations of a technical department. The administrative and the technical aspects of a department were so much bound together that the lack of understanding of technical aspects on the part of the generalist, far from being an advantage, became a decided disadvantage. Since the generalist administrators of technical departments depend mainly upon the officers of the Secretariat for the assessment of the proposals from the technical departments and, since half of the officers of the Secretariat Service admitted their inability to perform their functions effectively for lack of technical orientation, serious doubts are created about the effectiveness and the efficiency of the generalists, as administrative superiors of technical departments.

The general consensus of the opinions reported above is that the management of technical departments by generalists is not satisfactory. The generalists. being untrained in the technological aspects of their charges, are considered to be ill-suited and un-qualified to administer effectively technical government depart-ments.

The technical specialists contest the exclusive right of the generalists to be the administrative heads of all government de-partments for the personal and professional reasons that this arrangement relegates them to a position inferior in status to that of the generalists. In this complaint the technical specialists have, occasionally, received support from certain independent quarters. For example, it was admitted in the *First Five Year Plan* that the technician had not yet received the recognition due to him in the public administration of the country. It was conceded that he was not accorded the same status in the formulation of policy as was the generalist nor was he given equal position in terms of salary, prospects and official ranking. The authors of the Plan asserted that this invidious distinction resulted in heartburning, in frustra-tion and in the diversion of some talented technicians to non-technical jobs. [1]

Before the reorganization of the executive departments of the Government of West Pakistan, it often happened that the admin-istrative head of a department was far younger in years and less ripe in experience than was the executive head. The resentment of the technical specialist towards the generalist was exacerbated because the latter occupied a superior position in the hierarchy in spite of being younger in age and in experience. Professor Paul L. Beckett noted that in Pakistan the technical judgement of mature and well qualified technical personnel was generally sub-jected to modification by junior secretariat officers of very limited maturity and experience. He observed that he could think of few more effective ways in which to dampen the enthusiasm and to stifle the initiative of the specialists or to impede economic devel-

---

[1] Government of Pakistan, National Planning Board, *The First Five Year Plan, 1955-60*, Karachi, 1958, para. 95, p. 113.

opment programmes which must depend heavily on technical skills and judgements.[1]

A general practice in the Civil Secretariat of the Government of West Pakistan has been to attach to the generalist administrative head of a technical department some technical specialists as deputies under the generalist to help in the preparation and the evaluation of development schemes. It may be argued that, if the generalist head is ultimately dependent upon the advice of the technically qualified aides, it is useless to have a generalist as the head of the department. Conversely, that if it is desirable to have a generalist as the administrative head, it is almost equally useless to post technical specialists in the administrative departments. The general policy of keeping the technical specialist in a position subordinate to that of the generalist gives rise to the suspicion that administrative concepts in Pakistan are biased against the specialists.

Sometimes the appointment of generalists as administrative heads of government departments, technical, as well as non-technical, is criticized for the reason that ordinarily the generalists are transferred to different positions so rapidly that they fail to develop an interest in or an understanding of one particular branch of government activity. Since the generalists come to their posts untrained in the technical aspects of their work, their very brief association with one particular department prevents them from exercising effective supervision and co-ordination of their responsibilities.

At times, the preference for the generalist over the technical specialist is defended and advocated on the plea that he represents an intelligent layman who sees the problem as a whole and who evaluates and assesses its merits and demerits from the human viewpoint and not from a purely technical point of view. The advantages of this concept may be admitted, but its application results in duplicating the function which is assigned to the minister. It is the job of the minister to tell the specialist what the people

[1] Paul L. Beckett, *A Few Concluding Comments on Public Administration and Development in Pakistan*, a cyclostyled pamphlet, Karachi, 1957, pp. 7-8.

will not accept. On the basis of this argument, the generalist seems to have rendered himself superfluous.

One of the premises, upon which is based the thesis that the generalist is better qualified to be the administrative head of a technical department, is that the function of policy-making can be separated sharply from the execution of policy. Note has already been made of the analogy of the staff and the field officers in the army, which was first presented by Sir Richard Tottenham, and which the generalists are very fond of quoting in their support. The assumption of the analogy is that the duties of the generalist administrator correspond broadly to those of the general staff of the army organization and that the duties of the executive heads, who are, generally, technical specialists, correspond to those of the field officers in the army. The intent of the analogy is to prove that just as the field officers in the army do not perform staff functions, the executive heads who are normally chosen from among the technical specialists should not perform the functions of the administrative heads who are ordinarily drawn from the ranks of the generalists. Commenting upon this analogy, Professor Rowland Egger writes that, in the army, the general staff is not in the line of command and that the delegation of authority is invariably from the central command to the area of field command. On this analogy the delegation of authority in government should be from the minister to the technical specialist as the executive head and not from the minister to the administrative head or the generalist.[1]

It would seem that there is a need to water down the 'divine right' of the generalist to administrative leadership. There is also a need to modify the permanent and absolute ban on the technical specialist in the matter of assuming administrative leadership. Such a change of policy would be in conformity with the current trend in Pakistan and in other parts of the world. There was a time when the posts of the Director of Agriculture and of the Inspector-General of Police were held by generalists. With

---

[1] Rowland Egger, *The Improvement of Public Administration in Pakistan*, Karachi, 1954, para. 54.

increasing specialization, the generalists have been replaced by technical specialists. [1]

A compromise which may be suggested is that the key posts in government should be assigned to generalist specialists. A generalist specialist may be defined as a generalist who has had sustained practical experience in a single, well-defined, broad area of government activity. Conversely, a generalist specialist may be described as a technical specialist, who displays special aptitude for general management.

One way of producing a sufficient number of the required type of generalist specialists, as suggested by some of the respondents, is to create a pool of administrators. The proposed pool would be similar in nature to the Economic Pool which has been created by the Government of Pakistan. This pool is expected to ensure adequate representation of officers of all cadres in the administrative posts in government.

Another proposal aimed at finding a solution of the generalist versus the specialist controversy which deserves mention, is that each department should be headed by a committee, with one of the members, presumably the senior official, acting as the chairman. For the sake of illustration, if this proposal is applied to the Department of Irrigation, Communication and Works, the administration of the department would be headed by a committee of three technical specialists, one drawn from each area of administration.

A modified form of this proposal would be that the committee thus constituted, should act as an advisory body to a single administrative head of the department. A proposal along these lines has been offered by Professor Rowland Egger. The real intention of Professor Egger's proposal was to eliminate the secretaries to the government, who are administrative heads of departments, from the line of command. He has admitted that although his proposal would involve a break with prevailing practices, yet, in effect, it would mean a 'return to the basic principles upon which

[1] Government of India, *Report of the Royal Commission on Public Services in India*, London, 1916, para. 29, p. 21.

the administrative system in the sub-continent was established.'
Originally, it was not planned that the secretaries to the government were to be in the line of command, but as with the general
staff of the army, they were to be a staff agency, created only to
assist the minister. In the course of time the secretaries have
acquired operational functions. In order to restore the original
position Professor Egger recommended 'the building of strong
operating departments in which both executive and administrative
duties and responsibilities would be vested'. He hoped to give
these departments into the charge of generalist specialists who
would be on a parity with secretaries to government in the administrative hierarchy. As a consequence of this change, Professor
Egger foresaw the need of setting up 'ad hoc inter-departmental
committees to deal with matters involving more than one department'. The function which he assigned to the counsellor of the
minister was only to report the deliberations of the committee to
the minister and to offer his advice. The final decision would rest
with the minister. [1]

It is appropriate to mention another factor which influences the
position of the generalist and the specialist in government, namely
the shortage of trained specialists in the developing countries.
Most of these countries on gaining independence embark upon
large-scale, industrial development. In most cases it takes the form
of State enterprise which requires specialist administrators, and
the new governments are faced with a difficult choice, namely
either to accept foreign specialists as the heads of national State
enterprises or to appoint non-specialist administrators from its own
nationals.

In referring to the Indian solution of this problem a commentator noted that the Indian Government chose to fill specialist posts
in its State enterprises with officials of the highest category, namely
the Indian Administrative Service, the successor to the ICS. The
commentator observed that in view of their broad studies and
training, the officers of the IAS functioned remarkably well as
general administrators, judges and diplomats, but that as directors

[1] Rowland Egger, op. cit., para., 69 and 75.

of industrial works, not all proved equal to the task. [1]

The above observations apply *mutatis mutandis* to Pakistani experience as well. A lesson which may be learnt from this experience is that too much reliance should not be placed on the generalist, as a jack of all trades. It is imperative that the supply of a sufficient number of trained specialists is ensured to match the development needs of Pakistan. Out of this group of specialists a certain number of people who possess administrative leadership of a higher order will be able to make a significant contribution if the opportunities for promotion to top-ranking administrative posts are liberalized.

The Civil Service of Pakistan and other Cadres

Public service in Pakistan consists of a number of cadres which have been organized on a functional basis, such as the cadres for the Departments of Engineering, Health Services, Agriculture and the like. In addition, there are two more cadres which cannot be identified with any particular function. These are the Civil Service of Pakistan and the Provincial Civil Service. The officers of these two cadres are primarily charged with revenue collection and police-cum-judicial work in the districts and in the divisions. They are also appointed to the Civil Secretariat where they act as co-ordinators and general managers. Apart from these functions, most of the posts in the government which do not belong to any particular functional cadre are ordinarily assigned to the officers belonging to the Civil Service of Pakistan and the Provincial Civil Service.

Although both are regarded as cadres of general administrators or non-technical personnel a distinction is made between the Civil Service of Pakistan and the Provincial Civil Service. The former is considered to be superior in quality and is accordingly given a higher rate of remuneration. Furthermore, most of the positions of higher responsibility in the government are assigned to the CSP officers. Relatively, a far smaller fraction of posts and the less important positions in general administration are given to the

---

[1] E. N. Shaffer, 'Indian-Criterion for Developing Aid', an article published in *Wirtschaftsdienst*, Hamburg, (English Edition) No. 3, March 1962, p. 10.

officers of the cadre of Provincial Civil Service.

Since the posts to which the senior CSP officers are generally appointed entail a relatively higher pay-scale and higher responsibilities they enjoy a higher prestige. The large-scale development work which the State has taken upon itself after Independence has given these posts a fateful significance. Administrative leadership of the highest order is required to fill these posts. In this part of the study the question regarding the source and supply of this leadership has been considered. Should the leaders be picked from one single cadre or should they be chosen from all the cadres of the public service? The present policy of filling the top administrative posts is based upon the concept that non-technical or non-specialized personnel make the best administrators. This concept is stretched to the extent of claiming that every single public servant who may be described as a generalist by virtue of his non-technical training automatically makes the most suitable choice for all administrative posts and that all technical-specialists are inherently and absolutely unqualified to hold such administrative posts.

This concept is questioned mainly on two grounds. Firstly, that not all non-technical public servants make the best administrators nor do all technical personnel make poor administrative leaders. Secondly, it is wrong to presume, without evaluating the performance of individual public servants, that the personnel of one particular non-technical cadre always and in all cases make better administrative leaders than the personnel of other non-technical cadres.

In order to obtain the views of the various cadres on this issue the respondents were asked to comment upon the proposal that a certain percentage of the officers on the CSP cadre should be recruited from the non-CSP officers on the basis of their performance.

The figures in Table 33 indicate that the desire to share the top administrative posts with the CSP is strong in all the other cadres. This desire seems to be relatively stronger in the Provincial Civil Service, Police Service of Pakistan, Provincial Police Service, and the Engineering Service. It is significant that more than one-third of the officers in the Provincial Civil Service and the Police Service of Pakistan are not satisfied with a percentage of the top administrative posts only. They go a step further and demand the establishment of a single cadre of general administrators who are different from one another only in function, but not in status.

Moreover the desire for a larger share of the top administrative posts is almost unanimous among the officers of the Police Service of Pakistan and the Provincial Civil Service. It appears that among the technical specialists the Engineers and among the non-technical personnel the public servants in the Provincial Civil Service and the Police Service of Pakistan resent more intensely the near monopoly of administrative leadership by the Civil Service of Pakistan.

It is also notable that a little less than half of the CSP officers favour a certain amount of lateral recruitment into the CSP from the other cadres. If those CSP officers who favour the application of this policy only to the PCS, and not to all the non-CSP Cadres, are combined with those who agree to lateral recruitment with the CSP from all non-CSP cadres, the proportion of CSP officers willing to share their administrative leadership with other cadres rises to about three-fifths.

The position of the public servants who advocate or support lateral recruitment will become clearer when the reasons which they advanced in support of their proposals are examined. The reason most often put forth was that the experience and maturity of a public servant should be counted as the decisive factor for the purposes of filling top administrative posts and not the cadre to which he belongs. The second most frequently offered reason was that actual performance during his tenure should be the final deciding factor while choosing a public servant for a post of higher administrative leadership. This argument implies that the selection of administrators for top government posts should not be confined to any one or two cadres, but that such administrative leaders could be drawn from any cadre on the basis of ability and aptitude for the post concerned and that the assessment of their ability and aptitude should be made on their actual performance and not

Table 33
ATTITUDE TOWARDS THE INTRODUCTION OF PERSONNEL FROM non-CSP CADRES INTO THE CIVIL SERVICE OF PAKISTAN

Cadre	Agree	Disagree	Indifferent	Only PCS officers should be promoted into the CSP	One administrative service	Pool of administrators	Total
Animal Husbandry	13	3	—	2	1	—	19
	68.4	15.8	—	10.6	5.3	—	100.0
Engineering	75	7	3	—	5	—	90
	83.3	7.8	3.3	—	5.6	—	100.0
Health	53	8	6	2	1	—	70
	75.7	11.4	8.6	2.8	1.4	—	100.0
Police Service of Pakistan	7	—	1	—	4	1	13
	53.8	—	7.7	—	30.8	7.7	100.0
Provincial Police Service	29	1	1	—	2	1	34
	85.3	2.9	2.9	—	5.9	2.9	100.0
Secretariat Service	55	13	1	1	—	—	70
	79.4	18.8	1.4	1.4	—	—	100.0
CSP	15	11	1	4	—	—	31
	45.4	35.5	3.2	12.9	—	—	100.0
PCS	17	—	—	2	9	—	26
	65.4	—	—	2.6	34.6	—	100.0
Miscellaneous	60	14	4	2	—	—	80
	75.0	17.5	5.4	2.6	—	—	100.0
Total	323	57	17	11	22	2	432
	74.7	13.3	3.8	2.6	5.1	0.4	100.0

on the basis of their membership in a particular cadre.

The third reason, in order of frequency, was that if the positions of highest administrative leadership were to be permanently withheld from the vast mass of public servants, there would be no incentive left to excel in performance. In its place their would develop a feeling of frustration and demoralization which is most harmful for the efficient and effective running of administration.

The next reason, offered mainly by the PCS officers, was that a water-tight compartmentalization between the CSP and the PCS was unjustified. It was maintained that since both the CSP and the PCS officers performed essentially similar functions, the Provincial Civil Service might be compared to a sub-cadre of the Civil Service of Pakistan. For this reason it was demanded, that on the pattern of other services, recruitment to the Civil Service of Pakistan should also be made partly through direct entry and partly through promotion of the PCS officers.

Some other reasons offered in support of lateral recruitment to the Civil Service of Pakistan by a small number of the respondents were, firstly, that such a policy, if adopted, would help eliminate cadre-consciousness, in particular; it would remove a sort of superiority complex exhibited by CSP officers. Secondly, such a policy would enable the technical specialist of high administrative ability to enter the Civil Service of Pakistan and would make him available for appointment as head of a technical department. This proposal, in fact, amounts to the conversion of the Civil Service of Pakistan into a cadre which would represent the most gifted administrative talent of the body of the civil servants. At present it claims to be such, but this is not the case because certain highly-qualified, technically-trained people who possess excellent administrative ability are currently excluded. In the third place, it was alleged that most of the CSP officers were young and inexperienced but they were assigned to positions of higher administrative leadership just because they happened to be the members of the Civil Service of Pakistan. As against this practice senior and more experienced public servants in other cadres, especially the PCS, were compelled to stay for years in junior and less important positions.

The result was that, on the one hand, administration was affected adversely and, on the other, frustration, demoralization and heart-burning were common among the officers of other cadres. It was claimed that resentment would be eliminated and administration would improve if opportunities were provided for the non-CSP officers to move into the Civil Service of Pakistan.

Those who were opposed to any lateral movement between the CSP and other cadres advanced the following arguments. Firstly, it was held that the non-CSP officers, in general, and the PCS officers, in particular, lacked that comprehensive and liberal training which was given to the CSP officers. Secondly, it was asserted that the officers who had for the greater part of their tenure served in subordinate positions lacked the independence of judgement, self-confidence and freshness of outlook which was so essential for the holder of top administrative positions. Thirdly, it was feared that if a system for the introduction of a certain proportion of non-CSP officers were started it might be subjected to abuse. Instead of deserving officials, favourites might be moved into the top administrative posts. Fourthly, it was stated that recruitment to the Civil Service of Pakistan took place through an open competitive examination. All those who wanted to join the Civil Service of Pakistan were free to compete. If a person failed to enter that service by an open competition there was hardly any justification for promoting him later to the same cadre. Fifthly, it was said that if all the non-CSP officers, including the technical specialists, were to be made eligible on one ground or the other to the Civil Service of Pakistan, it would amount to misplacing and wasting the technical training, skill and experience of the technical specialists.

One thing common among all the non-CSP cadres is the questioning attitude towards the right of the Civil Service of Pakistan to monopolize the administrative leadership of the country. It has been already noted that there are two main under-currents in this rivalry: firstly, between the technical specialists on the one hand and the generalists, especially those in the Civil Service of Pakistan, on the other; and secondly, between the Provincial Civil

Service and the Civil Service of Pakistan. The first aspect of this
rivalry has been dealt with earlier. The second aspect will now be
discussed.

The nature of the jealousy on the part of the PCS towards the
CSP will become more intelligible if the history of the evolution
of the former is briefly reviewed. In 1886, on the recommendation
of the Aitchison Commission, the number of appointments ordinarily reserved for the covenanted service, as the Indian Civil
Service was then called, was reduced and the appointments thus
set free were assigned to a local service which was named the
Provincial Civil Service. This service, unlike the Imperial Services,
was to be separately recruited in India, in each province. Recruitment was to be made partly by promotion from the subordinate
civil service and partly by examination as far as the executive
service was concerned, and by direct nomination in the case of
the judicial service. The salaries of the members of the PCS were
to be fixed on independent grounds and were to have no relation
to those attached to Imperial Civil Service appointments.

The cadre of the Provincial Civil Service was created in response
to a mounting demand by educated Indians for positions in the
government. It was a clever device to appease the Indians and at
the same time to keep the substance of power in the hands of the
ruling elite. The British wanted to keep the substance of power
in their own hands because they did not trust the Indians. [1]

A notable illustration of such distrust was evidenced by the
Police Service of India which as late as 1917 laid down that, 'every
candidate must be a British subject of European descent'. Apart
from security considerations, the British were sceptical about the
ability and the integrity of Indians to hold positions of greater
responsibility. [2] As a precaution against these fears and doubts the
PCS officers were mainly assigned to those posts which were under
the direct and constant supervision of a member of the covenanted service which was then predominantly British in composition. That the PCS officers were primarily appointed as assistants

[1] *Report of the Pakistan Pay Commission*, 1949, Karachi, p. 4.
[2] Ibid, p. 4.

to the members of the Indian Civil Service is reflected in the designations of the posts they held such as Deputy Collector, Extra-Assistant Commissioner and Assistant Magistrate.

By virtue of the executive power that they were given and by virtue of their association with the ruling race as a part of 'the government', the PCS officers did enjoy considerable prestige with the people. However, in comparison with the ICS personnel, they enjoyed very little of the substance of power and prestige. In this manner the British were able to obtain the desired result, which was to give an impression to the educated Indians that they had been accepted into the power-elite and, at the same time, to withhold the real power from them.

Another factor which seems to have influenced the creation of the Provincial Civil Service is that it provided the British rulers with cheap trained manpower. [1] It has been stated earlier that on the recommendations of the Aitchison Commission it had been decided that the salaries of the PCS officers would be fixed on independent grounds and that they would have no relation to those attached to the Imperial Civil Service appointments. The salaries of the Imperial Civil Service posts were fixed at a very high rate, supposedly to attract the most talented British young men to serve in India. An additional consideration for the high pay scales of the Imperial Civil Service officers was that their standard of living was high. These two considerations did not apply to the Indians. Consequently, the salaries of the PCS officers, who were predominantly Indians, were fixed at a much lower scale.

The third notable feature about the composition of the PCS is that many of the PCS officials were recruited by promotion from subordinate service and by nomination. These two methods of recruitment provided the British with convenient tools of patronage and favouritism. It is commonly believed, perhaps not very incorrectly, that the consideration which influenced the recruitments by promotion and nomination was not so much ability and competence but loyalty to the British raj. Obviously, the British preferred to fill their government posts with men whom they trusted.

[1] Ibid, p. 26.

It is amusing to learn that while the Provincial Civil Service officers were recruited by nomination and were given positions of lesser responsibility with lower salaries, yet it was desired that they should 'as far as possible, be put on a footing of equality' with the members of the Imperial Services. In practice, as should have been expected, the PCS officials did not receive as much respect as did the ICS officers. In 1912 the Islington Commission on public services in India took note of this fact, but mistakenly attributed it to the use of the prefix 'Provincial' in the designation of the Provincial Civil Service, which in those days was used to indicate the lower rank of certain cadres. At that time, in many cases, the higher and the lower cadres of a single service were designated as Imperial and Provincial, respectively. The prefix 'Provincial' indicated the lower rank of cadre and not the fact that it had been recruited by the government of a particular province. After the creation of the Provincial Civil Service the prefix 'Provincial' was meant to indicate the fact that the cadre had been recruited, by a provincial government and not by the central government. It seems, however, that as a result of the meaning attributed to this word previously, it continued to be associated with an inferior cadre. In order to eradicate this feeling the Islington Commission recommended 'the services which lie between the higher and the subordinate services should no longer be designated "provincial" services. If they are organized provincially they should ordinarily bear the name of the province. If they are under the central government the term Class I and Class II should be used.'[1]

From the above interpretation it appears that the creators of the PCS had intended this service to occupy a status equal to that the Imperial Civil Service, later called the Indian Civil Service. But certain policies of the government indicate that this was not the intention. For example, the Islington Commission recommended that officers promoted from a lower into a higher service should ordinarily be given the same opportunities as the officers who had

---

[1] Government of India, *Report of the Royal Commission on Public Services in India*, London, 1916, para. 30, p. 21.

been directly recruited and should be eligible on their merits for appointments to any post in their service. The Commission also recommended that both classes of officers should be shown on the same list and should take seniority amongst themselves from their date of entry on the list. The Commission recommended the application of this principle to all services except the Provincial Civil Service.[1] As a result of this policy a PCS officer, even after his promotion to a post ordinarily held by an ICS officer, continued to be designated as a PCS officer. Although he performed the same duties as an ICS officer, he was not recompensed according to the ICS pay scale. The fact of the matter is that although it has been asserted that the Provincial Civil Service is not an inferior service it has certainly been treated in such a manner as to suggest inferiority.

This spirit is reflected in the procedure by which officers of the Provincial Civil Service were admitted to the higher administrative posts ordinarily held by the members of the ICS. On the demand of the Provincial Civil Service a certain percentage of the higher administrative posts were reserved for them. The members of the Provincial Civil Service who were promoted to those posts performed exactly the same functions as those which were performed by the members of the ICS. However, these officers were paid at a different rate and contrary to the principle, stated above, that the promoted officers and the directly recruited officers should be treated equally, these PCS officers were not accepted into the fraternity of the ICS. They performed the same functions which were ordinarily undertaken by ICS officers yet they were designated as listed post-holders and not as ICS officers. These facts show that unlike the practice in other services, the designation of the Indian Civil Service and that of the Provincial Civil Service was not supposed to reflect the functions these services performed but the manner in which they were recruited. The emphasis was more on origin than on the type of work performed by each service. It is hard to miss similarities between this attitude and the attitude which forms the basis of the caste system.

[1] Ibid. para. 27, p. 20.

The fact that a certain percentage of the PCS officers were eligible for appointment to posts ordinarily held by the ICS shows that the functions of the two services were essentially similar. It also shows that the PCS was treated for all practical purposes as the junior cadre of the ICS. In these circumstances, the differences in designations, pay scales and methods of recruitment appear to be an unsuccessful attempt at creating an artificial division between the two categories of public servants. This segregation seems still more undesirable in view of the circumstances in which and the reasons for which it was effected.

The continuation after Independence of the discrimination between the Provincial Civil Service and the Civil Service of Pakistan, the successor to the ICS, has given rise to an intense feeling of jealousy among the PCS officers towards the members of the Civil Service of Pakistan. This feeling has become still more acute in view of the rapid promotion of CSP officers to positions of higher responsibility. A member of the PCS must serve three or four times as long a period before he becomes eligible for such promotions. This is a very sore point among the PCS officers who have, in certain cases, served for a length of time which is roughly equivalent to the total age of a young CSP officer. In such cases jealousy induces resentment, frustration and demoralization. These feelings adversely affect inter-service relations and the amount and the quality of work.

The main cause of grievance on the part of the members of the PCS is that suitability for top administrative posts is determined by the aptitude and ability of a public servant not as demonstrated in actual performance but as demonstrated in a written examination held prior to the original recruitment. Furthermore, it is stated, that experience in administration is not given due consideration in making appointments of higher responsibility.

The members of the PCS who joined the service through competitive examination feel more demoralized because their prospects for positions of administrative leadership are conditioned by their membership in the Provincial Civil Service and not determined by their performance on the job. No matter how well they perform their jobs, since they happen to be members of the Provincial Civil Service they must hold inferior positions and receive a lower rate of salary. Such a situation, it is said, not only eliminates incentive and a sense of competition but creates demoralization. Some of the directly recruited PCS officers claim that they failed to enter the Civil Service of Pakistan because of the operation of the quota system. They might still have managed to rise to a higher administrative position had there been some provision for promotion based upon merit. Since there was no such provision they were condemned to remain in inferior positions in spite of the will and ability on their part to occupy places of higher responsibility.

The fact that the sharp segregation between the CSP and the PCS is artificial was demonstrated by the decision of the Governments of Pakistan and India to entrust a large number of administrative positions to the members of the PCS immediately after Independence, in view of the shortage of trained administrators. The performance of the PCS officers in both countries indicates that they did rise to the occasion in helping their governments through very difficult periods of their history. In Pakistan about eight to ten senior PCS officers were promoted as full members of the Civil Service of Pakistan during the fifties. In India, such lateral recruitment has been on a far larger scale. One observer states that in 1960 two-fifths of the officers in the Indian Administrative Service were selected or promoted from the State Services. Other sources of personnel for the IAS were the Defence Forces and *ad hoc* recruits from outside the ranks of the public service. The directly recruited personnel in the IAS formed only one-third of the total.[1]

All this evidence lends support to the need for greater integration of the two cadres, the CSP and the PCS. One of the means suggested for the implementation of this proposal is to increase the opportunity for the PCS officers to be promoted to the cadre of the Civil Service of Pakistan. The members of the PCS thus moved into the CSP would be considered as full members of the

[1] T. C. A. Srinivasavardam, 'Some Aspects of the Indian Administrative Service' published in the *Indian Journal of Public Administration*, January-March, 1961, Vol. VII No. I. p. 26.

Civil Service of Pakistan and would be designated as such. It has been noted earlier that more than half of the CSP respondents were in agreement with this proposal. This position has also been accepted by the Provincial Administration Commission which was appointed in 1959. The Commission recommended that 10·0 per cent. of the vacancies in the Civil Service of Pakistan should be filled regularly by the promotion of young Provincial Civil Service officers who are below thirty years of age and who have shown exceptional promise. The Commission also recommended that PCS officers appointed to higher administrative posts which are ordinarily held by the CSP officers should be treated as members of the Civil Service of Pakistan.[1]

One justification for such a change in policy is that the political reasons, for which the British Government of India created the PCS and for which it enforced a segregation between the PCS and the ICS, are no longer valid. The political reason of the British Government was to keep the substance of power in British hands. In the beginning this objective was easily achieved by concentrating all power in the members of the ICS who were predominantly British. It was claimed openly that as members of a free and conquering race, British officers were better suited to occupy government positions of higher responsibility and authority than were Indians, a conquered race. At this time, the concentration of all key government posts was justified openly on the grounds of the racial superiority of the British.

Sir John Strachey quotes the Duke of Argyll, the Secretary of State for India in 1870, in support of this position. The Duke, writing to the Government of India on the question of giving a larger share to the 'natives of India' in the administration of their own country offered the warning:

'It should never be forgotten, and there should never be any hesitation in laying down the principle that it is one of our first duties to the people of India to guard the safety of our dominion ... In the full belief of the beneficial character of administration, and of the great probability that on its cessation

[1] Government of Pakistan, *Report of the Provincial Administration Commission*, Lahore 1960, p. 145.

anarchy and misrule would reappear, the maintenance and stability of our rule must ever be kept in view as the basis of our policy, and to this end a large proportion of British functionaries in the more important posts seems essential.'[1]

Replying to the criticism of the monopolization of the top administrative positions by the British, Sir John Strachey wrote that the differences of race could not be ignored. He rejected the demand for the holding of competitive examinations for the ICS in India which were at that time held only in England on the plea,

'Although this system (competitive examinations) has, on the whole worked well with Englishmen, it is open even with them to objections and drawbacks, and to think of applying it to the Native of India is nothing less than absurd. Not the least important part of the competitive examination of young Englishmen was passed for him by his forefathers, who, as we have a right to assume, have transmitted to him not only their physical courage, but the powers of independent judgement, the decision of character, the habits of thought, and generally those qualities that are necessary for the government of men and which have given us our empire.'[2]

With the increase in the number of educated Indians a demand arose for the Indianization of the higher public service in India. Instead the British created the Provincial Civil Service. This was an attempt to accommodate educated Indians in a relatively inferior cadre, as it was less of a security risk, and to keep the ICS predominantly British in composition. Since some Indians had also joined the ICS through open competition, concentration of administrative leadership in the members of the ICS could not be justified on racial grounds. It was of great importance for the British government to reserve all power in the hands of this exclusive cadre whose members were still nearly all British. This time the justification was derived from a concept similar in nature to the Platonic idea. The concept upon which the ICS was built envisioned the 'recruitment of young men of presumably tested intellectual attainment in humane letters, aloof from politics and devoting their lives to the interests of the State.'[3] Professor Ralph

[1] Sir John Strachey, *India: Its Administration and Progress*, London, 1903, p. 79.

[2] Ibid., p. 494.

[3] Ralph Braibanti, op. cit., p. 262. et seq.

Braibanti tells us also that this system relied too optimistically upon the 'fixation of virtue in malleable youth'. This system, in its over-confidence resembles predestination. Originally, a predestined superior role for a particular cadre of public servants was based upon racial superiority, while later it was based upon academic excellence. In both instances each argument was basically a cover for the political needs of the ruling race. After Independence these considerations have ceased to exist so that a sharp segregation between the Civil Service of Pakistan, which has been created in the image of the ICS, and the Provincial Civil Service is unjustified.

After Independence, officers of the Provincial Civil Service, like the CSP, have been largely recruited by open competition on the basis of the results of a written examination and of a *viva voce* test, the justification being Macaulay's famous assertion that the persons who excel over others in academic learning also excel over them in other walks of life. But although the basic principle for the selection of the two categories of public servants is essentially the same, the persons with the highest achievement in one examination are considered superior to the persons with the highest achievement in the other.

As the basis of selection in both cases is academic excellence, a single examination should be sufficient. The standard of performance indicated by the written test could be used to make initial assignments of positions in the hierarchy. If the separate examination for the PCS is supposed to ensure representation of the provincial population, the same objective can be achieved by reserving the number of seats for each province as is already done in the case of the Civil Service of Pakistan itself. The advantage of such an arrangement is that it would promote the sense of belonging to a common service. As a result of the exclusively separate existence of the Civil Service of Pakistan and the Provincial Civil Service, cadre-consciousness is intense. This consciousness is healthy when it is possible for the members of the inferior cadre to achieve membership in the superior cadre by hard work and outstanding performance. Cadre-consciousness is fatal for the effectiveness and the morale of the public service if opportunities for such upward mobility are permanently closed. It is common knowledge that cadre-consciousness is extremely acute between the CSP and the PCS, but under the existing circumstances, it does not act as an incentive.

Whether or not a single service of general-purpose administrators is created, a change in the designation of the Civil Service of Pakistan seems to be necessary as it is a definite misnomer. The present designation seems to cover all personnel employed in the non-military establishments, of the entire public service of Pakistan though, in fact, it connotes only one small cadre of the total public service. To denote this particular cadre there appears to be every justification for reverting to the designation, Pakistan Administrative Service, which was used after Independence as the name for the former Indian Civil Service. The Government of India has also changed the designation of the ICS to Indian Administrative Service. The designations of all other Services indicate the functions they perform rather than the source of recruitment. The designation suggested above is more appropriate in describing the function which this cadre performs. This designation removes the confusion which the present designation creates. The CSP is not the 'Civil Service', but only a small part of it.

There is a general tendency for public servants to display their cadre designations after their names. Although this tendency is a symptom and not the cause of cadre-consciousness, yet perhaps it might have a good effect if public servants were forbidden from displaying their cadre designations. A deputy secretary is a deputy secretary no matter whether he is from the CSP, PCS, or GAR.[1] Similarly, a deputy commissioner is a deputy commissioner no matter whether he is from the CSP or PCS. There is a need to cultivate an identification of the public servant with the specific function he is performing rather than with the manner in which he was recruited.

Side-jobs for Public Servants

According to the classical concepts of public service a public ser-

[1] General Administrative Reserve.

vant is expected to offer absolutely undivided and exclusive service to his employer, the State. He is not allowed to serve a second employer, nor to work for payment during his spare time. This prohibition applies equally to participation by him in business transactions. In general, two main objections are advanced against side-jobs for public servants, firstly, that the public servant is likely to abuse his special position in a side-job or a side-business and secondly, that as a representative of the State which is supposed to reflect the interests of all groups, the public servant should not be, nor should he appear to be, associated with any particular interest. This second consideration has gained so much significance that the modern State has imposed restrictions even upon the freedom of speech of its permanent professional servants and also upon their behaviour in a non-official capacity in public.

However, in practice the idea of allowing public servants to utilize their spare time in gainful activities is not unknown. For example, the servants of the East India Company were allowed by law to pursue private trade. In Pakistan, certain categories of public servants, for example doctors, are allowed to undertake private practice over and above their official duties. Subordinate employees of the Postal Department have also been granted permission to do insurance work.

There appear to be two considerations behind the policy of allowing officers of certain categories to take up jobs in addition to those which they are holding under the government. In the case of the low-paid public servants the primary consideration is to provide them with an opportunity to supplement their incomes. In the case of skilled and specialized public servants the reason may be to make maximum use of their training and also to meet the shortage of trained persons.

This subject is of special interest in Pakistan because on the one hand there is a general feeling current among the people that a considerable proportion of public servants are engaged in some business activity, while on the other hand many public servants think that their salaries are so inadequate that they should be permitted to undertake part-time work.

The attitude of the respondents on this controversial subject is presented herewith. About three-fifths of the public servants, or 60·2 per cent., do not see eye to eye with those who think that public servants should be free to take side-jobs or to undertake business concurrently holding posts in government employ. About two-fifths of the public servants, or 38·9 per cent., are of the view that they should be allowed to take up side-jobs.

The officers who disapproved of allowing the public servants to undertake part-time work did so on the basis of three main reasons. In the first place, it was feared that side-jobs would divide the attention and the loyalty of the public servants. It was maintained that government servants were so preoccupied with official work that it would be impossible for them to spare time for side-business. In such circumstances, if allowed to pursue side-business, the public servants would use office time for private work to the neglect of their official work.

The second argument against side-jobs for the public servants was that they would be tempted to utilize their prestige and power as public servants to promote their private interests. Such behaviour would compromise the position of the public servant as a disinterested agent of the State. Such conduct on the part of the public servant would shake the confidence of the people in the government and might also lower the prestige of the public service.

Some of the public servants thought that instead of allowing public servants to take up side-jobs or side-business it would be better to increase their salaries. This measure would not only provide them with a decent income but would also ensure undivided loyalty and attention to a single employer and a single type of work, namely the government and official work.

A relatively larger proportion of officers who were fortunate enough to be in the high income group was against the permission of side-jobs for the public servants. For example, 77·3 per cent. of the officers whose monthly income from all sources was three thousand rupees or more were opposed to the introduction of side-jobs for the public servants. Only 42·0 per cent. of those officers whose monthly income from all sources ranged between three hundred and four hundred rupes shared this opinion.

The officers who belonged to Class II were relatively more in-clined to allow the public servants to undertake additional jobs than were the officers of Class I or the unclassified rank. For example, 47·3 per cent. of the Class II officers were in favour of side-jobs while 35·9 per cent. of the unclassified and 34·0 per cent. of the Class I officers were in favour of side-jobs.

More than half of the officers in the Electricity Department, or 52·7 per cent., and a little less than half of the officers in the Department of Co-operative Societies, or 46·2 per cent., approved of side-jobs for public servants. In the Department of Health, 43·8 per cent., and in the Public Relations Department, 45·9 per cent., were in favour of providing opportunities for the public servant to supplement his income. A comparatively small proportion of the officers of the Civil Service of Pakistan, 19·1 per cent., were in agreement with this proposal.

The most frequent argument advanced by the supporters of side-jobs was that not only were the salaries of the public servants in-adequate to begin with, but that the salaries had not been in-creased to balance the increase in the cost of living. The respon-dents stated that it was impossible for any public servant to meet his expenses with the income earned through lawful means. In fact a public servant was obliged to take recourse to unauthoriz-ed methods of supplementing his meagre income. In many cases, he was obliged to resort to corrupt means as well. Quite a number of the respondents said that some of the public servants were al-ready engaged in side-jobs in violation of the rules. Why not recognize the *de facto* position, they argued, and provide them with lawful and honest means of supplementing their income rather than compel them to use unlawful and corrupt methods?

Some of the supporters of side-jobs for public servants took an-other position. They said that Pakistan was an underdeveloped country, and was short of trained manpower. In this situation, it was not advisable to restrict the application of the skill of trained personnel. In order to make the maximum use of the skill of the public servants, especially in the case of a specialist such as a doctor or an engineer, he should be encouraged to apply his knowledge on a wider scale. This policy, it was believed, would contribute materially to the national development effort.

Quite a few of the respondents maintained that by permitting a skilled public servant to practice his skill in a private capacity, his experience would be widened.

About three-fourths of the supporters of side-jobs for public servants extended unqualified support to this idea. The remaining supporters offered conditional support. Some of them said that public servants should be allowed to find additional means of income only if these did not interfere with their official work. A few said that only the low-paid public servants should be allowed to supplement their income in this way. A few suggested that it should not be a universal right but should be granted on an individual basis. A small number of officers said that some hobbies fetching small incomes should be allowed. The examples of hobbies mentioned were writing, painting, photography, gardening and the like.

When asked to say what was the actual practice of the public servants in this respect a vast majority of the respondents, 82·6 per cent., replied that some of the public servants had actually taken up some side-business in addition to their government jobs. Whereas 5·8 per cent. of the respondents were of the opinion that none of the public servants had taken up a side-business, 4·6 per cent. of the public servants maintained that most of the public servants had done so. Seven per cent. of the officers were unable to say anything on this matter.

The respondents were not asked to state what type of public servants were engaged in side-business. An impression, however, gained by probing here and there, is that the majority of the public servants who had undertaken side-jobs are to be found among the low salaried, non-gazetted officials. For example, some peons, after working-hours, sell newspapers, work as gate-keepers in cinema halls or act as part-time domestic servants. In their free hours some clerks take up insurance work, keep accounts or files for private firms, or, in a very small number of cases, take up tuition work. Some of the steno-typists work as part-time personal assistants or typists to private individuals or to private firms.

The public servants who occupy the next higher place to those mentioned above are, in certain cases, engaged in small-scale business such as running a shop or a small factory such as a hosiery manufacturing establishment. More often than not such a business is conducted in the name of a relative who is either actually a partner or who acts as a front.

A few of the respondents who thought that many of the higher public servants were engaged in a large-scale business stated that such officials were actively engaged in business under the names of their wives, sons or other relatives. As it was not possible to test this assertion a statement with any amount of certainty cannot be made. However, it is possible to give figures for the respondents who possessed sources of income in addition to their salaries. Reputedly for public servants there is no restriction upon owning land, buildings or shares in limited companies so that there was no difficulty in getting information about such additional sources of income from the respondents.

Some additional source of income was possessed by 24·8 per cent. of the respondents. A little over half of this group of respondents owned land as a predominant additional source of income. A little less than half of them owned buildings, the rents of which provided them with some additional income. In the case of a very small fraction some contribution was made by their sons or wives when and if they were employed. A relatively larger proportion of officers in the Police Department, Civil Secretariat and the Civil Service of Pakistan possessed one or another additional sources of income. In the first two categories of officers those with additional sources of income formed about two-fifths of the total number and, in the last category formed one-third of the total.

As we have seen, an overwhelming majority of the respondents were of the view that some of the public servants were constrained to exploit sources in addition to government employment to meet the growing costs of the basic needs of life. About two-fifths of the respondents felt that they should be permitted to supplement their income in one way or another. About a quarter of the respondents were not living entirely upon their salaries but had to meet their needs from additional sources of income such as land or buildings.

It is certain that the salaries of public servants are inadequate since a fair number have had to find means of making up the deficiency. Some have been lucky enough to inherit additional sources of income. Some by frugal living, almost on a subsistence level, have saved enough to establish some kind of income-producing activity. The public servant is basically not different from other men, but by virtue of his position as a servant of the public, different things are expected of him, the public tends to be more shocked by amoral behaviour on the part of public servant than by similar behaviour on the part of a private citizen. Regardless of the type of employment, as long as salaries remain inadequate the chances are that a man who may be public servant will augment his income by unlawful or corrupt means.

Touring by District Officers

The District Office Manual specifically prescribes the number of days on which the district officer should tour the areas under his care. The purpose of this regulation is twofold, firstly, to supervize the work of the subordinate staff and, secondly, by bringing the officer into close contact with the people to give him firsthand knowledge of the difficulties which beset the common people.

Government leaders have laid great emphasis, especially after Independence, on the ideal of 'establishing a living human fellowship' between the official and the people. Touring is considered to be an effective method of achieving this objective. For example, the Report of the Council for Administration of West Pakistan recommended that 'the old rules in respect of village touring by officers should be revised and strictly enforced. Every officer should spend at least ten nights in a month away from his headquarters and submit a tour note to his immediate superior officer.'[1] In May 1961, the Government of West Pakistan enforced new rules for

[1] *Report of the Council for Administration of West Pakistan*, February, 1955, para. 25, p. 9.

travelling allowances, abolishing the practice of the payment in a lump sum of travelling allowance to touring officers. Under the new rules the officials were to get travelling allowance for actual touring done by them. This decision was taken in order to encourage extensive touring by public servants.[1]

In an editorial on the new rules, the *Pakistan Times* commented, 'the change will be welcomed by all interested in the improvement of administration, for it is well-known that inadequate touring by officers is one of the main causes of laxity and inefficiency at the lower levels'.[2] The editorial even suggested that the performance of his touring duties should be made a part of the regular service record of a public servant.

Laxity in touring by officers, especially the district officers, has often come under criticism. A number of research studies indicate that omission of touring responsibilities has occurred in some instances. In one study the example of a village was given, as an extreme case, which was only visited by the deputy commissioner after seventeen years.[3] In another study it was noted that one sub-division in Rawalpindi Division was not visited by a commissioner for seven years.[4]

In order to study this aspect of public administration a question was designed for the officers who had served either as sub-divisional officers or as district officers. The number of these officers in our sample was twenty-eight, all of whom belonged to the Civil Service of Pakistan. None of them was working as a sub-divisional officer or a district officer at the time of interview. This consideration limited the scope of the question which asked them whether or not their desk-work at headquarters had left them enough time to go on tour for the prescribed number of days.

A little more than half of the officers replied in the affirmative and a little less than half replied in the negative. Among the first

[1] *The Pakistan Times, Lahore,* 16 May 1961.

[2] *The Pakistan Times, Lahore,* 18 May 1961.

[3] A. H. Aslam, *The Deputy Commissioner,* Lahore, 1957, p. 26.

[4] M. Javaid Ilyas, *Divisional Commissioner, A Study in Public Administration* (typescript), p. 56. (A study presented to the Graduate School of Business Administration, Karachi University, 1961).

category of officers the majority had worked as sub-divisional officers only or had worked in small districts. That is to say, the areas in their charge were small and also their responsibilities were not so numerous or pressing as were those of a district officer with a large area to cover. Only one-third of the officers who had worked as district or divisional heads of large areas had been able to fulfil their touring commitments. This information suggests that it is relatively easier for an officer to leave his headquarters for the purpose of an inspection tour when he is in charge of a smaller area.

Among the officers who had not been able to tour the areas in their charge for the prescribed period, three had held the position of a district or divisional head of a relatively large-sized district or division, five had held the charge of average-sized districts and another five had worked only as sub-divisional officers. One district officer from the second category maintained that he had not been able to tour his district for the required period because he had not been provided with a sub-divisional officer to assist him. The sub-divisional officers stated that although they had been able to fulfil the requirement for touring it had been possible only with the greatest difficulty. The experience of these officers confirms the previous findings.

Not only is the area under the care of a district officer very large, his work is so varied and heavy that it is humanly impossible for him to devote adequate attention to office work and to the work in the field. If the participation of the district officer in field work is to be increased and improved either the size of the district should be reduced or the district officer should be relieved of some of his routine duties. One way of reducing the size of the district was suggested in 1960 by the Provincial Administration Commission, which recommended that districts in West Pakistan should be divided into sub-divisions on the pattern of East Pakistan. It was maintained that this would 'result in the creation of an effective administrative unit even closer to the people than the district and would relieve the district officer of a great deal of routine work'.[1]

[1] *Report of the Provincial Administration Commission*, Lahore, 1960, p. 189.

Another or an additional means of achieving this effect was suggested in *The First Five Year Plan*. The Plan suggested that in order to relieve the district officer of formal and routine functions additional district officers and revenue assistants should be appointed in all the districts.[1]

Transfer Policy

Writing about the government policy of transferring public servants to different posts, districts or departments, an adviser to the Government of Pakistan on public administration commented as follows:

Skilled and experienced manpower is certainly one of Pakistan's scarcest commodities. Yet a habit pattern seems to have been built up under which there is such constant and frequent movement in and out of key government posts, especially among district officers and in the Secretariat, that it cannot fail to affect the efficiency of the government system as a whole, and particularly, of course, the efficiency of individual agencies and officers. I remember encountering on one occasion a young deputy secretary in West Pakistan who had held something like fourteen different posts within the space of about five years. And, on another a secretary who had served as secretary of five different departments in about a year and a half. It does not take much imagination to visualize some of the evil results of this degree of job instability.[2]

This problem has been singled out by some other observers as well. Professor Bernard L. Gladieu, an expert on public administration, who was invited by the Government of Pakistan sometime in 1954 to offer advice on improving its public administration, maintained that district officers had played a minor role in development programmes, partly for the reason that they had been transferred too frequently. Frequency of transfers was responsible for a lack of continuity in administration, for the consequent inefficiency of administration in general, and for an absence of sustained effort at development in particular.[3] The same criticism

[1] Government of Pakistan, National Planning Board, *The First Five Year Plan, 1955-60*, Karachi, 1958, p. 102.

[2] Paul L. Beckett, *A Few Concluding Comments on Public Administration and Development in Pakistan*, A mimeographed pamphlet of eighteen pages, Karachi, 1957, p. 11.

[3] Bernard L. Gladieu, *Re-orientation of Pakistan Government for National Development* (Presented to the Planning Board, Government of Pakistan), Karachi, 1955.

was later repeated in *The First Five Year Plan of Pakistan*.[1] The Provincial Administration Commission, appointed on 12 February 1959, by the Government of Pakistan, also touched upon this subject. One of the recommendations of the Commission was that frequent transfers should be avoided as a matter of administrative policy, particularly in the case of divisional and district heads of departments, including commissioners and districts officers, to enable them to perform effectively their important role in the new set-up.[2]

The quality if not the amount of evidence presented above proves that the transfer policy of the government is an important source of the organizational problems of administration in Pakistan. However, it emphasizes only one unfavourable consequence of rapid transfers. The other unfavourable consequence is the impact of rapid and frequent transfers on the personal life of the public servant. Rapid rotation more often than not was accompanied by the displacement of the official from one district to another. It is not difficult to visualize the inconveniences which may, and generally do, arise in transporting one's belongings and in making adjustments to new people and places. In large towns comfortable accommodation becomes an extremely expensive affair, while the relatively less expensive accommodation suffers from the absence of most of the basic amenities for living. Accommodation provided by the government is stated to be inadequate for all types of public servants. Moreover, the machinery responsible for allotment of government accommodation is alleged to be slow and susceptible to patronage.

In certain cases, other personal problems are involved. For example, a public servant whose children are enrolled in institutions of higher education may be appointed to a place where there are no such educational facilities.[3] In such circumstances, the public servant must choose between taking his children with him

---

[1] Government of Pakistan, National Planning Board, *The First Five Year Plan of Pakistan, 1955-60*, Karachi, 1958, p. 101.

[2] *Report of the Provincial Administration Commission*, Government of Pakistan, Lahore, 1960, p. 147.

[3] *The Pakistan Times*, Lahore, 10 September 1960.

to the detriment of their education or incurring the additional expense of housing his children in a hostel. In some cases it is reported that the transfer is ordered at a time of the year when it is difficult to gain admission for children in local schools. Directions exist to the effect that every possible care should be taken to ensure that transfers coincide with the beginning of academic sessions in the schools. Commendable as this measure is, it gives recognition to the fact that public servants are frequently transferred in accordance with remote, impersonal regulations without due consideration of their special qualifications or their special needs. If a public servant has to suffer frequent physical dislocations, accompanied as they usually are by other inconveniences, he will be clearly unable to concentrate fully on his work.

With a view to assessing the importance of this problem, the respondents were asked to give the number of occasions on which they had been transferred during their period of service following Independence. They were also asked to state whether the transfer was from one district to another, from one post to another, or from one department to another. They were asked to give the reasons for the transfers as well.

Forty-five respondents were unable or unwilling to give this information. Sixty-one officers, all of whom were employed in the Civil Secretariat, were not liable to transfer. The rate of transfer in the cases of the remaining 326 public servants is given in the table below. Slightly less than one-half of the public servants who were working at posts from which they were liable to be transferred had been transferred once in less than three years. As the general rule is that a public servant should preferably not be transferred in less than a minimum period of three years, we may conclude that in 47·9 per cent. of the cases transfers had taken place more rapidly than prescribed. It may also be observed that transfers had been more frequent in the case of Class I officers than in the case of Class II officers. Only 6·4 per cent. of the respondents had been transferred in accordance with the regular, prescribed interval of three years.

Another feature of the transfer policy which calls for attention is that more than two-fifths of the officers who were posted on transferable posts had, in a period of four to fifteen years, not been transferred at all or had been transferred once only. Perhaps it shows a problem in the reverse direction, that is to say, that certain officers are allowed to stay on in their posts for far longer periods than is considered desirable.

The consequences of frequent transfers become more harmful depending upon the nature of and the reason for a transfer. The first point taken up is the nature of a transfer as it can result in an unwholesome effect on the public servant.

Broadly speaking a transfer may take three basic forms. It may be a transfer to a new post or to a new district or to a new department. Arithmetically more forms are possible by the combination of any two of the basic forms or by a combination of all three of them. In practice, however, in most of the departments and cadres, the transfer usually takes place between districts so that the public servant concerned continues to work in the same department. Such departments are Engineering, Health, Police and the like.

In a few cadres, the public servant is not only rotated between districts, but also between departments. Quite often this rotation may be accompanied by a change in the post as well. Transfers of this type generally take place in the case of officers of the Civil Service of Pakistan and those of the Provincial Civil Service. The officers of these two cadres are popularly known as generalists, by which it is meant that they are not specialists like doctors or police officers. These generalists are rotated, as a matter of policy, from the district to the Secretariat in order to provide them with experience in the two types of work which are different but interrelated. In addition, the generalists are appointed to different departments within the Secretariat and also to a good number of other miscellaneous posts such as those in the autonomous corporations and the semi-government departments. The officers of the Civil Service of Pakistan, by virtue of belonging to an All-Pakistan cadre, are liable to appointment anywhere within Pakistan. In practice, they are alternately appointed for a certain amount of time in each of

Table 34

RATE OF TRANSFERS OF OFFICERS OF DIFFERENT CLASSES

Class	No transfer took place in 3 or less than 3 years	No transfer in 4-15 years	One transfer in 1 year or less	One transfer in more than 1 but in less than 2 years	One transfer in 2 or more than 2 years but in less than 3 years	One transfer in 3 years	One transfer in more than 3 but in less than 6 years	One transfer in 6 or more years but in less than 16 years	Total
Class I	15 / 14·0	27 / 14·6	4 / 2·2	45 / 23·3	47 / 25·4	15 / 8·1	24 / 13·0	23 / 12·4	185
Class II	—	29 / 21·3	6 / 4·4	29 / 21·3	20 / 14·7	6 / 4·4	19 / 14·0	12 / 8·8	136
Unclassified	—	—	—	2	3	—	—	—	5
Total	15 / 4·6	—	10 / 3·1	76 / 23·3	70 / 21·5	21 / 6·4	43 / 13·2	35 / 10·7	326

the two wings of the country and also in the provincial or the central government.

The impact of the transfers of the types described above is two-fold, firstly, on the public servant, and, secondly, on the departments. The transfers which are purely between districts affect primarily the public servant. In the type of transfers to which the generalists are subject the impact is mainly upon the department. Apart from physical dislocation, the public servant is denied an opportunity to familiarize himself, to the desired extent, with any one area of administration. As a result, in the words of Professor Gladieu, 'the generalists in the ICS-CSP tradition have breadth without depth in terms of governmental experience, particularly in development subjects'. Professor Gladieu goes on to point out that technological development and the increasingly specialized activities of government no longer permit an administrator to 'get by' with only general or superficial knowledge of the subject-field he is supposed to administer. He invites us to note that some of the best of the generalists in Pakistan had attained excellence by successfully steeping themselves in the substance of the pro-gramme they were administering. A public servant can apply sustained interest and attention to a particular branch of knowledge or field of activity only if he is allowed to stay at a particular job for a reasonable length of time.

As to the reasons for transfers the findings are as follows.

Leaving out the officers who were working at non-transferable posts and those who were unable or unwilling to supply information about transfers, the remaining 326 officers offered 342 reasons for their transfers. The number of reasons is higher than the number of officers because some of them gave more than one reason for their transfers.

As should be clear from Table 35 in a vast majority of cases the transfers were ordered because of administrative considerations. The officers did not prescribe the precise circumstances which caused their transfers. However, it is possible to identify one specific situation in which the entire process of transfers is set in motion when one public servant decides to go on long leave.

Table 35

REASONS FOR TRANSFERS AND FREQUENCY OF TRANSFERS

Reason of transfer	Number of transfers									Total
	1	2	3	4	5	6	7	8	9 or more	
Administrative expediency	27	36	26	38	39	32	25	15	37	248
Promotion	48	18	1	—	—	—	—	—	—	67
Police considerations	9	6	1	—	1	—	—	—	—	17
Departmental friction	8	1	1	—	—	—	—	—	—	10

The temporary absence of one public servant necessitates the transfer of another to fill his place. The transfer of the second public servant requires the transfer of the third, that of the third requires the fourth to be transferred and so on.

Another reason which is responsible for transfers in some cases, is the promotion of a public servant to a higher post. Sometimes the higher post is available in the same district, but in most cases the public servant has to be transferred to a new district for this purpose. Another reason, somewhat resembling promotion, is the transfer of an outstanding public servant to a larger and a more important district. At times, an officer is transferred in view of his special qualifications and experience in order to deal with a special situation. It will be interesting to quote the case of a senior public servant who had experienced frequent rotation of offices for this reason. This officer had once received his transfer orders to a metropolitan city as its chief executive. In view of the frequency of transfers which had been his lot he was unwilling to accept the latest transfer. In order to persuade him, his superior officer told him that he should consider his appointment as the chief executive of a metropolitan city as a feather in his cap. The unhappy officer retorted that he had collected so many feathers of that kind that by now he looked like a Red Indian Chief.[1] We feel that this officer has, in humourous vein, expressed the feeling of many public servants who have been the victims of frequent 'displacements', but who might not react so good humouredly.

It will be observed that a very small proportion of officers offered political considerations and departmental friction as reasons for their transfers. The reason for the reticence of the respondents can be well imagined because these considerations are extremely sensitive. None of the public servants in the Department of Co-operative Societies, Jails, Local Fund Audit, Public Relations and the Civil Secretariat was transferred on political considerations. Officers who were transferred on this ground were the largest, or 12·9 per cent., of the CSP officers.

[1] Reported to the writer in a personal interview. The remark is being reproduced with the permission of the officer concerned.

Indications are available that governmental leaders are aware of the need of reorganizing the transfer policy on a more rational basis. In September 1960 the Government of West Pakistan distributed an eleven point questionnaire among the officers of the Provincial Civil Service in order to obtain information about their qualifications, experience, interests and personal affairs. It was hoped that this information would help the government in finding the right type of officers for specialized jobs and also in posting an officer to a district or a position in keeping with the qualification, interests and needs of that officer.[1]

[1] *The Pakistan Times*, Lahore, 10 September 1960.

CHAPTER 11

THE PASSING OR THE PERMANENCE OF THE POWER OF THE PUBLIC SERVANT

The President of Pakistan speaking on the inauguration of the Pakistan Administrative Staff College, said, 'As you are no doubt aware, human society developed from the stage of a cave man to the family structure, from family structure to feudalism, from feudalism to capitalism and from capitalism it has blossomed into diverse material channels like communism, socialism and the concepts of a welfare state. In Pakistan we have not yet reached the stage of capitalism. We have, therefore, to make a big jump and develop into a social welfare state, which in fact is the inevitable demand of the ideology on the basis of which we can reach this target expeditiously and is the real touchstone of all our developmental programmes and administrative reforms'. [1]

This statement coming from such a high source sums up Pakistan's immediate objective, namely to transform the rural-agri-

[1] *The Pakistan Times*, Lahore, 25 December 1960.

cultural pattern of her society into a predominantly urban-industrial one. The statement quoted above also implies a certain amount of impatience with the rate at which this transformation is taking place.

In the same speech, the President emphasized the need for giving dynamic dimensions to the 'static administration' inherited from the colonial days. From the conjunction of the President's two statements it can be easily discerned that the public service is identified as the major agent of change. This concept is not peculiar to one particular regime in Pakistan. Almost all governments have envisioned a similar role for the public service. In fact, there seems to be a general tendency among most of the new states to rely more and more upon professional, salaried government employees for the implementation of plans to accelerate the socio-economic changes in their societies.

The new functions assigned to the civil servant indicate a significant departure from the traditional role commonly associated with him. The traditional role of a public servant is concisely summed up in the motto of the British Civil Service, 'Poverty, Obedience, Anonymity' which implies that the classical civil servant is only a servant of the political superior and remains in the background. In the new role, the public servant is very much in the public eye in presiding over all types of development activities both in the public and the private sector. The role of the public servant in the new states is based on the premise that private citizens are incapable, at the moment, of producing leadership which, therefore, must be provided by the State, through its public servants.

In order to illustrate this trend of thought in Pakistan it is appropriate to quote from a senior administrator who for some time has been the head of a training institution for public servants. In an article devoted to a description of the functions of the training institution, he writes:

We can, no doubt, learn small lessons from other countries, but we must remember that conditions here are different. While in developed countries public administration systems grow with the growth of the people, here a system was imposed upon a people who had yet to grow. If we examine this fact alone, a little minutely, we will quickly come to the conclusion that for this single reason some of the principles of public administration recognized as basic in other countries are not applicable to conditions obtaining here. It will, for example, be a matter of surprise for the administrators of countries which have not been subjected to to colonial rule that administrators under certain conditions have to be used for creating political consciousness in the people and educating them in the art of self-government. We had to violate some universally accepted concepts of impersonalized bureaucracy because our culture, which had been ruthlessly trampled upon, demanded it. Here we have dared to make a bold, departure and we are proud of it in spite of the inveterate critic who cannot but find faults. [1]

In the last part of the article, the author describes the 'bold departure' as follows: 'The challenge is first to convert the administrator trained in Western type of bureaucracy to the new line of thinking and to make him a proud Pakistani citizen from a disinterested and inert tool which he had become.'[2]

Some might contest the assertion that the people have failed to produce leaders of stature from among themselves. However, even if this assertion may be accepted, there are serious doubts that the civil servant can adequately provide this leadership or that the civil servant is the only substitute.

The people who expect the civil servant to provide leadership subconsciously presume that he is something like a worker of a political party who, having identified himself with certain basic political and economic ideals, is pledged to work for their propagation and promotion.

This may be the case in one-party governments in which political affiliations may form an influential consideration for the selection of administrators. In multi-party systems, political considerations, as a matter of principle, are not allowed to influence the recruitment of the civil servant. The reason is probably that in multi-party systems no unanimity, supposed or real, exists on basic po-

1 Raja Muhammad Afzal, 'A Year of Village Development Academy: The New Concept', an article published in *The Civil and Military Gazette*, Lahore, 15 October 1960.
2 Ibid.

litical and economic goals. It is all the more true in the new states where the differences are more basic than those present in the older states. As a result, in multi-party systems, civil servants are supposed to be politically neutral. It is considered as misconduct on their part if they allow themselves to be identified with the objectives of one particular political party.

Under such circumstances, the 'average civil servant is likely to be an agent who propagates certain ideas because he is paid to do so and not because he himself believes in them. It is also entirely possible that a government functionary who is appointed to promote the practice of a certain principle such as, for instance, co-operative farming may not have any faith in this system or that he may be basically opposed to it.

Let us take the example of the Village Agricultural and Industrial Development movement which was started in this country some time ago. As should be evident from its name, the purpose of this endeavour was to break the static traditions of village society. This task was entrusted to a hierarchy of paid servants of the State. The most important position was occupied by the V-aid worker who was in the closest contact with the village. This worker was regarded as a 'listening post' for the government and as a transmitter of government directives. It was difficult, however, to find in him the characteristics of a missionary or a revolutionary. His chief failing was that he himself was not involved in the process. The role described above is not suited for the paid public servant but for the voluntary political worker. If we expect the former to play the latter's role we are being unfair to both.

A student of the development problems of the new states observes, 'To perform all its functions properly, an Asian bureaucracy must not merely be on proper terms with its politicians, it must be competent, honest, and have a proper *esprit de corps*. It is an advantage if it also has some passion for the country's advance.'[1] This passion is in fact what distinguishes the voluntary political worker from the indifferent paid servant of the State. The State servant has been described as indifferent because he is not

[1] Maurice Zinkin, op. cit., p. 88.

supposed to identify himself with any ideology. As described above the political neutrality of the civil servant is considered to be his chief virtue, whereas that is exactly what disqualifies him to act as a leader of men.

In Pakistan the civil service has generally played a leading role in the government of the country. As noted in earlier chapters, this situation was partly a result of the British tradition of bureaucratic rule in India. Khalid Bin Sayeed informs us that this tradition was so powerful that it was possible for the chief secretary of a province, a civil servant, to annual the orders passed by the provincial minister of finance and commerce. He also tells us that the politicians of that particular province alleged that the chief secretary used to send fortnightly reports on the activities of the provincial ministers to the central government.[1]

The ascendency of the civil servants was also due to the poverty of leadership among the politicians. Two civil servants were able to reach the position of the head of State. Two of them held the office of Prime Minister. Many others held the positions of ministers in the central and in the provincial governments, and a few became the chief ministers of certain provinces. The posts of provincial governors were ordinarily filled by civil servants.

Originally, it seemed, the civil servants were assigned to high political offices as an *ad hoc* arrangement. Later developments show that the civil service became conscious of its power and tried to retain it by deliberate policy. General Iskander Mirza's remark on the assumption of the office of Governor-General, that the politicians will not be allowed 'to make a mess of the things' is indicative of the growing consciousness on the part of the civil service of its powerful position. The political history of Pakistan from 1954 onward clearly shows the weakness of the politicians if not the greater power of the civil servants. Khalid Bin Sayeed has well summed up the position of bureaucracy in the power structure of Pakistan. He writes, 'The Government of Pakistan could be described as a pyramid carved out of a single rock and, it has been shown how the civil servants captured the apex of the

[1] Khalid Bin Sayeed, op. cit., p. 385.

pyramid. Below the apex were several layers of authority descending downwards from the Secretariat level to the base of the pyramid, the district administrators.'[1]

Certain other people have also come to a similar conclusion. In reply to the questionnaire of the Constitution Commission in 1960, nineteen religious leaders wrote in a pamphlet,

Up to the year 1953 the feeling grew and developed in the Services that they were the real holders of power and that the political leaders were ruling the country with their support only. A factor which contributed more than anything else to give this feeling of the Services a practical shape was the fact that after the death of Mr. Liaquat Ali Khan, the office of the head of the State fell to the lot of a member of this class and thereafter members of this very class continuously held this office.[2]

In view of the fact that the civil service has held the substance of power and also because there is a definite move to provide this situation with a philosophical rationale, it becomes important to examine the characteristics of the civil service personnel in order to determine what is the nature of the leadership of the country.

Considering the background information of the respondents the following general observations may be made. The higher public servants, in general, represent the middle class. Those who belong to the cadres which are better paid and enjoy a higher public esteem form part of the upper middle class in the social hierarchy, while those with lower pay scales represent the lower middle class. A vast majority of the higher public servants are drawn from the group of people with an urban background. As compared to the general population, the educational attainment of the higher public servants is very high. A characteristic of this education is that it is generally influenced by the values of Western Europe and North America.

Taken together, all these basic characteristics present the image of a rising middle class. This middle class is the product as well as the promoter of a social change as evidenced by increasing in-

---

[1] Khalid Bin Sayeed, op. cit., p. 390.

[2] *Answers to Constitution Commission's Questionnaire unanimously formulated in a Meeting of nineteen Ulema held at Jamia' Ashrafia, Lahore, on 5 and 6 May 1960*, Lahore, 1960, p. 6.

dustrialization and its effect upon social and economic affairs. Similar to the middle classes of other cultures the Pakistani middle class, of which the higher public servants form a significant part, is also the harbinger of an abrupt break with the values of the pre-industrial era. The conservative elements of society, as is natural, bemoan the passing of the old order. They blame the rising middle class for the decline of pre-industrial values and customs which they feign to believe to be the national culture of Pakistan. The following quotation is typical of this attitude.

The emergence of the middle class was the most significant contribution of the British rule on the sub-continent. Designed to be the interpreters of the West to the East they became in fact the oracles of the East on the strength of their Western knowledge and so the potential supplanters of the British. These were the lawyers, the doctors, the teachers and the professors. Indian and Pakistani political leadership came from this class. Significant influences on the lives of the older generations of the middle class were Shakespeare, Milton and the Bible, Burke, Mill and Macaulay, Magna Carta and the Long Parliament, in fact the whole liberal gospel of the nineteenth century. While in this generation there were some who had also roots in the oriental tradition of piety and learning and helped to evolve the Anglo-Muslim synthesis of culture of which we have spoken, the younger generations were almost completely alienated from the indigenous tradition. Our universities have produced and continue to produce men and women, 'pathological egoists', who have lost their roots in society, who care neither for the learning of the East nor of the West, who are feebly affected by the mass culture of the West on its vulgar and sensate (*sic*) side and have no appreciation whatsoever of the spiritual or cultural values of the East. Such culturally displaced persons, we have remarked, are occupying positions of power and responsibility in the life of the country and dictate the future cultural pattern of our society. They generally agree with the communists in regarding religion as the 'opium of the people' or 'the pie in the sky' and regard education merely as a means of 'getting on' economically and acquiring social prestige. Characteristically, they are exclusively interested in manufacturing 'man-power' for the national services and not creating men and women who would aspire to be God's vice-regents on earth. Persons more crassly materialistic than this class would be difficult to find in the East or the West.

Greatest confusion is caused by the half-educated, half-Westernized member of the middle class, who has fallen between two cultural stools. He has alienated himself from sources of Muslim culture and Western culture has affected him only on its superficial and sensate sides. This class of faintly atheistic, egoistic and aggressive anarchists is rapidly increasing in numbers and setting the pattern of our society. There are large numbers of civil servants, educationists and others who are similarly culturally displaced and normally split, but are highly influential in moulding the national policies.

The public service in Pakistan represents modern values. In this sense it is not the representative of the general population. The social milieu in Pakistan is basically rural and the economy which it supports is predominantly agricultural. A truly representative leadership chosen through elections must reflect the values of a rural-agricultural society. The dilemma of the intelligentsia is that if they insist upon a truly representative form of government they risk placing the destiny of the country in the hands of a conservative and reactionary group of people. If they allow the public servants to govern the country with the hope of accelerating the modernization of an underdeveloped society they feel that the ideal of a representative form of government would have to be abandoned and that further progress in democratic practices would be retarded. In other words, they tacitly lend support to the view that it is legitimate that the judgements about what is good for the people should be made for the people and may be carried out by a small minority.

Another risk which is involved in accepting the civil service as the legislator and the executor of national policies is that the civil service may not always represent liberal ideas. This fear springs from two considerations. Firstly, that bureaucracy is inherently conservative. In certain respects it represents the liberal forces of the modern world, but not necessarily to the desired extent. The civil service may be more progressive than the general population but it may not be progressive enough to achieve the basic goals before Pakistan.

The second consideration is the relatively advanced age of the top administrators in Pakistan. Old age is commonly associated with conservatism. In Pakistan it also means past association with a system of government which was authoritarian in operation and negative in purpose, namely the colonial administration under the British. The fear is that the senior administrators may not only be slow in accepting change but that they may also not be well-orientated to or in sympathy with the needs of a free people who are eager for speedy social and economic development.

If the public service is accepted as the leading agent of change it may be necessary, as a first step, to increase the representation of the younger generation. Such a move is important in order to make bureaucracy more representative of the new generation and in order to make it more responsive to the demands of a new era. Old age is reputed to possess the advantage of mature experience. The advantage held by youth is its orientation to the needs and the aspirations of the new times. So far the first consideration has dominated the thinking of government leaders in choosing admin-istrators for all types of situation. There is an urgent need to accord equal recognition to the second point of view. Apart from the benefits to be gained by this, the appointment of more young administrators has been advocated for another consideration as well. It has been pointed out 'that having a wrong man in a posi-tion of power merely because he was of a superior age was every bit as wasteful as having the wrong man in a position of power merely because his parents were of a superior class. In an open society the few who are chosen out of the many who are called should be chosen on merit; age is as much an irrelevant criterion as birth.'[1]

That the supremacy of old age results in the demoralization of the young and that this issue is not purely of academic interest to Pakistan was shown by the decision of the Government of West Pakistan in November 1960, which laid down that the heads of departments were not to be allowed to serve beyond the normal period of their tenure. The government made this decision after noting that, although the posts of heads of departments were tenure posts, each lasting for three years, yet heads of departments were allowed to continue for a second term lasting for five years. This

[1] Michael Young, *The Rise of the Meritocracy, 1870-2033, An Essay on Education and Equality*, London, 1958, p. 62.

practice blocked promotions on different subordinate levels and caused frustration among the junior officers. On some occasions, subordinate officers have been tempted to indulge in intrigues against the head of a department when they thought that he might continue for more than one term.'[1]

So far we have attempted to study the background of the public servant and the role he is expected to play in the government. Now it is proposed to examine the position which the public servant occupies in society.

Public service is one of the very few sources of employment available to educated Pakistanis. Although public esteem for public service has shown some decline with the increasing prospects of employment in industry and commerce and in independent professions, yet certain positions in the public service continue to confer tremendous prestige. The outstanding example is the position of a deputy commissioner. The deputy commissioner, who was formerly called the collector, exercises considerable executive and judicial power. He is the chief executive of the district, which is the basic and the most important unit of administration. In this capacity, he co-ordinates the activities of all other government departments at the district level. As a result of the policy of increased delegation of power to the field and regional officers the powers of the deputy commissioner have been further reinforced. Apart from his legal powers, the deputy commissioner is accepted as a leader in all private spheres of activity. He is invited to preside over prize distribution functions in the educational institutions in his district, to inaugurate new business and industrial enterprises and to address the conferences and seminars of voluntary welfare associations. He is generally invited to be the patron or a member of informal private boards or committees devoted to the promotion of social and cultural matters. These powers and the accompanying status invest the office of the deputy commissioner with immense prestige, so much so that it has become the cherished dream of almost all educated young men in Pakistan.

The high prestige attached to the office of the district officer is

1 *The Pakistan Times*, Lahore, 21 November 1961.

also partly a result of the traditional aura of authority and status which was attached to this office during British rule. The following quotation from a letter written by a young Englishwoman to her friend in England in describing her life in India, gives us some idea of the prestige which the office of the collector (deputy commissioner) enjoyed in the nineteenth century:

Twenty-first December, 1837. You ask what our visitors say, if ever they say anything? That, you know, depends upon taste; there is anything and anything—'fagots et fagots'. However, some of them are very sensible and agreeable; and when I have them alone, they talk very well, and I like their company, but as soon as three or four of them get together they speak about nothing but 'employment' and 'promotion'. Whatever subject may be started, they contrive to twist it, drag it, clip it and pinch it, till they bring it round to that; and if left to themselves, they sit and conjugate the verb 'to collect': 'I am a collector—he was a collector—we shall be collectors,—you ought to be a collector—they would have been collectors'; so, when it comes to that, while they conjugate 'to collect' I decline listening.[1]

The description in the above quotation might well have been written by a Pakistani about certain of his countrymen.

The image of the public servant as a ruler, developed during British rule, is still present in the public mind. A change in this image is taking place, though at a tardy pace, yet it is important that this change is occuring at all. The rate of this change grows apace proportionally to the spread of political consciousness and to the rise in the status of the business executive in trade and in industry.

With the spread of education the proportion of well-educated people is increasing as is the number of highly-educated and well-travelled persons outside the ranks of the public service. This situation is not the result of a pronounced aversion on the part of the highly-educated men and women to employment in public service, but is due to the limited capacity of the public service to accommodate all or most of them. Public service, especially the highly

[1] Hilton Brown (ed.) *The Sahibs, The Life and Ways of the British in India as Recorded by Themselves*, London, 1948, pp. 127-28.

responsible administrative positions, are still the first preference
of nearly all educated Pakistanis. However, the increase in the
number of intelligentsia outside the public service, counter-balan-
cing those who are inside the public service, is exercising significant influence in sizing down the image of the public servant.

Furthermore, the growth in status of the top-ranking executives
in business and in industry is producing a corresponding deflation
of the overblown prestige of the administrator. In order to study
the relations of the public servant with the public, we may use
the classification of the public as devised by Frank Dunnill. He
divided the public into two broad categories, namely the organized
public and the unorganized public. By the first category he means
the industrialists, the businessmen, journalists and the like. The
second category denoted the average lay citizen. The greater effectiveness of the impact of the former as compared to the latter is
understandable. The impact receives added strength from the general policies of the government which professedly aim at inculcat-
ing a spirit of public service in the public servants as against the
tradition of authoritarianism which they inherited from the colonial past of the country.

The sudden and relatively rapid expansion of industry and commerce in Pakistan is also exerting severe pressure on the methods
and procedures of Pakistani bureaucracy. Apart from making due
adjustments in the balance of power which was till recently heavily
weighted in favour of the bureaucracy, there is an urgent need to
reorganize bureaucratic policies and practices in response to the
changed socio-economic conditions.

The following quotation sums up the attitude of the industrialist
on this issue.

The real problem is that the bureaucracy, from its very nature,
is restricted by red-tapism. The expanding industries, on the other
hand require an initiative and efficiency which are beyond the
present capacity of the members of bureaucracy with all their good
intentions. The solution is that the industrial organizations should
more and more be officially recognized as authoritative and responsible advisers to the departments concerned. [1]

[1] Mian Muhammad Shafi, 'Modernizing Bureaucracy' an article published
in *The Civil and Military Gazette*, Lahore, 29 June 1961.

The public service is finding itself more and more under pressure to adjust its concepts to a changing social and economic scene. This is shown by the increasing attention being given in public discussions to the problem of the relationship between the industrialist and the public servant. The social distinction which the public servant enjoyed as a person without equal in his social milieu is giving place to a situation in which the public servant is being obliged to recognize the rise of people who, if not his superiors, can be a match for him.

The following quotation from a letter written in 1857, describing the sharp distinction which existed in the social status of the administrator as compared to other professionals, reveals the deep-rooted tradition against which the struggle for status is waged. The quotation reads :

The social distinctions are by no means lost sight of in India; on the contrary, they are perhaps more rigidly observed here than at home (England), and the smaller the society the broader are the lines of demarcation. Each man depends on his position in the public service, which is the aristocracy ... The women depend on the rank of their husbands. Mrs. A—the wife of a barrister, making £4,000 or £5,000 a year, is nobody as compared with the wife of B—who is Deputy Commissioner, or with Mrs. C—who is the better-half of the station surgeon. Wealth can do nothing for man or woman in securing them honour or precedency in their march to dinner ... A successful speculator, or a 'merchant prince' may force his way into good society in England ... but in India he must remain for ever outside the sacred barrier which keeps the non-official world from the high society of service. [1]

These comments were true of the period to which they referred. They continued to be valid, for the most part, until more recent times. However, these comments cannot be applied to the present-day conditions without reservations. The 'merchant prince', the business executive, the barrister and the physician are now forcing their way into 'good society'. Not infrequently the young administrators belonging to the cadre of the Civil Service of Pakistan discover the bitter truth that the above-mentioned *nouveau riche* can spend more in the clubs and in smart restaurants than they can. Similarly, they are surpassed in the procurement of everyday

[1] Hilton Brown, op. cit., pp. 126-7.

comforts of life. In wooing the ambitious daughters of the upper classes for marriage the public servant has now to face stiff competition.

Sometimes a fear is expressed that if the trend described above continues bright and outstanding young men may cease to seek careers in the public service and may instead prefer to join industry and business. This fear seems to be unfounded because, on the one hand, opportunities of employment for educated young men outside government service are very limited and, on the other hand, the number of highly-educated people in need of employment is constantly on the increase. Although the number of well-educated young men may increase considerably, the public service will continue to attract most of them.

The Pakistan Pay Commission in 1949, in reducing the pay scales of the higher public servants, advanced the following argument:

We do not think it to be a right policy for the State to offer such salaries to its servants as to attract the best available material. The correct place for our men of genius is in private enterprise and not in the humdrum career of public service where character and a desire to serve honestly for a living is more essential than outstanding intellect. We cannot, therefore, prescribe our pay scales with the object of attracting to public service all the best intellect in the country.[1]

It is significant to note that in spite of the drastic cuts in the salaries of the higher public servants, for the last many years the best university students have annually entered a 'gruelling competition for the sake of getting a place in the limited number of seats of the superior cadres of the public service. Most of the aspirants value a place in the coveted cadres so highly that they start intensive preparations years ahead of the competitive examination. Some of the candidates carry their preparations to the extent of craziness. Surrounded by books they confine themselves to their rooms for months at a stretch, memorizing facts about everything under heaven, ranging from the mysteries of mysticism to the latest discoveries of outer space.

[1] *Report of the Pakistan Pay Commission*, Karachi, 1949, p. 27.

The methods of preparation adopted by the candidates for the Civil Service of Pakistan resemble closely those which were used in the past by Indian candidates for the I.C.S. It is not uncommon, for example, for some of the candidates to make a pilgrimage to a foreign university, generally in Britain or in the United States of America, to improve their chances of selection. The most popular method of preparing for the *viva voce* test is still a rigorous study of current periodicals. *The Times* of London which was the favourite source of general information of the I.C.S. candidates has, however, given way to *Time* magazine, published in U.S.A. The I.C.S. candidates embarked upon a deliberate attempt to emulate as nearly as possible the dress and deportment, the style and manner of a European gentlemen even before appearing in the competitive examination. In the case of the C.S.P. candidates such intensive preparations follow rather than precede selection. [1]

Students of bureaucracy have often stressed the potential dangers of the inherent tendency in bureaucracy to resist policies which it does not like or to promote policies which it likes. In Pakistan a test case would be the attitude of the higher public servants towards a representative form of government. Ever since the creation of Pakistan representative government has had a chequered history. On many occasions, the public servant superseded the politician for long periods of time. On other occasions, when he worked with the politician who was supposed to be his political superior, the public servant discovered that the politician was not superior to him in terms of personal ability or experience. In certain cases the public servant has also suffered at the hands of the politician.

Against this background, voices were raised against the representative form of government and in its place the introduction of authoritarian systems such as 'controlled democracy' and 'benevolent dictatorship' was advocated. The attitude of the public service on this issue must naturally be crucial.

The question which arises is whether the higher public service supports a representative form of government in Pakistan, which,

[1] See p. 7 *supra*.

by its nature, must consign the public servant to a secondary place, or whether it is more favourable to the alternatives suggested above, which imply a more pronounced share for bureaucracy in the power of the State. To put it bluntly, it amounts to asking, 'Is the public service in Pakistan power hungry?'

The findings of this study are that a vast majority of the public servants in Pakistan profess a sincere devotion to the representative form of government. As a part of the Western-educated middle class they show guarded enthusiasm for a representative form of government because it has the potential of degenerating into rule by pressure groups. But when it is a question of preference, the average public servant supports the representative form of government. It seems that the impact of nineteenth century liberalism, which in most cases has formed the attitudes of educated Pakistanis, is more enduring than any other influence. If the civil service has exercised extraordinary influence upon the fundamental policies of the State, it has not been basically as a result of a desire to capture power but mainly in response to the need to fill the vacuum left by the occasional failure of the politician and to stop things from drifting.

In certain cadres of the public service resistance to the introduction of policies which are intended to change the conditions of service of the higher public servants has been strong. Apparently, this resistance has been no more than a form of self-defence, and not an attempt to aggrandize the power for bureaucracy. Nevertheless it is difficult to rule out completely the possibility that the resistance to change in this direction may in part be the result of desire for power. The reason for drawing the above inference is stated below.

The organization of the administrative system in Pakistan is so intimately related to the organization of the public service that no reform is possible in one without upsetting the other. As a consequence, if the public service opposes reform in its own organization, it is indirectly opposing reform in the administrative system. It is in this sense that certain cadres in the public service of Pakistan act as the preservers of the *status quo*.

The following example will amplify this point. The Secretariat system of administrative organization and procedure has been criticized repeatedly for being 'extraordinarily cumbersome in its operation and for being extremely productive of time-wasting frictions.' Another defect which has generated controversy and criticism was that one single cadre has almost monopolized every top Secretariat position. A reform in this system would affect adversely the position of the privileged cadre which had offered powerful, concerted resistance to the proposed reform. This resistance, therefore, has not been in self-defence, but has become identical to the opposition against the modernization of the whole administrative system. The comments of a foreign observer on the issue support the above inference; he wrote, 'taken together, I was constrained to conclude, as I became more familiar with Pakistan's government and its problems, the two institutions (the Secretariat and the Civil Service of Pakistan) constitute the prime citadels of resistance to needed administrative change.'[1]

It is Pakistan's good fortune that, ever since its creation, government leaders have been conscious of the need for the re-examination of its administrative framework and for its adjustment to the new requirements which have emerged following the achievement of Independence. Many different Pakistani governments have appointed inquiry commissions to assess the adequacy of the existing apparatus for the accomplishment of increasing development work. These measures were considerably stepped up under the regime of Martial Law. This spirit of 'self-criticism and reconstruction' evoked the praise of a foreign student of Asian governments, who wrote, 'A State which engages in such deliberate, rational, self-analysis and which introspectively seeks answers in its own cultural traditions may be said to be mature intellectually.'[2]

The two major types of administrative reforms undertaken during the past few years are the programme for the reorientation

---

[1] Paul L. Backett, op. cit. p. 6.

[2] Ralph Braibanti, 'The Philosophical Foundations of Bureaucratic Change', *The Pakistan Times*, Lahore, 27 December 1961.

of the attitudes of the public servants towards the people and the reorganization of the administrative procedures to achieve the development of social welfare.

A great deal has been said in the preceding chapters about the nature of the problem involved in changing the attitudes of the public servant. At this stage the whole issue is summed up along with a brief description of some of the measures which have been taken to find a remedy to the problem.

In order to neutralize the effect of the colonial mode of administration in the sub-continent, the primary need is to replace the colonial administrative policies, which were animated by the concept of 'rulership', with democratic concepts of administration which are inspired by a sense of public service and which accept the mass of the lay citizens as the ultimate political sovereign. The second need is to modify the administrative organization and the accompanying procedures so as to establish better communication and co-operation between the official and the private citizen.

A variety of methods have been pressed into service in order to realize the two objectives stated above. A powerful propaganda campaign is one. During the last many years reams of circulars, directives and instructions have been issued by the various governments calling upon the government servants to change their outlook towards the people. For illustration are reproduced below the five important instructions which were issued by the Central Police Office to its personnel in all districts and units. The instructions read:

1. Don't be discourteous. Courtesy creates goodwill and makes your task easier.

2. Don't keep a visitor waiting a moment longer than is necessary. It is apt to be irritating.

3. Don't overlook to offer a seat to any one who visits you with a complaint or a request. A person who is made to feel easy presents problems in a reasonable frame of mind.

4. Don't shout at members of the public, rich or poor. It destroys the feeling that you are their friend and protector.

5. Don't hurt the self-respect of a citizen by a public exhibi-

tion of his arrest or crime. It instils hatred in him for the organization you represent.[1]

Similar instructions were issued to the heads of departments, commissioners of divisions and the district officers by the government of the former Punjab. One circular advised the district officers to make sure that the public had easy access to their offices. It suggested that certain times should be fixed in which to hear the grievances of the public.[2]

Another method adopted for the reorientation of the attitudes of the public servants towards the people has been the organization of seminars in which the public servants and the public representatives, who are seated side by side, are by this close proximity enabled to communicate to each other their side of the argument. Training academies for public servants are being utilized to create a new spirit of service among the public servants of all ranks. The Academies for Village Development deserve special mention in this respect. The main objective of the Academies is to instruct the public servants in the methods of the implementation of development programmes.

This objective is sought to be achieved by educating the public servants in social sciences primarily to enable them to gather basic social data for the purpose of developing greater understanding of the cultural background of the people, which is needed in obtaining fuller participation of the people in the development efforts of the government. In short the objective is to produce 'an ideal-oriented public servant in the place of a career-oriented bureaucrat'.[3]

A more concrete attempt at establishing better relations between the public servant and the people is the introduction of the system of basic democracies. The system may be described as a pyramid of representative bodies rising from the union, representing four or five villages through the next administrative units, namely the

[1] M. Shariff Khan, 'Reforms in Police Administration', *The Pakistan Times*, Lahore, 27 October 1960.

[2] Director Public Relations, Punjab, *The Punjab, 1947-53, A Review of the First Six Years*, Lahore, 1954.

[3] M. A. Salam Ansari, 'Development Needs : Training of Administrators' *Dawn*, Karachi, 23-4 December 1960.

tehsils which are sub-divisions of a district, the division, and the province up to the central government. A common characteristic of the representative bodies at the tehsil, the district and the division level is that public servants form an integral part of the councils. They participate in the discussions and answer questions put to them by non-official members, but they do not have the right to vote.

The purpose which the basic democracies were supposed to serve was expressed in the following words by the President of Pakistan, in a letter addressed to the governors of the provinces:

It is one of the primary objectives of basic democracies to develop a new government-people relationship for tackling the tasks that face the country today. For this purpose, government officials have been associated with people's representatives not in any superior capacity but as equals. Officials are there to help the local communities not to domineer over them. In fact, it is intended that government operations should be discussed in the councils, so as to make the administration accountable to the people and responsive to their actual needs and aspirations. [1]

The President had expressed similar views in the earlier letter addressed to the chairmen of the basic democracies on 15 May 1960. [2] These statements suggest that a wind of change is blowing. It is, however, felt that it will be long before a real improvement takes place in the attitude of the public servant towards the people. In order to achieve this objective more concrete measures than mere exhortations and appeals will have to be taken. The basic democracy is an institutional innovation which, in certain ways, goes further than mere talk in bringing about a new relationship between the public servant and the people. The greatest potentiality for an evolution of this type appears to be present at the tehsil and the district level of the basic democracies.

The device which has been utilized for the purpose of establishing a closer liaison between the public servant and the public representative is the time-honoured parliamentary practice which enables public representatives to put questions to the public servants representing the government. Previously, this privilege was

[1] *The Pakistan Times*, Lahore, 6 December 1960.
[2] *The Pakistan Times*, Lahore, 19 May 1960.

enjoyed only by the members of the national assembly and of the provincial assemblies. The extension of this right to the thousands of basic democrats is a decision of momentous significance. This device not only keeps the public representatives well-informed about government policies but also tends to make the public servant accountable to and more responsive to the needs of the people.

In a meeting of one of the tehsil councils the writer observed that one of the official members of the council whose department was under fire from almost all the non-official members for its unsympathetic attitude towards the people was absent from the meeting. In a conversation with one of the members of the council after the meeting, the writer learnt that this incident illustrated the strength, and not the weakness, as some might conclude, of the system of basic democracies. The government official had absented himself because he was unable to face the criticism. Before the introduction of basic democracies, the public servant hiding behind the curtain of anonymity was under no obligation to explain his conduct to anyone except his immediate superiors. In the question hour of the national and provincial legislatures the civil servants themselves did not appear before the legislators. Under the system of basic democracies, the public servant has not only to answer the questions of the people's representatives, but is obliged to be present at the time of interpellations. As is illustrated by the incident described above, it is not easy to face the people when one is not in the right. It is hoped that the psychological impact of the face-to-face encounter with the people's representatives will act as a check upon the excesses of the bureaucrats.

It is, however, not intended to suggest that all is perfect with the basic democracies. The basic democracies do have their shortcomings, some being inherent in the scheme and some springing from the limitations of the members of these bodies. However, the constitution of the basic democracies at the tehsil and district level suggests that these bodies have the potential to develop into a reasonable check upon the bureaucracy.

The government in Pakistan has devoted considerable attention to the orientation of the public servants to welfare development. The object is to involve the public servant more and more in development work. At one time it was believed that the public service was merely a means for the carrying out of certain policies for which it should not show any partisan interest or enthusiasm. In the words of Professor Appleby, political neutrality on the part of the civil servants was 'made to appear to extend to programme neutrality'.[1]

The government leaders in Pakistan, however, were not too late in realizing that, for speedy development of the resources of the country, it was necessary to convert the public servant into an ardent votary of the development programme of the government. It was an area in which he must with profit be a partisan. The various training academies for the public servants were utilized to produce this effect. The institutions which merit special mention are the National Institutes of Public Administration and the Pakistan Administrative Staff College. The three Institutes, in Lahore, in Karachi and in Dacca, were established in early 1961. The main objective of these institutes is to train public servants of the intermediate level in management development so that they can play an effective role in a 'programme of accelerated social and economic development'[2] to which Pakistan is committed.

The Pakistan Administrative Staff College was inaugurated on 24 December 1960. The establishment of such a college had been recommended by experts in Public Administration from time to time. Professor Rowland Egger was the first to make such a proposal. The proposal was repeated by Professor Bernard L. Gladieu, by the Council of Administration for West Pakistan and more recently by the Commission on the Provincial Reorganization.

The college is a residential institution. It provides an opportunity to selected senior government officers and business executives to study intensively the plans and problems of Pakistan's nation-building programme with special reference to development

[1] Paul H. Appleby, op. cit. p. 25.
[2] Government of West Pakistan, *National Institute of Public Administration*, April 1961, a souvenir issue, Lahore, 1961, pp. 7-8.

administration. It is hoped that the intermingling of the public servants and business executives will enable them to understand each other's manner of working and to appreciate each other's difficulties. The training offered by the college is designed to widen the experience of the administrators occupying senior positions in government, in the public corporations, and in the private sector of industry and commerce who are likely to be considered for posts of greater responsibility. The college will provide the opportunity for such officers to obtain a better understanding of the new and vigorous environment in which they work, to study the administrative problems involved in the national development programme to which Pakistan is dedicated, to examine some of the individual plans and projects now underway, and to develop their awareness of the complexity of development administration and the importance in this whole process of personal initiative and enterprise.

The Government of Pakistan has decided to make administrative training a prerequisite for the public servant who wishes to retain a high governmental position or to qualify for promotion to a higher position. [1]

The most striking feature of the public service system in Pakistan today is that it is passing through a process of change. The impulse for this change originates partly from within the system itself and partly from outside due to the impact of the newly-emerging, socio-economic forces in the Pakistani society. The first aspect of the change is visible in the broad government policy to review and to reassess the entire administrative system. In this context, the large-scale research sponsored by the government in the public service training institutions, the appointment of inquiry commissions into public service matters and the reinvigoration of the organization and method units inside the government apparatus mark the trend in the thought process of the government leaders.

Among the social forces, growing industrialization is exercising an indirect but influential impact upon the composition and the status of the public service. As a result of the expansion of industry

[1] *The Civil and Military Gazette*, Lahore, 5 December 1961.

the lower middle class has become socially mobile. This group is gaining a share in power in the form of representation in business, industry and in government. With the emergence of competition from industry and commerce the bureaucracy is slowly yielding ground as the *primus inter pares* with regard to other social groups. This social change however has just begun. It has yet a long way to go.

APPENDIX I · THE QUESTIONNAIRE

Strictly Confidential

This questionnaire is being issued by the Social Sciences Research Centre of the University of the Panjab to determine the attitudes of the higher Public Servants in Lahore towards selected departmental, social and other adjustment problems in the Public Service of Pakistan. All the information obtained in this questionnaire shall be kept strictly confidential and shall be used only for the purposes of research.

THE QUESTIONNAIRE TO DETERMINE THE ATTITUDES OF THE
HIGHER PUBLIC SERVANTS IN LAHORE TOWARDS SELECTED PROBLEMS

Date _____ Place of interview: Home/Office/Other

Name of the interviewer _____

  1. (*a*) Department_____

     (*b*) Title of Post_____

  2. To which service do you belong? _____

3. Class   Senior Class I   Junior Class I

                     Class II   Unclassified

4. Age_____

5. Are you Refugee?_____Local?_____

6. (*a*) Place of birth_____

    (*b*) Province or State or Area to which you belong at present?_____

    N.B. (If the officer belongs to West Pakistan ask him to give the name of the former Province/State/Area which now forms part of West Pakistan)_____

7. Where did you live most of the time before you were 15 years old? In a village_____In a town_____

8. Religion_____

9. (*a*) Sect

    (*b*) Do sectarian considerations influence the conduct of public servants in the performance of their official duties?

    Yes_____No_____Don't know_____

    (*c*) If yes, in what way?

10. (*a*) Caste

    (*b*) Do caste considerations influence the conduct of public servants in the performance of their official duties?

    Yes_____No_____Don't know_____

    (*c*) If yes, in what way?

11. (*a*) Do regional considerations influence the conduct of public servants in the performance of their official duties?

    Yes_____No_____Don't know_____

    (*b*) If yes, in what way?

12. Please name the college which you attended for the longest period.

13. When did you join the government service?

14. What positions in the government service have you held prior to your present post after the establishment of Pakistan? Please give dates and tell me which posts you obtained as a result of promotion?

(Note to interviewers: Indicate promotions by printing letter 'P' against the post to which the respondent was promoted.)

Serial No.	Date	Title of the post	Department

15. Please give me the number of occasions, with dates, on which you were transferred during the period from August 1947 to the present time. Please state whether the transfer was from one district to another, from one post to another, from one department to another and the like. Also give reasons for the transfers, such as administrative expediency, political considerations or promotion and the like.

Serial No.	Date	District		Post		Department		Reasons
		From	To	From	To	From	To	

16. Do you have any family members[1] and/or near relatives[2] who are or have been in government service? If 'yes', please give the following information about them.

Serial No.	Relationship	Post held	Department

[1] Family members include your parents, children, brothers and sisters.
[2] By near relatives we understand father-in-law and brother/s-in-law.

17. Please give the following information about those of your family members and/or near relatives who are not in government service.

Serial No.	Relation-ship	Occupa-tion	Name of the establishment in which employed	Position held in the establishment

18. (*a*) According to rules, are you required to go on tour for a specific number of days?

Yes _____ No _____

N.B. (If the answer is 'No' skip to Question 19.)

(*b*) If 'yes' for how many days in a year, are you supposed to go on tour?

(*c*) Does your desk-work in office leave you enough time to go on tour for the required number of days?

Yes _____ No _____

19. Father's education

20. Mother's education

21. Wife's/husband's education

22. Father's monthly income when you were 15 years old. Please include income from all sources such as salary, land, buildings, investment and the like.

23. Why did you decide to accept government service instead of some other kind of job? (Probe.)

24. What other occupation would you have taken up if you had not entered government service? Please specify the occupation. (Probe.)

25. (A) (*i*) If you had to recommend to somebody (for example your own children) one of the following employments

what would be your preference?

(a) Government service.

(b) Employment in a Pakistani private concern.

(c) Employment in a foreign private concern.

(d) Employment in a private concern no matter Pakistani or foreign.

(ii) What are your reasons for that?

(B) (i) What would have been your own preference at the time of first seeking employment?

(a) Government service.

(b) Employment in a local private concern.

(c) Employment in a foreign private concern.

(d) Employment in a private concern no matter local or foreign.

(ii) What are your reasons for that?

(C) (i) If the choice were to be made now what would be your preference?

(a) Government service.

(b) Employment in a Pakistani private concern.

(c) Employment in a foreign private concern.

(d) Employment in a private concern no matter Pakistani or foreign.

(ii) What are your reasons for that?

26. I will read three statements to you. Please tell me with which you agree.

(Note for interviewers: Ask for reasons for each opinion.)

(a) The people in Pakistan are qualified to run a democratic form of government. Therefore the task of policy-making must be done by the elected representatives of the people and the public servants should confine themselves to the implementation of the policies.

(b) The people in Pakistan are not yet ready for a democratic form of government. Therefore, until they are ready for it, they should leave the tasks of policy-making and administration in the hands of the public servants.

(c) The people in Pakistan are not qualified and never will be to run a democratic form of government. Therefore, they should leave the tasks of policy-making and administration in the hands of the public servants.

27. Now I will read out to you an imaginary situation. When
I have finished reading I will ask you some questions relating to
this imaginary situation.

A public servant was entrusted with the task of diverting the course
of an inundation *nullah* in order to protect a number of villages
from floods. He was authorized to obtain voluntary manual labour
from the villagers to complete the project. The public servant,
having failed to enlist the co-operation of the villagers, used physical force, through the police, to compel them to work on the project. The project was completed.

(A) Do you think the public servant was justified in using
force?

Yes_____ No_____

(B) If the answer is 'yes', why do you think so?

(*a*) Because in all cases the end justifies the means.

(*b*) In this particular case, the co-operation of the villagers, even if obtained by compulsion, was for the good
of the villagers themselves.

(*c*) The people should not be allowed to oppose the authority of the public servants.

(*d*) Any other (specify).

(C) If the answer is 'no', why do you think so?

(*a*) Because it is opposed to the principles of human dignity.

(*b*) Because the use of force creates hatred towards the
government in the minds of the people.

(*c*) Because it discourages the habit of self-help among
the people.

(*d*) Any other (specify).

28. Here is another imaginary situation followed by a number
of questions.

A public servant is assigned the task of issuing permits to the
public for the purchase of foreign made bicycles of which only a
limited number is available. One of his relatives asks him to grant
him a permit. The public servant has already received a large number of applications. He can favour his relative only at the cost of
one of the applicants. Please state what will be the reaction of the
relative if the public servant does not agree to oblige him.

(*a*) He will consider the public servant a timid officer.

(*b*) He will speak ill of the public servant among his relatives and friends.

(*c*) He will come to respect the public servant as an officer who is not influenced by the considerations of family ties in the discharge of his official duties.

(*d*) Any other.

29. Kindly try to imagine the situation I am going to read out to you. On finishing reading I will ask you some questions relating to this imaginary situation.

At a given time during elections a minister asks a certain public servant to overlook the illegal practices of the supporters of a certain candidate or to muster support for that candidate or to harass his opponents. What in your opinion should the public servant do?

(*a*) Yield to the influence of the minister.

(*b*) Apparently agree to oblige the minister but in practice perform his duty in an impartial manner.

(*c*) Ask for a transfer to another post or place.

(*d*) Apply for sick/long leave.

(*e*) Refuse to oblige the minister.

(*f*) Any other.

30. If the public servant refuses to oblige the minister what treatment may he expect from the minister? (Probe.)

31. Which of the statements that I am going to read to you best conveys the attitude of the people towards an officer?

(*a*) The people look upon an officer as a person who is above them and who is there to rule them.

(*b*) As a person who is a servant of the State and whose main job is to protect the interests of the State.

(*c*) As a person who is a servant of the public and whose main job is to safeguard the interests of the public.

(*d*) As a person who is a leader of the people and whose main job is to guide and educate the people.

(*e*) Any other.

32. (*a*) Do you have some Service/Staff Association in your department?

Yes_____   No_____

(*b*) If 'yes' please give the name of the Service/Staff Association:

(c) Are you a member of the Service/Staff Association?
Yes_____ No_____

(d) Is there any membership fee for becoming a member of the Service/Staff Association?
Yes_____ No_____

(e) If 'yes' how much is it?
Per month_____ or per year_____

(f) Please state whether the Service/Staff Association is
Active only when faced
Active_____ with some specific issue_____ Inactive_____

(f) If there is a Service/Staff Association and you are not a member of it please give some of the reasons for this:

33. Do you think public servants should form their own Service/ Staff Associations?
(a) Yes_____ No_____ Indifferent_____ Don't know_____
(b) Why do you think so? (Probe.)

34. (a) Do your friends/colleagues visit you in your office during office hours on private business?
Yes_____ No_____
(b) If the answer is 'yes', please state how many of them come per day on the average?
(c) What is your attitude towards this practice?
Approve_____ Don't approve_____ Indifferent_____

35. (a) Do you think the government should permit all public servants to hold other jobs or to undertake side-business in addition to their posts in spare time?
Yes_____ No_____ Indifferent_____ Don't know_____
(b) Why do you think so? (Probe.)

36. Which of the statements I am going to read to you describes most correctly the actual state of affairs?
(a) None of the public servants has taken up some side-business in addition to his government job.
(b) Some of the public servants have taken up some side-business in addition to their government jobs.
(c) Most of the public servants have taken up some side-business in addition to their government jobs.
(d) Almost all the public servants have taken up some side-

business in addition to their government jobs.

37. Do you think that decisions relating to policy matters should be taken

(*a*) by the officer in charge of a department, without inviting or taking into consideration the views of his subordinates;

(*b*) by the officer in charge of the department in consultation with all the senior members of the department no matter whether they are or are not directly concerned with that particular policy decision;

(*c*) by the officer in charge of the department in consultation with all those members of the department who are directly concerned with that particular policy decision no matter whether they are senior or junior?

38. Do you think that decisions relating to the methods of implementation of a given policy should be taken

(*a*) by the officer in charge of a department, without inviting or taking into consideration the views of his subordinates;

(*b*) by the officer in charge of the department in consultation with all the senior members of the department no matter whether they are or are not directly concerned with that particular policy decision;

(*c*) by the officer in charge of the department in consultation with all those members of the department who are directly concerned with that particular policy decision, no matter whether they are senior or junior?

39. Do you think that decisions relating to internal office administration (for example seating arrangements, distribution of work, fixation of working hours, etc.) should be taken

(*a*) by the officer in charge of a department without inviting or taking into consideration the views of his subordinates;

(*b*) by the officer in charge in consultation with all the senior members of the department;

(*c*) by the officer in charge in consultation with all the members of the department excluding Class IV employees;

(*d*) by the officer in charge in consultation with all the members of the department including all the Class IV employees?

40. Do you think that decisions relating to staff welfare (for example the opening of a canteen or a co-operative store or the introduction of a benevolent fund scheme) should be taken

(*a*) by the officer in charge of a department without inviting or taking into consideration the views of his subordinates;

(*b*) by the officer in charge in consultation with all the senior members of the department;

(*c*) by the officer in charge in consultation with all the members of the department excluding Class IV employees;

(*d*) by the officer in charge in consultation with all the members of the department including all the Class IV employees?

41. (*a*) Do your superior officers offer you a chair when you visit their offices?

Yes_____ No_____

(*b*) Do you offer a chair to your subordinates when they visit your office?

Yes_____ No_____

(*c*) (*i*) Do you think an officer should offer a chair to his subordinates when they visit his office?

Yes_____ No_____ Indifferent_____

(*ii*) Why do you think so? (Probe.)

42. A clerk is transferred, or retired, from his department. His colleagues arrange a farewell party in his honour. They extend invitations to their gazetted officers as well. Should these officers attend the party?

(*a*) Yes_____ No_____

(*b*) If the answer is 'yes', should the officers

(*i*) attend the party as a gesture of their goodwill and leave soon;

(*ii*) stay but keep a distance from their subordinates;

(*iii*) stay throughout the party and mix freely with their subordinates?

43. (*a*) Suppose an officer is sitting alone in a restaurant and one of his Class III subordinates walks in. The officer is aware that no other table is free. Should the officer ask his sub-

ordinate to come and sit with him?

Yes_____ No_____

(b) What are the reasons for your opinion?

44. As you know, the policy of the government is to appoint CSP officers to a diverse variety of important posts. Do you think that in the modern age of specialization

(a) the specialist posts should go to a specialist only, no matter whether he is a CSP or non-CSP;

or (b) arrangements may be made that the CSP officer should receive previous training in the field of specialization of the post to which they are being considered for appointment? (Interviewers should ask for reasons in each case.)

45. (a) As you may know, at present all CSP officers are recruited directly. If it is proposed that a certain percentage of the CSP cadre should be recruited from the non-CSP officers on the basis of their performance, would you

agree_____ disagree_____ be indifferent_____?

(b) May I know some of the reasons for your opinion?

46. (Note. The first three questions are not applicable to women.)

(i) Do you like to go dancing?   Yes_____ No_____

(ii) Do you accept an alcoholic drink when offered?   Yes_____ No_____

(iii) Do you offer alcoholic drink to your guests in your own home?   Yes_____ No_____

(iv) Do your womenfolk (i.e. mother, wife, sisters, daughters) observe purdah?

All do _____Some do_____None does_____

(v) Do you think that a father should allow his son to choose his wife himself?   Yes_____ No_____

(vi) Would you send your children rather to a Western-type school than to other schools?   Yes_____ No_____

(vii) Do you preferably converse in

English with those of your friends
and relatives who can speak Eng-
lish and Urdu equally well?   Yes_____ No_____

(*viii*) Do you usually read foreign
newspapers or magazines in the
English language?   Yes_____ No_____

(*ix*) Do you usually prefer to see
foreign films in the English lang-
uage?   Yes_____ No_____

(*x*) Do you think that a father
should allow his daughter to
choose her husband herself?   Yes_____ No_____

(*xi*) Would you allow your women-
folk to have clipped hair?   Yes_____ No_____

(*xii*) Do you think that a father
should allow his daughter to attend a co-educational college or
university?   Yes_____ No_____

47. (*i*) What is your monthly income? Please include monthly
income from resources other than your salary, such as buildings, land or investments of any kind.

(*ii*) Number of dependents i.e. members of your own family
and other relatives economically dependent on you.

(*iii*) Your education:

(*iv*) How many domestic servants do you have excluding
those given to you in your official capacity?

(*v*) Do you have a radio set?   Yes_____ No_____

(*vi*) Do you have a motor car of
your own?   Yes_____ No_____

(*vii*) Do you have a telephone at
your residence?   Yes_____ No_____

(*viii*) Do you have a refrigerator?   Yes_____ No_____

(*ix*) Do you have an air-conditioner
or a cooler in your house?   Yes_____ No_____.

(*x*) Do you have a radiogram or a
phonogram?   Yes_____ No_____

(*xi*) Do you have a tape-recorder? Yes_____ No_____

(*xii*) Do you own a house?   Yes_____ No_____

(*xiii*) Do you have flush system in
the house in which you are living
at present?   Yes_____ No_____

(*xiv*) (*a*) Are you a member of
some (cultural, social or
sports) association(s)?   Yes_____ No_____
(*b*) Please give the name(s) of
the association(s).   _____
(*c*) Do you hold office in any
association?   Yes_____ No_____

(*xv*) (*a*) Are you a member of a
club?   Yes_____ No_____
(*b*) Please give the name of
the club.   _____
(*c*) Do you hold office in the
club?   Yes_____ No_____

(*xvi*) (*a*) Is your wife/husband a
member of some associa-
tion(s)?   Yes_____ No_____
(*b*) Please give the name of
the association(s).   _____
(*c*) Does she/he hold office in
any association?   Yes_____ No_____

(*xvii*) (*a*) Is your wife/husband a
member of any club?   Yes_____ No_____
(*b*) Please give the name of
the club.
(*c*) Does she/he hold any of-
fice in the club?   Yes_____ No_____

48. Would you like to make any comments about this questionnaire or about any point I may have missed?

APPENDIX II·THE LETTER OF AUTHORITY

COPY
From

  Mr. M. M. Ahmed, T.Pk., C.S.P.,
  Addl. Chief Secretary to Government,
  West Pakistan.

To

  1. All Administrative Secretaries to
  Government, West Pakistan.
  2. All Heads of Attached Departments
  in Lahore.

  Memorandum No. S.VIII-9-17/61, dated Lahore,
    the 15th February 1961.

Subject: Questionnaire to determine the attitude of the higher
  public servants in Lahore towards selected problems.

  Mr. Munir Ahmed, Assistant Research Officer in the Social Sciences Research Centre, University of the Panjab, is conducting
research to determine the attitude of higher public servants towards selected departmental, social and other adjustment problems
in the public service in Pakistan. He proposes to approach different officers of the Provincial Government for obtaining answers
to the questionnaire formulated by him.

  2. It has been decided that he may be afforded full assistance
and co-operation in the matter and officers working under you
may be directed to answer the whole questionnaire or a part there-
of provided the provisions of the Government Servants Conduct
Rules and the Official Secrets Act are not violated.

    Sd/- Section Officer VIII,
    for Addl. Chief Secretary to Government,
    West Pakistan.

APPENDIX III · CONSTRUCTION AND EVALUATION OF THE WESTERNIZATION INDEX

In order to test certain common suppositions about the influence of Westernization on attitudes it was decided to construct an index to assess roughly the degree of Westernization of our respondents. Twelve items were considered important for this purpose. These items are listed in question 46 of the questionnaire in Appendix I.

In order to calculate the total score of a respondent the following method was adopted. On the basis of possession-non-possession principle each 'yes' answer was given 1 score and each 'no' reply zero score. In the case of the fourth item of the index which related to the *purdah* observing practice of the womenfolk of the respondent's family to which three different answers were possible the following scores were given. If all women in his family observed *purdah* the respondent was given a zero score. If none or only some of the women did so the respondent earned 1 score.

The maximum score which a respondent could obtain was 12. In order to determine whether the respondent was high, low, or in the middle on the index the maximum score was divided into three equal intervals by simple division. A respondent who obtained 0-4 score was categorized as least Westernized, he who scored between 5-8 was categorized as semi-Westernized and a person obtaining a 9-12 score was rated as highly Westernized.

In the case of women public servants a similar method of scoring and evaluation was used as for men with the exception that the first three questions on the index were not applicable to women. These questions relate to drinking and dancing. Social disapprobation against women's participation in these activities is extremely rigorous.

As a result of this modification the total number of items on the Westernization index for women was reduced to 9. The high, middle and the low positions of women on the Westernization index were accordingly calculated on the basis of a maximum score of 9. Women public servants who scored 0-3 were considered to be the least Westernized, those who scored 4-6 were adjudged as semi-Westernized and those with a score of 7-9 were regarded as highly Westernized.

APPENDIX IV · CONSTRUCTION AND EVALUATION OF AN INDEX OF SOCIO-ECONOMIC STATUS

The socio-economic status is also, like Westernization, supposed to exercise some influence upon the attitudes of people. For the purpose of finding out what correlation did exist between the attitudes of our respondents and their status we decided to prepare an index of socio-economic status.

Seventeen items were taken up for this purpose. In selecting items which we expected to have an intimate relationship with the socio-economic status of our respondents, advantage was taken of the experiences of a sociological study of the causes of mass failure of college students in examinations in West Pakistan.[1] The authors of this study had developed a S.E.S. Index and had selected the items after laborious statistical calculations. The items selected for the S.E.S. Index are given in question 47 of the questionnaire in Appendix I.

In order to calculate the final score of the respondents the principle of possession-non-possession was applied. Every 'yes' answer was given 1 score and every 'no' answer a zero score.

In order to rate the income per capita of a respondent the following method was adopted. Zero to thirty rupees income per capita carried a zero score, 31 to 200 rupees income per capita carried 1 score and 201 and more income per capita carried 2 score.

In evaluating the education of the respondent the following procedure was adopted. Undergraduates including those who had also received some training in a foreign country scored a zero, graduates scored 1 and postgraduates along with graduates with some foreign training scored 2.

[1] J.J. Manglam and others, *Study of Student Mass Failure*, Department of Sociology, University of the Panjab, Lahore, (cyclostyled) pp. 62-9.

The education of wives was evaluated as follows. Matriculates and below earned a zero score, undergraduates and graduates 1 and postgraduates including graduates with some European training 2.

The respondents who had not employed a domestic servant scored zero, those who had employed 1 to 2 domestic servants scored 1 and those who had employed three or more domestic servants earned a score of 2.

The maximum score which a married respondent could obtain was 21. In order to determine the position of our respondents on the S.E.S. Index the maximum score was divided into three equal parts by simple division. The respondents who scored between 0-7 were considered to occupy a low status, those who scored between 8-14 were rated as occupying a middle-class status, those who scored between 15-21 were considered to possess an upper-class status. For the sake of a more detailed evaluation the respondents scoring between 8-14 were further subdivided into two equal halves. The respondents who scored between 8-11 were rated as lower middle and those scoring between 12-14 as upper middle.

The maximum score which an unmarried respondent both male or female could earn was 15. This was because a few items on the S.E.S. Index which were related to the wives or husbands of the respondents became inapplicable in the case of the unmarried respondents. The low, lower middle, upper middle and the upper class status of the unmarried respondents was assessed by a corresponding score of 0-5, 6-8, 9-10 and 11-15 respectively.

In the case of the married women public servants the education of the husband was counted in evaluating their socio-economic status. The education of husbands was assigned scores at the same rate as in the case of the education of the male respondents.

BIBLIOGRAPHY

GENERAL PUBLICATIONS

Marshal Edward Dimock, *Public Administration*, New York.

Marshal Edward Dimock, *Administrative Vitality*, New York, 1960.

Frank Dunnill, *The Civil Service: Some Human Aspects*, London, 1956.

A. Dunsire, (ed.) *The Making of an Administrator*, London, 1956.

H. R. G. Greaves, *The Civil Service in the Changing State*, London, 1947.

Lord Hewart, *The New Despotism*, London, 1945.

H. J. Laski, *A Grammar of Politics*, London, 1938.

J. D. Millet, *Management in the Public Service: The Quest for Effective Performance*, 1954.

John M. Pfiffner, *Public Administration*, New York, 1956.

Peter du Sautoy, *The Civil Service*, London, 1957.

Max Weber, *The Theory of Social and Economic Organization*, (ed. by Talcott Parsons), New York, 1947.

L. D. White, *Introduction to the Study of Public Administration*, New York, 1955.

GENERAL PUBLICATIONS ON PUBLIC SERVICE IN FOREIGN COUNTRIES

Asoka Chanda, *Indian Administration*, London, 1958.

Paul Appleby, *Public Administration in India, A Report of a Survey*, New Delhi, 1956. Conducted for the Cabinet Secretariat, under Ford Foundation, a re-examination of India's administrative system with special reference to administration of the government industrial and commercial enterprises.

Morroe Berger, *Bureaucracy and Society in Modern Egypt, A Study of the Higher Civil Service*, Princeton, 1957.

Sir John Craig, *A History of Red Tape*, London, 1955.

T. A. Critchley, *The Civil Service Today*, London, 1951.

R. Dwarkadas, *Role of the Higher Civil Service in India*, Bombay, 1958.

A. D. Gorwala, *Report on Public Administration*, New Delhi, 1951.

A. D. Gorwala, *Of Matters Administrative*, Bombay, 1958.

R. K. Kelsall, *Higher Civil Servants in Britain*, London, 1955. This book contains an exhaustive bibliography on civil servants in Britain, spread over ten pages.

S. S. Khera, *District Administration in India*, New Delhi, 1960.

B. B. Majumdar, *Problems of Public Administration in India*, Calcutta, 1956.

Herbert Morrison, *Government and Parliament: A Survey From Inside*, London, 1959.

Northcote, *Trevelyan Committee on the Organization of the Permanent Civil Service*.

William A. Robson, (ed.) *The Civil Service in Britain and France*, London, 1956.

N. C. Roy, *Civil Service in India*, London, 1958.

K. A. V. Sastri, *Principles of District Administration in India*, New Delhi, 1957.

Kenneth Younger, *Public Service in New States*, Oxford, 1960.

HISTORY OF PUBLIC SERVICE IN BRITISH INDIA: GENERAL BOOKS

Sir Edward Blunt, *The Indian Civil Service*, London, 1937.

Hilton Brown (ed.), *The Sahibs: The Life and Ways of the British in India as Recorded by Themselves*, London, 1948.

Sir Bampfylde Fuller, *Studies of Indian Life and Sentiment*, London, 1910.

Sir Percival Griffith, *The British Impact on India*, London, 1952.

G. N. Joshi, *Indian Administration*, London, 1953.

Lajpat Rai, *The Political Future of India*, New York, 1919.

L. S. S. O'Malley, *The Indian Civil Service 1601-1930*, London, 1931.

Sir Michael O'Dwyer, *India As I Knew It, 1885-1925*, London, 1925.

N. C. Roy, *Civil Service in India*, London, 1958.

T. G. P. Spear, *The Nabobs*, London, 1963.

Sir John Strachey, *India, Its Administration and Progress*, London, 1903.

Philip Woodruff, *The Men who Ruled India*, Vols. I, II, London, 1953-4.

Cambridge History of India, Vols. V, VI, British India, 1955-8.

HISTORY OF PUBLIC SERVICE IN BRITISH INDIA:
OFFICIAL PUBLICATIONS

As most of the official publications were in the form of Commission Reports it was not possible to identify their authors nor was it possible to list them alphabetically. The official publications, therefore, have been listed in chronological order.

A Collection of Statutes Relating to India, (in two volumes), Calcutta, 1913.

Aitchison Commission, *Report of the Royal Commission on Public Services in India, 1886-87*.

Islington Commission, *Report of the Royal Commission on the Public Services in India, 1916*.

Montagu-Chelmsford Report, *Report of the Indian Constitu-*

tional Reforms, 1918.

Lee Commission, *Report of the Royal Commission on the Superior Services in India*, 1924.

Punjab Settlement Manual, Lahore, 1930.

Simon Commission, *Report of the Indian Statutory Commission*, Vols. I, II, 1930.

Police Rules, 1934, (*Punjab*), 1937.

Government of India Act, 1935. (As adopted in Pakistan.)

Wheeler Committee, *Report of the Government of India, Secretariat Committee*, 1937.

District Office Manual (*Punjab*), contains rules and regulations governing the procedure in the offices of Commissioners and Deputy Commissioners and takes the place of Standing Order No. 5, etc., 1942 (second edition).

Tottenham Report, *Report on the Reorganization of the Secretariat of the Government of India*, 1946.

HISTORY OF PUBLIC SERVICE IN PAKISTAN: GENERAL BOOKS

The bibliography on public service in Pakistan is not confined to those publications which were used in the preparation of this study. An attempt has been made to list all possible publications which have some bearing on Pakistani public service.

Anisuddin Ahmad, C.S.P., *Civil Service and Social Changes in Pakistan*, a short essay presented to Cambridge University as a part of training in Public Administration, 1956, (typescript).

A. H. Aslam, *The Deputy Commissioner, A Study in Public Administration*, Lahore, 1957.

M. Aslam Khan, *The Organizational Survey of the Services and General Administration Department, The Government of West Pakistan*, a thesis presented to the Institute of Public and Business Administration (now called the Graduate School of Business Administration), University of Karachi, Karachi, 1958, (typescript).

Barkat Ram Kalia, *A History of the Development of the Police in the Punjab*, Lahore, 1929.

A. Bertrand, 'The Civil Service Academy and the Training of

the Members of the CSP', published in *International Social Science Bulletin*, Vol. VII, No. 2, 1955.

Ralph Braibanti, *The Civil Service of Pakistan: A Theoretical Analysis*, Lahore, 1961.

Keith Callard, *Pakistan: A Political Study*, London, 1957.

Muhammad Jawaid Ilyas, *The Divisional Commissioner, A Study in Public Administration*, a Master's thesis presented to the Graduate School of Business Administration, University of Karachi, 1961, (typescript).

Muhammad Iqbal, *Ranking of Successful Candidates in Superior Services Examination*, Karachi, 1961, (cyclostyled).

Khalid Bin Sayeed, *Pakistan: The Formative Phase*, Karachi, 1960.

Mushtaq Ahmad, *Government and Politics in Pakistan*, Karachi, 1959.

Muzaffar Ahmad Chaudhuri, *The Civil Service in Pakistan: (The Centrally Recruited Civil Service)*, a thesis submitted for the Degree of Doctor of Philosophy to the University of London, 1960, (typescript).

Salim A. Jilani, *The Civil Service of Pakistan*, an M. A. thesis submitted to the Political Science Department of the University of the Panjab, 1956, (typescript).

Seminar on the Expanding Role of the Public Servant in Pakistan's Democratic Structure, a report prepared by the Social Sciences Research Centre and published by the Bureau of National Reconstruction, Lahore, 1960.

Virgil H. Stevens, *Public Administration in Pakistan, Organization and Personnel Management of the Central Administration*, Karachi, 1960, (cyclostyled).

Notes on the Civil Service in Pakistan in the Report of the U.N. Seminar on the Organization of Personnel, 1951.

Papers read at the *Seminar on the Police and the Citizen*, organized by the Bureau of National Reconstruction, West Pakistan, in October 1961.

United Nations, *A Handbook of Public Administration*, New York, 1961.

HISTORY OF PUBLIC SERVICE IN PAKISTAN: OFFICIAL PUBLICATIONS

The publications are, as far as possible, listed in a chronological order.

Report of the Central Secretariat Committee, 1947-48.

Government of Pakistan, *Report of the Committee appointed by the Legislative to review the organization, the structure and the level of expenditure of various ministries, departments and offices of the Government of Pakistan.*

Reports of the Economy Committees, 1948-58.

Reports of the Public Accounts Committees, 1948-58.

Report on Pakistan Pay Commission (three vols.), Karachi, 1949.

Statement showing the Total Number of Persons, employed under the Government of Pakistan, belonging to different Provinces, States, etc. of India, Karachi, 1950.

Report on the General Election to the Punjab Legislative Assembly, 1950-51, Lahore, 1952.

O and M in Pakistan, a pamphlet published by the Establishment Division, Cabinet Secretariat, Government of Pakistan, Karachi, 1952.

Report of the Economic Appraisal Committee, Vols. I, II, (1952-53).

Government of Pakistan, *Report of the Administrative Enquiry Committee,* Karachi, 1953.

Government of East Bengal, *Report of the Police Enquiry Committee, 1953.*

Rowland Egger, *The Improvement of Public Administration in Pakistan,* Karachi, 1954.

Report of the Sargodha District Board Election, 1952-53, Lahore, 1955.

Report of the Court of Inquiry constituted under Punjab Act 11 of 1954 to enquire into the Punjab Disturbances of 1953, Lahore, 1954.

Bernard L. Gladieu, *Reorientation of Pakistan Government for National Development,* Karachi, 1955.

Report of the Council for Administration of West Pakistan, Feb-

ruary 1955, Lahore, 1955.

Report of the Federal Re-organization Committee, Karachi, 1956.

Paul L. Beckett, *A Few Concluding Comments on Public Administration and Development in Pakistan*, Karachi, 1957, (cyclostyled).

Government of East Pakistan, *O and M in the East Pakistan Government*, a report prepared by L. Parnwell, M.B.E., of the O and M Division of the U.K. Treasury, Dacca, 1958.

Provincial Administration Commission Report, Lahore, 1960.

Questionnaire for the Provincial Administration, issued by Pay and Services Commission, 1960.

STATUTES AND RULES

Civil Service Rules (Punjab), Vols. I, II, III.

Government of Pakistan, *The Civil Service (Classification, Control and Appeal) Rules*, Karachi, 1951.

Civil Service of Pakistan (Composition and Cadre) Rules issued from time to time by the Establishment Division of the Cabinet Secretariat for the Rules issued in 1954, see *Gazette of Pakistan*, 18 June 1954.

The Constitution of the Islamic Republic of Pakistan, 1956.

The Second Constitution of Pakistan, 1962.

The Police Act, 1862.

The West Pakistan Government Servants (Efficiency and Discipline Rules), January 1960.

The new form introduced for writing confidential reports (May 1960).

GAZETTE NOTIFICATIONS

Separation of Executive from Judiciary in the Office of the Deputy Commissioner. *The Pb. G. 'Letter No. 10993-53-5G/Gazette'*, 28 December 1953.

Cabinet Secretariat, Resolution No. F-25/4/50-Ests. (S.E.T.) 8 November 1950, published in the *Gazette of Pakistan*, 8 November 1950, pp. 829-835, also *Gazette of Pakistan*, 18 June 1954, and *Gazette of Pakistan*, 12 November 1954.

Notification No. F-25/47/49-SEI, Cabinet Secretariat, Establishment Division, 15 June 1954.

Gazette of Pakistan, 25 June 1954.

REPORTS OF THE PUBLIC SERVICE COMMISSIONS

Second Report of the Pakistan Service Commission for the Period from 1st January to 31st December 1949, Karachi, 1956.

Third Report of the Pakistan Public Service Commission for the Period from 1st January 1950 to 31st December 1951, Karachi, 1957.

Fifth Report of the Pakistan Public Service Commission for the Period from 1st January to 31st December 1952, Karachi, 1957.

Report on the Central Superior Service Examination held at Karachi, Lahore, Dacca, London, Washington, in January/February, 1953, containing Reviews, Rules, etc., Karachi.

Seventh Report of the Pakistan Public Service Commission for the Period from 1st January to 31st December, 1954, Karachi.

Eighth Report of the Federal Public Service Commission for the Period from 1st January to 31st December 1956, Karachi, 1959.

Ninth Report of the Federal Public Service Commission for the Period 1st January to 31st December 1957, Karachi, 1959.

Annual Report of the Sind Public Service Commission for the year 1947-48, Karachi, 1951.

Annual Report on the Working of the Sind Public Service Commission for the year 1951-52.

Annual Report on the Working of the West Pakistan Public Service Commission for the period from 14th October 1955 to 31st December 1956, Lahore.

Annual Report on the Working of the West Pakistan Public Service Commission for the period from 1st January 1957 to 31st December 1957, Lahore, 1959.

Debates in the Legislatures.

Publicity literature published by the Information Department of the Government of Pakistan.

Sir Eric Franklin, *Careers in Pakistan C.S.S.*, Karachi, 1954.

The Punjab, 1947-53, A Review of the First Six Years, Lahore, 1954.

First and Second Five Year Plans of Pakistan.

JOURNALS AND PERIODICALS

American Political Science Review.
The Indian Journal of Public Administration.
The Journal of the American Society of Public Administration.
Pakistan Management Review, Journal of the Institute of Personnel Training, P.I.D.C., Karachi.

FICTION AND LIGHT ESSAYS DESCRIBING BUREAUCRATIC ATMOSPHERE

Balachandra Rajan, *The Dark Dancer*, London, 1959.

H. E. Beal, *Indian Ink*, London, 1954.

Compton Mackenzie, *The Red Tapeworm*, London, 1941.

Northcote Parkinson, *Parkinson's Law or the Pursuit of Progress*, London, 1958.

MISCELLANEOUS

A. K. Brohi, *Fundamental Law of Pakistan*, Lahore, 1958.

Herbert Feldman, *A Constitution for Pakistan*, Karachi, 1955.

Alan Gledhill, *Pakistan: The Development of its Laws and Constitution*, London, 1951.

E. W. R. Lumby, *The Transfer of Power in India 1945-7*, London, 1955.

I. H. Qureshi, *Pakistan: Islamic Democracy*, Karachi.

Richard Symonds, *Making of Pakistan*, London, 1950.

Maurice Zinkin, *Development for Free Asia*, London, 1956.

INDEX